# FREEBIES AND WELFARE SCHEMES A FISCAL DISASTER & SUGGESTED FRAMEWORK FOR ELECTION FINANCING

By

Prahalad Rao

© Prahalad Rao 2023

**All rights reserved**

All rights reserved by author. No part of this publication may be reproduced, stored in a retrieval system or transmitted in any form or by any means, electronic, mechanical, photocopying, recording or otherwise, without the prior permission of the author.

Although every precaution has been taken to verify the accuracy of the information contained herein, the author and publisher assume no responsibility for any errors or omissions. No liability is assumed for damages that may result from the use of information contained within.

First Published in February 2023

**ISBN: 978-93-5704-970-2**

**BLUEROSE PUBLISHERS**
www.BlueRoseONE.com
info@bluerosepublishers.com
+91 8882 898 898

**Cover Design:**
Yash

**Typographic Design:**
Tanya Raj Upadhyay

**Distributed by:** BlueRose, Amazon, Flipkart

# DISCLAIMER

Views expressed by the author in this book are based on his personal understanding of the past and perception of the present. This book neither intends nor suggests any attribution of whatsoever nature to anyone or to any policy or program or system existing or envisaged nor this book intends or suggests to hurt sentiments of any person or state or political bodies or religious bodies or political or religious leaders or body of any other nature or defame any of them whatsoever and any construction of the writings in this book otherwise is sole to the person so construing. The author or the publisher will not be liable for any civil or criminal proceedings under the laws of the country.

# GRATITUDES

My gratitude to Dr. Sharda, K.Ananth Raman, Royal Hotel, Hyderabad, V.Laxma Reddy, T.S.Murthy, A.R.Venkataraman, P.P.S.Puri, A.S.Dhupia, R.B. Mathur and Lalit Chand, whose guidance, benevolence and humanism in my initial years of service will shine in my heart for ever, C.V.Nair, D. Sankaraguruswamy, Dr. Uddesh Kohli, B.M. Pant, M. Prasad, T.N. Thakur, A.A. Khan, Dr. K. K. Govil and Raji Phillips who gave confidence and lent support to me during my most testing time of life.

My gratitude to senior Indian Administrative Officers (IAS) who headed the organizations, account and audit service officers, eminent engineers, eminent finance & legal experts with whom I had the opportunity to work in one capacity or the other during my thirty years of service in public sector Financial Institutions. Gratitudes to A.K.Sah and Shahzad Bahadur for giving me opportunity to develop my career as a consultant post retirement. My gratitude and special thanks to Dr.J.T.Verghese who offered me chance for continuity of my consultancy job with continued guidance and advice. My association with all of them helped imbibe in me their direction, dedication to the cause of economic development, virtues, values, compassion and affection that became bedrock of my life.

My gratitude to Scholars, Journalists, Thinkers, Philosophers, Historians, Bankers, Economists, Professionals, Socialists and Environmentalists within and outside the country whose writings on Google website helped me to understand the width and depth of subjects selected for this book. Author has disclosed the sources of valuable writings relied upon under "References", also stated in the book at some places. No copyright infringement is intended. Author reiterates his grateful thanks to all of them.

My special thanks to Google for providing inspiration with invaluable sources of information that helped me in completing this book.

In particular, my gratitude to Arun Kumar Sarna who gave me strong standing support during my association with him in service in multi-national consultancy Services Company as well as throughout thereafter.

My gratitude to K. G. Dewan, Sadiq Shafiq and Boben Anto whose ever helping hand remained a sustainable strength to me.

Grateful thanks to M/s BLUE ROSE PUBLISHESERS PRIVATE LIMITED, the Publishers without whose cooperation, guidance and advice, this book wouldn't have reached the readers.

Thanks to my friends, relatives and my family members for their continued encouragement. Their suggestions and support were a great strength for me in completing this book.

8$^{th}$ November, 2022  Prahalad Rao

# TABLE OF CONTENTS

*DISCLAIMER* ............................................................................................... *iii*

*GRATITUDES* ............................................................................................... *v*

PART 01 INTRODUCTION .............................................................................. 1

PART 02 SUGGESTED FRAMEWORK FOR FINANCING ELECTIOINS IN INDIA .... 34

PART 03 FREEBIES AND WELFARE ................................................................ 59

PART 04 THE FISCAL DISASTER ................................................................... 123

PART 05 SPURRING THE FISCAL DISASTER ................................................. 160

ABOUT THE AUTHOR .................................................................................. 199

# PART 01
# INTRODUCTION

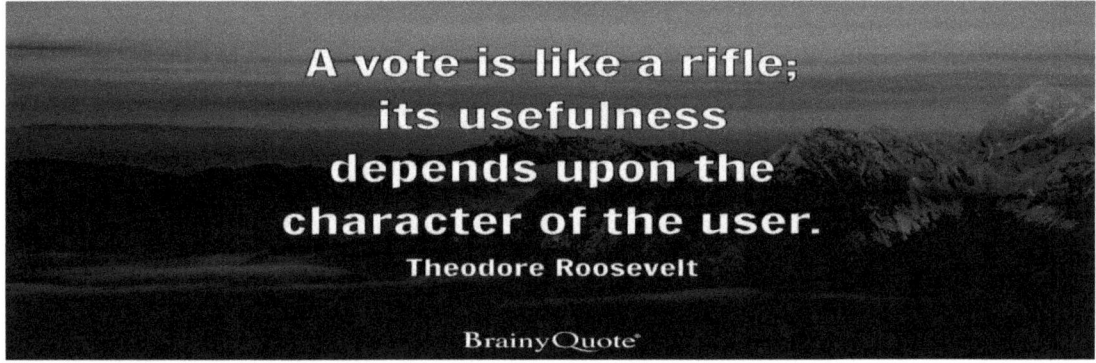

Constituent Assembly debates throw some light on election financing. It is a different matter there was no unanimity and, in the wisdom of the founding fathers, this was left open for the future generations to consider and evolve a healthy election financing system. This loophole became very handy for the succeeding generations to twist the election financing as suited best to each party that ruled the country. The enormity of corruption rise is directly attributable to the faulty and highly questionable method justified and adopted by the parties as permitted by the central government. Once a new party assumed power, it found it necessary to introduce more fairness transparency and continued to change election funding laws and rules not realizing that the transparency and fairness advocated was altogether absent therein.

"It is very relevant and timely to reproduce below what one of the Learned Members of the Constituent Assembly {CAD} had said about the financing of elections, as also what could happen if that is not done:

".... a voter shall have the right to election and the cost of election shall be met by the State--I say so, because to come to the Assembly is not a profession or a profiteering business. If that is the concern of the State and if a person who comes to the Assembly comes to serve the people, it is necessary that the State must see that his election expenses are borne by the State. Otherwise some landlords and some capitalists will build up a party to set up candidates and those candidates will be returned. Let us say here is a poor man, a good worker, an honest man; but he has neither the money nor the party backing. The result is he cannot stand for election. If he stands, he comes to ridicule. If you say that the election is as much in the interest of the State as the President or the Ministers or the bureaucracy, you must say that in the same manner as they are brought to being, legislative members should also come to the Assembly, the State bearing their election expenditure in a regulated and therefore in the least expensive and most organized manner. This may be laughable, but this is just and fair and unless we make such a provision no sincere, honest and real worker can be returned at least for the next fifteen or twenty years. If we do not do so now, we invite only revolution. And revolution will make everything topsy-turvy. It will have to be done, then by the fire of the people instead of our intelligent understanding, if we chose it now. Therefore, the cost of the elections must legitimately and in fairness to the cause be borne by the State because election as such is a State affair and is not a private concern. It need not stagger us now. We must not allow members to come calculating profit and loss, calculating how much money they will be making in five years and therefore how much they may beg, borrow or steal for this parliamentary investment." (Lokanath Misra, Member of the Constituent Assembly (29th November, 1948)"

The constitution makers did not make the related provisions in the constitution, but empowered the parliament on any matter in respect thereof {See Art.327} nor by those who inaugurated the republic process as the first council of ministers sooner the country became republic and put into action thought of the urgent need for the laws governing the political parties and election financing besides the Representation of Peoples' Act, 1950 and 1951, amendment in progress thereafter only to that extent to which the political parties are more and more benefitted; that only touched the surface of the political systems that resulted in widening space in loosened control and functioning of political parties. This may not be an unintended mistake but the parties that ruled and ruling the country until now nor the parliament itself ever remembered to bring forth laws governing the political parties system including election financing in the country. In my personal opinion, that was a democratic blunder that lead to seeping of increasing mud into the working of the political parties making more and more difficult for others to enter that area that lead and continues to be so to chaotic conditions that is what we are witnessing today.

It was like an engine filled with full steam and rolled out on the rails without the driver. The political parties mushroomed causing incalculable damage to the democratic structure with their invention of loopholes for defections from one party to another party just to enrich overnight. Today's political arena has become self-shaming and our democracy a jocosity. The victim continues to be the people, the economic development and the security of the country. The poverty and miserability of the poorer and the poorest of the poorer, which the rulers of the country thought would make them self-learning, self-earning and living with self-dignity, could only do gold coating that is now showing up the results.

Today, we are in the seventy second year of our country becoming Republic. First elections were held in 1951. There was no time to think how to evolve the election financing process, leaving the matter open ended that continued for seventy two years with maneuveuring both by the government and the political parties; what is discernable is government desire to loosen the control over the election financing while the political parties not only engaged, also embraced the funding the elections using money stashed through illegal means such as corruption, black money, money laundering, fake notes, drug trafficking, to mention few. This is continuing in the seventy second year of democracy, none bothered to look back other than by the Hon'ble Supreme Court of India, the Law Commission and the Election Commission of India. It is not disputed the efforts made by these great institutions to bring reforms and transparency in the election means and methods whereby the election system in our country could be said to be learnt to stand up on its own legs except as far as financing the elections,

A brief account of the efforts made on the election financing front so far is given below:

**Law Commission Report - Report No.255 on Electoral Reforms - GOVERNMENT OF INDIA - Electoral Reforms – March 2015 [Excerpts]:**

CHAPTER II ELECTION FINANCE REFORM

"……….2.1 Electoral reforms often contain proposals for reforming election funding, and candidate and party expenditure. This Chapter discusses the issue under three broad sub-groups: limits on political contributions and party and candidate expenditure; disclosure norms and requirements; and funding of elections. These issues are governed by the provisions of the RPA, the Conduct of Election Rules, 1961 (hereinafter "Election Rules"), the Companies Act, 2013, and the Income Tax Act, 1961 (hereinafter "IT Act").

2.2 The Current Law: A Summary Snapshot

2.3 The law regulating election finance in India has to be ascertained after examining the provisions of the RPA and Election Rules, the Companies Act, the IT Act, and the Foreign Contribution (Regulation) Act.

B. Need for Election Finance Reform

2.4 It is now well established that money plays a big role in politics, whether in the conduct, or campaigning, for elections. The Election Commission of India (hereinafter "ECI"), in its guidelines issued on 29th August 2014, recognised that "concerns have been expressed in various quarters that money power is disturbing the level playing field and vitiating the purity of elections. "What gives rise to these concerns about the role of big money in politics? These are not mere theoretical debates but are actual problems afflicting the electoral process in India. Money, often from illegitimate sources, results in "undisguised bullying" when it is used (both authorised and unauthorised) to buy muscle power, weapons, or to unduly influence voters through liquor, cash, gifts. Currency notes come first in containers, then in truckloads, moving to wholesale/small retail forms, and finally to suitcases and in people's pockets. Mr. Qureshi, in his book, documents instances of Returning Officers and Chief Electoral Officers in Tamil Nadu seizing crores of rupees in cash, bundles of saris and dhotis and hundreds of gas stoves. It is evident that money is used in myriad of forms in today's election process, but what are its consequences? Why is there a need for election finance reform? The answers to these questions are articulated below.

2.5  First, is the undeniable fact that financial superiority translates into electoral advantage, and so richer candidates and parties have a greater chance of winning elections? This is best articulated by the Supreme Court in Kanwar Lal Gupta v Amar Nath Chawla (hereinafter "Kanwar Lal Gupta"), when it explained the influence of money as follows: "...money is bound to play an important part in the successful prosecution of an election campaign. Money supplies "assets for advertising and other forms of political solicitation that increases the candidate's exposure to the public." Not only can money buy advertising and canvassing facilities such as hoardings, posters, handbills, brochures etc. and all the other paraphernalia of an election campaign, but it can also provide the means for quick and speedy communications and movements and sophisticated campaign techniques and is also "a substitute for energy" in that paid workers can be employed where volunteers are found to be insufficient. The availability of large funds does ordinarily tend to increase the number of votes a candidate will receive. If, therefore, one political party or individual has larger resources available to it than another individual or political party, the former would certainly, under the present system of ECI, Guidelines on Transparency and Accountability in Party Funds and Election Expenditure, No. 76/PPEMS/Transparency/2013, 29th August 2014, conducting elections, have an advantage over the latter in the electoral process".

2.6  The Supreme Court, in its 2014 decision in Ashok Shankarrao Chavan v Madhavrao Kinhalkar (hereinafter "Ashok Shankarrao Chavan"), repeated this line of reasoning, where it highlighted how money was used to buy votes:

"55. In recent times, when elections are being held it is widely reported in the Press and Media that money power plays a very vital role. Going by such reports and if it is true then it is highly unfortunate that many of the voters are prepared to sell their votes for a few hundred rupees.

...... This view of ours is more so apt in the present day context, wherein money power virtually controls the whole field of election and that people are taken for a ride by such unscrupulous elements who want to gain the status of a Member of Parliament or the State Legislature by hook or crook."

2.7 Second, and connected to the above point is the issue of equality and equal footing between richer and poorer candidates. This can be explained with the help of the Court's observations in Kanwar Lal Gupta on the rationale behind expenditure limits:

"...it should be open to individual or any political party, howsoever small, to be able to contest an election on a footing of equality with any other individual or political party, howsoever rich and well financed it may be, and no individual or political party should be able to secure an advantage over others by reason of its superior financial strength."

2.8 Similarly, in Ashok Shankarrao Chavan, 11 the Supreme Court noted that:

"...it is a hard reality that if one is prepared to expend money to unimaginable limits only then can he be preferred to be nominated as a candidate for such membership, as against the credentials of genuine and deserving candidates."

2.9 The Court's observations are not made in vacuum. A simple perusal of the Lok Sabha 2014 candidates reveals that 27% (or 2208 candidates) of all the candidates were "crorepati candidates," and the average asset of each of the 8163 candidates was Rs. 3.16 crores. The percentage of crorepati candidates increased from 16% in 2009 Lok Sabha elections. Third, in complete contravention to the various laws and ECI notifications, there is widespread prevalence of black money, bribery. [ SCC 99. 10 (1975) 3 SCC 646. 11 (2014) 7 SCC 99.]

"48. It is common knowledge as is widely published in the Press and Media that nowadays in public elections payment of cash to the electorate is rampant and the Election Commission finds it extremely difficult to control such a menace. There is no truthfulness in the attitude and actions of the contesting candidates in sticking to the requirement of law, in particular to Section 77 and there is every attempt being made to violate the restrictions imposed in the matter of incurring election expenses with a view to woo the electorate concerned and thereby, gaining their votes in their favour by corrupt means viz by purchasing the votes.....

56. It is unfortunate that those who are really interested in the welfare of society and who are incapable of indulging in any such corrupt practices are virtually side-lined and are treated as totally ineligible for contesting the elections." ...........

2.12 Candidates and political parties have devised ingenious ways to disguise the illegitimate sources and expenditure of money by holding community feasts, organising birthday parties and marriages, giving costly gifts, or topping up mobile phones. Money is sometimes transferred through cash packets slipped in newspapers, through rural moneylenders, pawnbrokers or by organising 'fake aartis'. In fact, Tamil Nadu gained notoriety for the "Thirumangalam formula", when Rs. 5000 was paid per voter in Thirumangalam in Madurai in the 2009 bye-elections and other methods were used to distribute money and earn votes.

2.13 Fourth, the current system tolerates, or at least does not prevent, lobbying and capture, where a sort of quid pro quo transpires between big donors and political parties/candidates. While the problem of bribery, corrupt practices and black money are important, to some extent, they have distracted from the larger problem of election finance and the capture of government by private individuals and interest groups. The Supreme Court, citing a note from Harvard Law Review on campaign finance regulation, articulated this concern in Kanwar Lal Gupta observing:

"A less debatable objective of regulating campaign funds is the elimination of dangerous financial pressures on elected officials. Even if contributions are not motivated by an expected return in political favours, the legislator cannot overlook the effects of his decisions on the sources of campaign funds."

2.14 Similarly, Justice Kennedy in McConnell v Federal Election Commission very well, when recognising the problem of solicitation as a corruption, said:

"The making of a solicited gift is a quid both to the recipient of the money and to the one who solicits the payment (by granting his request). Rules governing candidates' or officeholders' solicitation of contributions are, therefore, regulations governing their receipt of quids.

2.15 Unregulated, or under-regulated, election financing leads to two types of capture: the first involves cases where the industry / private entities use money to ensure less stringent regulation, and the money used to finance elections eventually leads to favourable policies. The second involves cases of "deeper capture", where through their disproportionate and self-serving 16 Qureshi; supra note 1, at 263-267.

2.16 Thus, lobbying and capture give undue importance to big donors and certain interest groups, at the expense of the ordinary citizen and violates what the Indian Supreme Court terms, "the right of equal participation [of each citizen in the polity]."22 In Kanwar Lal Gupta, the Supreme Court expressed its views on this issue when it stated:

"The other objective of limiting expenditure is to eliminate, as far as possible, the influence of big money in electoral process. If there were no limit on expenditure political parties would go all out for collecting contributions and obviously the largest contributions would be from the rich and the affluent who constitute but a fraction of the electorate. It is likely that some elected representatives would tend to share the views of the wealthy supporters of their political party, either because of shared background and association, increased access or subtle influences which condition their thinking.

2.17 Finally, the argument for election finance reform is premised on a more philosophical argument that large campaign donations, even when legal, amount to what Lessig terms "institutional corruption", which compromise the political morality norms of a republican democracy. Here, instead of direct exchange of money or favours, candidates alter their views and convictions in a way that attracts the most funding. This change of perception leads to an erosion of public trust, which in turn affects the quality of democratic engagement..................

29.4 The first committee to deal with the issue of public funding was the Dinesh Goswami Committee on Electoral Reforms in 1990, which advocated for partial state funding of elections in the form of limited in-kind support for vehicle fuel (which is a primary campaign expense); rental charges for microphones; issuance of voter identity slips; and additional copies of electoral rolls.

29.5 In 1993, the Confederation of Indian Industries constituted a Task Force that recommended that elections be funded in effect, through a tax on the industry. This would involve the funds to be raised either through a cess on excise duty, or through corporate contributions to an election fund pool managed by the State, which would then be distributed via a pre-decided formula based on vote and seat share.

29.6 The 1998 Indrajit Gupta Committee Report on State Funding of Elections endorsed state funding of elections, seeing "full justification constitutional, legal as well as on ground of public interest" in order to establish a fair playing field for parties with less money power. The Committee envisaged a phased introduction of public funding, given the economic conditions of the country in 1998, beginning with in-kind state subsidies (and no cash) such as rent-free office space, free telephone facilities, electoral rolls' copies, loudspeakers, specified quantities of fuel, food packets, and airtime (both on state and private media). Gradually, the Committee envisioned a transition to full state funding, along with monetary provision via the creation of a central-governed Election Fund, whose funding would be provided by the Centre and the states together. However, the Committee excluded independent candidates from the benefits of state funding and required parties to submit audited accounts and tax returns to avail the benefits.

29.7 This was followed soon after by the Report of the Law Commission in 1999 on the Reform of Electoral Laws, which endorsed the Government of India, REPORT OF THE COMMITTEE ON ELECTORAL REFORMS, May 1990 (hereinafter "Dinesh Goswami Report"), Government of India, COMMITTEE ON THE STATE FUNDING OF ELECTIONS, December 1998. Ideas of the Indrajit Gupta Committee Report on partial state funding, as a first step towards total funding given that the latter was not "feasible" in light of the "prevailing economic conditions". However, the Commission clarified that given that the underlying premise of state funding was the elimination of the influence of money power, corporate funding and black money support, it was:

"... absolutely essential before the idea of state funding (whether partial or total) is resorted, the provisions suggested in this report relating to political parties (including the provisions ensuring internal democracy, internal structures) and maintenance of accounts, their auditing and submission to Election Commission are implemented.....The state funding, without the aforesaid pre-conditions, would merely become another source of funds for the political parties and candidates at the cost of public exchequer."

29.8 In 2001, the NCRWC {National Commission to review the working of the Constitution} concurred with the 1999 Law Commission report that the question of permitting state funding "should not even arise" without: "an effective systemic acceptance of full audit of party funds including a full audit of campaign funds, deletion of explanation 1 to section 77(1) of the Representation of People Act 1951, a fool proof mechanism to deter expenditure violations, and until the government is convinced that these improvements have been institutionalised and are no longer being breached."

29.9 To do so otherwise, would simply add to the burden on the Exchequer and taxpayers without any public or systematic benefit. The NCRWC's views were premised on the failure of the existing mechanisms of partial or indirect state funding in reducing campaign expenditure and the need to bring in transparency mechanisms first.

29.10 Similarly, the ARC's 2007 {Administrative Reforms Commission} Report on "Ethics in Governance" also recommended partial state funding of elections to reduce the scope of "illegitimate and unnecessary funding" of elections expenses.

U.S.A.120 • No direct or indirect public funding for political parties • No public subsidy for congressional elections • Partial public funding available for Presidential primary candidates in the form of primary matching grants (up to $250 by an individual) and general elections grants (to the individual candidates) - this results in a ceiling on expenditure • On 3rd April 2014, Present Obama signed a law (Public Law No. 113- 94) to end public funding of national nominating conventions to eliminate taxpayer financing of political party conventions.

U.K.12

• Modest public funding of political parties • Political parties receive direct public funding over each financial year for policy development purposes up to a total of £2mn on the basis of current legislative representation • Indirect support is provided to parties based on the number of candidates put forward in the election, which includes free broadcasting time for party political broadcasts, free postage, meeting rooms, and mail shot to electors.

German • Public funding to national political parties with tax credits, matching grants (of the amount earned by parties from transparent, private sources), and flat grants to parties based on their past performance • Absolute ceiling of public subsidy to all parties, with no subsidy for local party organisations or individual candidates • The state "request[s] partial approval" of public subsidy from the tax payers or party supporters, although threshold for access to public funding is "lower than anywhere else in the world" • Public subsidies not earmarked for any specific purpose • Indirect support in the form of free media access based on the duration and continuity of electoral participation; exemption from income, inheritance, and property tax; and caucus subsidies Italy124 • Public subsidies are a "major source" of funding elections, although have been restricted to election campaign activities since 1993 • Funding is distributed according to the votes polled and is given to candidates • The state "request[s] partial approval" of public subsidy from the tax payers or party supporters • Indirect, in-kind subsidy in the form of free media access and state aid for radio and newspapers, and reduced rates for sending electoral propaganda material by post to voters.

Sweden • "High level" of public subsidies exist for parties at various levels, with each party being given a base amount at the sub-national level, along with additional state aid to party sub-organisations and to party media based on part performance and current representation • General subsidy is given to parties, their secretariat and party groups in Parliament alongside regional and local subsidies • Public subsidies are given for general party administration and are not earmarked for any specific purpose • Indirect subsidies include media access and the party affiliated press receive public support

Australia • Political parties receive direct public funding during the election period and between elections • Funding is not ear-marked for a specific purpose and depends on the performance of the party at the previous election.

(iii) Recommendations

2.30.1 A quick perusal of the recommendations of various committees on state funding of elections and comparative provisions makes it clear that complete public funding of elections or political parties in India is not a practical option; instead, indirect state subsidy is a better alternative for various reasons provided below.

2.30.2 First, prevailing economic conditions make it impossible for complete state funding of elections. Full funding should prohibit candidates and parties from accessing alternative sources of money both during election campaigns and in the inter-election period. If full funding is a seen as a replacement for the pervasiveness of big money in elections, then it will have to be substantial enough to stop the prevalence of black money. Given the amount being spent on elections today, and the alternative use of money on poverty reduction, health, education, food etc.; it seems highly unlikely that the centre can provide such money.

2.30.3 Second, for similar reasons of financial burdens, monetary constraints, and weak enforcement, a system of matching grants as in Germany and the United Kingdom are not possible. Corporate grants are often enormous and hence will be difficult to match, while a lot of big donors give money in black, and hence will only to serve to increase the amount of total funding available with parties.

2.30.4 Third, currently, there is no clear picture on the cost of financing elections given the weak disclosure of expenditure by political parties and contributions by corporates and big donors. A system of complete monetary state support will work only if it replaces the actual demand for money in election campaigns and day-to-day administration of political parties. Hence any state support has to be in kind support, and not in cash because unless the current system satisfies the total requirement of parties, monetary support will only serve to increase party spending and invite uninterested or opportunistic candidates and parties.

2.30.5 Fourth, as the Law Commission Report in 1999 and the NCRWC Report in 2001 acknowledge, reforms on state funding of election have to be preceded by campaign finance reform; improvement in transparency, disclosure and audit provisions; decriminalisation of politics; and the introduction of inner party democracy. Funding parties (instead of candidates) with little internal democracy will only strengthen the power of the leadership and the benefits of public funding might not extend to the rank and file of the party.

2.30.6 Fifth, there are various associated problems with state funding such as the possible undermining of the independence of the parties due to their financial reliance on the exchequer, and can be especially problematic for new parties. Even otherwise, the distribution of public money may reduce party incentives to maintain their social base and generate funds through political mobilisation. Moreover, as the comparative table shows {Author's Note: Not reproducible}, in most countries subsidies are determined on the basis of past performance or current representation, and thus automatically discourage new (and weaker) parties. In case of current representation, money will have to be given upfront and subsequently, overpaid parties will have to reimburse the State, while underpaid parties will be reimbursed by the state after the results.

2.30.7 Finally, public funding of elections, including existing provisions on partial in-kind funding only extends to registered parties and hence excludes independent candidates, whilst simultaneously encouraging frivolous candidatures, with the sole intention of gaining access to public funds.

2.30.8 Instead, as the Indrajit Gupta Committee noted in its 1998 report, efforts should be made to curb the costs of campaigning by limiting or regulating the use and location of cut outs and banners; hoardings and posters; the number of public meetings; the use of vehicles during campaigns, and the publicity from moving vehicles. This will help reduce the cost of elections, although it may not reduce the incentives to raise election funds and abuse power.

2.30.9 With respect to indirect in-kind subsidy, reference should be made to the British practice to increase the quantum of such subsidies to include free broadcasting time on private channels, free postage and meeting rooms, access to public town halls, the cost of printing, and even provision of specified quantities of fuel and food packets. Thus, by providing a "financial floor" to parties and candidates, it reduces the cost of elections, without providing parties with liquid cash to spend in addition to their resources.

2.30.10 On the basis of the above, the following recommendations are suggested:

1. Currently, a system of complete state funding of elections or of matching grants, wherein the government matches the private funding (by donors or corporates) raised by political parties, are not feasible given the economic conditions and developmental problems of the country.

2. Given the high cost of elections and the improbability of being able to replace the actual demand for money, the existing system of giving indirect in-kind subsidies instead of giving money via a National Election Fund, should continue.

3. The wording of Section 78B of the RPA permits the Central Government, in consultation with the ECI, to supply certain items to the electors or the candidates and this provision can be used to expand the in-kind subsidy to include free public meeting rooms, certain printing costs, free postage etc.

4. Any reform in state funding should be preceded by reforms such as the decriminalisation of politics, the introduction of inner party democracy, electoral finance reform, transparency and audit mechanisms, and stricter implementation of anti-

corruption laws so as to reduce the incentive to raise money and abuse power………………………".

**"Political Funding In India**

Across the world, political parties need access to money in order to reach out to the electorate, explain their policies and receive inputs from people. And in order to do the same, parties resort to political party funding. One of the primary sources of this funding is voluntary contributions made by individuals. Besides this, corporates pay hefty donations to parties in different forms. Foreign aid is another source.

What is Political Funding? ♣ Political Funding implies the methods that political parties use to raise funds to finance their campaign and routine activities. ♣ A political party needs money to pitch itself, its objectives, its intended actions to get votes for itself.

Statutory Provisions: ♣ Section 29B of the Representation of the People Act (RPA) entitles parties to accept voluntary contributions by any person or company, except a Government Company. ♣ Section 29C of the RPA mandates political parties to declare donations that exceed 20,000 rupees. Such a declaration is made by making a report and submitting the same to the EC. Failure to do so on time disentitles a party from tax relief under the Income Tax Act, 1961.

Methods that Indian Political Parties use to raise the funds: ♣ Individual Persons: Section 29B of RPA allows political parties to receive donations from individual persons. ♣ State/Public Funding: Here, the government provides funds to parties for election related purposes. State Funding is of two types: Direct Funding: The government provides funds directly to the political parties. Direct funding by tax is prohibited in India. Indirect Funding: It includes other methods except direct funding, like free access to media, free access to public places for rallies, free or subsidized transport facilities. It is allowed in India in a regulated manner.

Corporate Funding: In India, donations by corporate bodies are governed under the Companies Act, 2013. Section 182 of the Act provides that: A company needs to be at least three years old to be able to donate to a political party. Companies can donate up to 7.5% of average net profits made during three simultaneous preceding financial years. Such contributions must be disclosed in the company's profit and loss account. Approval of the Board of Directors needs to be obtained for the contribution. If a company violates said provisions, it may have to pay a fine up to 5 times the amount contributed and every officer of the company who is in default shall be punishable with imprisonment for a term which may extend to six months.

Note: The government has removed the cap of 7.5% (seven point five percent) on corporate contributions to the political parties with the Finance Act, 2017. The same Act also removed the obligation to report such contributions in the company's profit and loss account.

Electoral Trusts: A non-profit company created in India for orderly receipt of voluntary contributions from any person like an individual or a domestic company. According to the Election Commission Guidelines, all electoral trusts formed after January 2013 are required to declare details of the money received and disbursed. The Central Government rules mandate these firms to donate 95% of their total income to registered political parties in a financial year.

Issues with Political Funding: ♣ One of the biggest disadvantages of the corporate funding is the use of fake companies to route black money. ♣ Influence of people and companies over political parties to which they provide funds. ♣ There are various gaps in Indian rules, the benefit of which political parties take to avoid any kind of reporting. ♣ Hidden sources of funding lead to more spending of funds in election campaigns, thus impacting the economy of the country.

Recent Steps Taken: ♣ In March, 2018, the government passed a key amendment to the Foreign Contribution Regulation Act, 2010 allowing foreign companies to fund political parties in India. ♣ Introduction of Electoral Bonds: The government notified the Electoral Bond Scheme on 2nd January, 2018 to establish and cleanse the system of political funding in the country. An electoral bond is a bearer instrument like a Promissory Note. It can be purchased by any citizen of India or a body incorporated in India to donate to the political party of their choice. Donor's name is not there on the bond. These bonds can be used for making donations to the political parties registered under Section 29A of the Representation of the People Act, 1951 and which have secured not less than one per cent of the votes polled in the last general election to the House of the People or a Legislative Assembly.

CORPORATE FUNDING OF ELECTIONS: A QUICK SNAPSHOT The history of corporate funding of political parties in India goes back to the freedom movement. The Birlas were one of the leading donors of the Indian National Congress. After Independence, the business class as a whole secured some leverage over the shaping of the Congress government's economic policy. It contributed the majority of donations towards poll spending in the post-independence era. In the 1960s, the Congress and the Swatantra Party — the latter started by C. Rajagopalachari as a party advocating free enterprise — were the main beneficiaries of donations from big conglomerates such as the Tatas and the Birlas, who together accounted for 34 percent of the total company contributions between 1962 and 1968.

In 1969, the Indira Gandhi government imposed a complete ban on corporate funding (via deletion of the Section 293A of the Companies Act) to break the nexus between politics and businesses and also to check the popularity of the centre -right Swatantra Party by drying it off finances. However, this proved counterproductive. To beat the ban, political parties started raising funds by publishing souvenirs, in which advertisements were placed by the business houses. Businesses also resorted to tax evasions, black-market operations and other illegal mechanisms due to political compulsions and the threat of selective raids and nationalisation. This period also saw the rise of "briefcase politics" through which vast amounts of black money was transferred into the Congress Party account. In the era of license permit raj, this arrangement also suited the businesses. However, a forward-looking Rajiv Gandhi government, intending to end the culture of license permit raj, took a crucial decision of lifting the ban in 1985.

Recent changes on corporate funding laws: The post-liberalisation period has witnessed a steady rise in the corporate funding of elections through both the traditional route of contributing directly to political parties and through other institutional innovations like electoral trusts. A major change affecting corporate donations was brought in 2013 by amending the Companies Act. This legislation raised the earlier 5 per cent limit to 7.5 per cent, allowing corporates to donate up to 7.5 percent of the net average profits earned in the preceding three years. While this was done to allow more funding space for political parties, the 2017 Finance Act, brought by the current National Democratic Alliance (NDA), removed the earlier limit (by amending the Section 182 of Companies Act 2013). In addition, changes were made in the Foreign Contribution Regulation Act (FCRA), 2010 via the 2018 Finance Bill to allow foreign companies registered in India to make political donations. Two other recent important developments with direct links to corporate funding are the legal basis for Electoral Trusts and Electoral Bonds. While the electoral trusts scheme was floated as early as 1996 by the Tata Group, this innovative form of corporate donations received legal sanctity in 2013 by bringing these entities under the Section 25 of the Companies Act, 1956. The electoral bonds scheme was introduced through the Finance Act 2017. It allows anyone, including corporates, to donate to political parties via electoral bonds. To sum up, laws and institutional forms related to corporate donations have gone through massive transformations since 2013.

Key trends in corporate donations: How are corporates/businesses funding political parties in India? Where do major political parties stand in terms of donations from corporates and businesses? A quick glance at the data compiled by the Association of Democratic Reforms (ADR) makes it easily discernible that in the last decade, corporate donations are on an upswing. From a measly Rs 26 crore in 2004-05, total donations through various corporate sources have climbed up to Rs 422 crore in 2017-18 (see Figure 1). Six national political parties — the BJP, the Congress, the Nationalist Congress Party (NCP), the Bahujan Samaj

Party (BSP), the Communist Party of India (Marxist) and the Communist Party of India (CPI) — are the major recipients of corporates' political generosity (Figure 2).

Figure 1. Flow of corporate donations 2004-05 – 2017-18

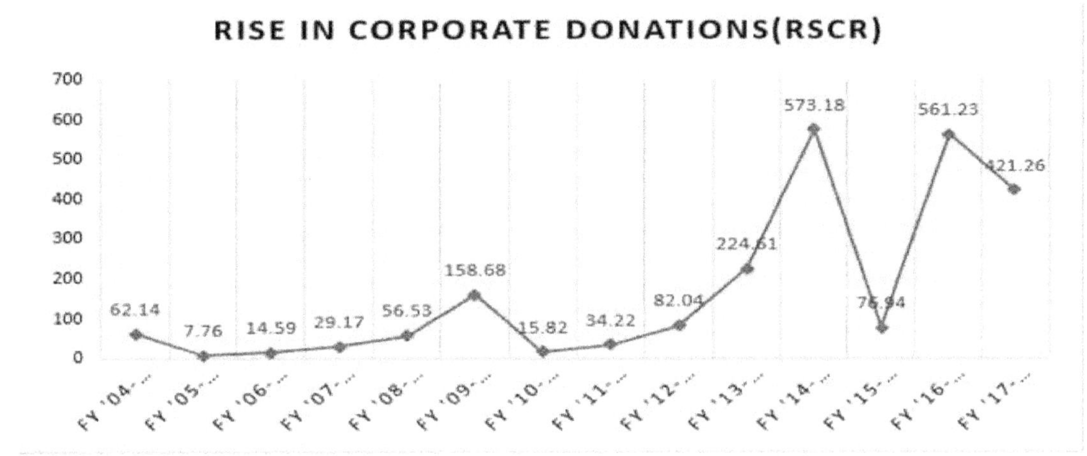

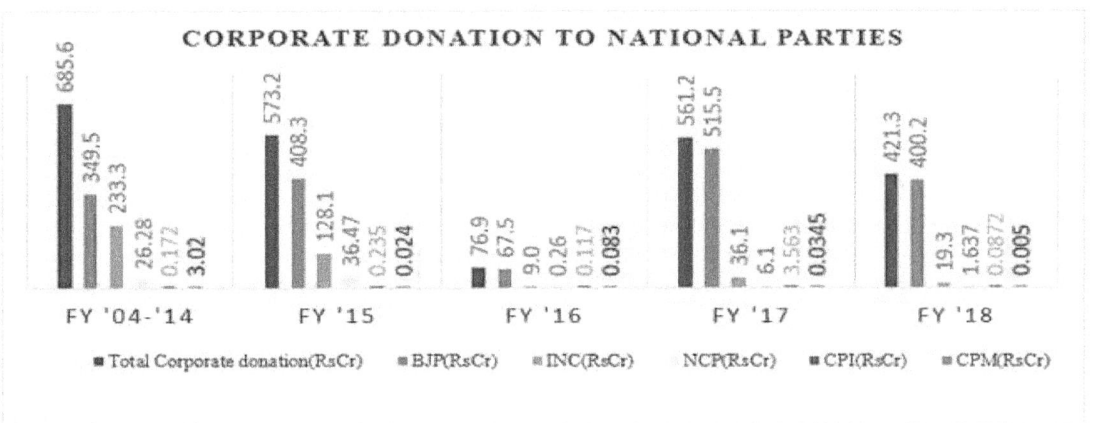

Source: Computed from ADR Data

Figure 2. Corporate donation to major national parties

Source: Computed from ADR Data

In terms of comparative figures of major parties, the BJP continues to have the lion's share in the entire pool of corporate funding (figure 2). The ruling party has captured as much as 92% of the total corporate donations in 2017-18. To interpret this in another way, corporates/businesses donated a mammoth 12 times more money to the ruling BJP than to other national parties in 2017-18. A comparison of the two principal national parties — the BJP and the Congress — makes it even more interesting. The BJP received as much as Rs 400 crores of corporate donations while the Congress received only Rs 19 crores in 2018 (figure 3). Surprisingly, the BJP has been maintaining a complete domination over the Congress even when the latter was in power in the 2004-2014 period, while the gap between the parties have grown massively since 2013-14 (coinciding with the phenomenal rise of Narendra Modi).

One of the key reasons for this growing asymmetry in corporate donations is the fact that some of the richest electoral trusts have been donating generously to the BJP, than to other national parties (figure 4). It must be noted that the biggest share in corporate donations come from 18 registered electoral trusts. With electoral bonds (where more than 99.9% donations are from corporate donors) emerging as the popular channel of donations since its introduction in 2018, the asymmetry in corporate donations may widen to an unsustainable level (figure 4).

**Reason for public funding**

It is well known in political finance literature that excessive reliance on corporate funding can turn political and democratic processes into a plutocracy in the longer run. The recent changes in laws — particularly the removal of the 7.5 per cent cap in corporate donations, the amendment of the FCRA, 2010 allowing foreign companies registered in India to make political donation and the introduction of electoral bonds without the mandatory donors' identities — is likely to push the country toward a plutocracy. And even more worrisome is the growing asymmetry in corporate donations to major political parties. This will have much more serious implications for the health of democracy in India in the near term. There are sound empirics to suggest that money plays a disproportionate role in determining election outcomes in India and elsewhere. This is the precise reason why many democracies have gone for public funding mechanisms to provide a level playing field to all political parties — big, small, old and new ones. Equity in political finance is a hallmark of a healthy democracy. It is high time Indian policy makers take note of this worrisome development.

**Figure 3 Corporate Donations: the BJP vs. the Congress**

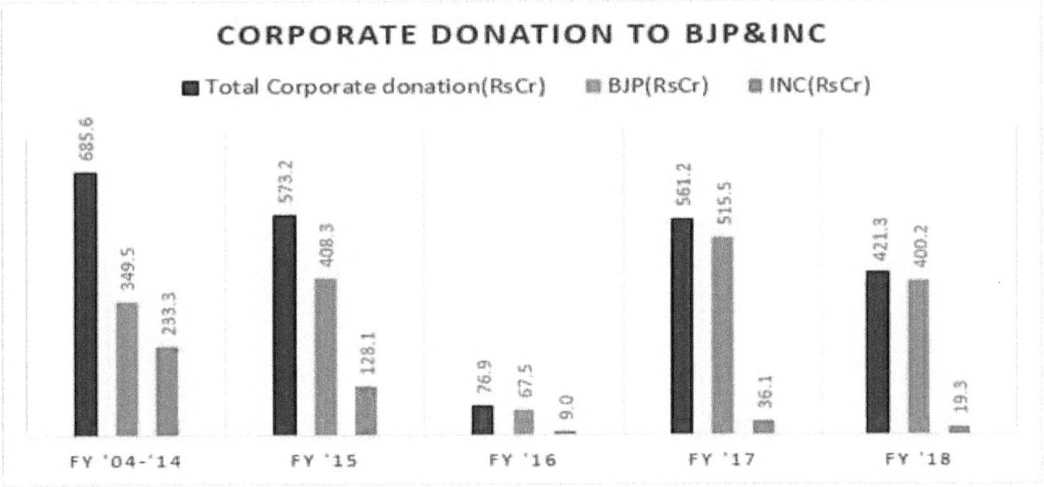

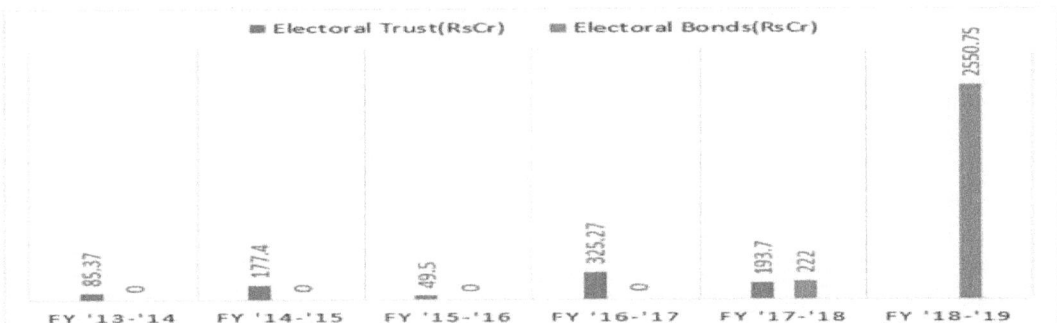

**Figure 4. Electoral Trusts vs. Electoral Bonds**

Source: Computed from ADR data" {Original Source: Dr. Bhim Rao Ambedkar College}

**Political finance needs tighter regulation and enforcement** {Financing Democracy {Published on February 04, 2016 Also available in: French - In series: OECD Public Governance Revi} posted on OECD Website. Excerpts:

Funding of Political Parties and Election Campaigns and the Risk of Policy Capture:

The recent debate on the role of money in politics has shed the light on the challenges of political finance regulations. What are the risks associated with the funding of political parties and election campaigns? Why are existing regulatory models still insufficient to tackle those risks? What are the links between money in politics and broader frameworks for integrity in the public sector? This report addresses these three questions and provides a Framework on Financing Democracy, designed to shape the global debate and provide policy options as well as a mapping of risks. It also features country case studies of Canada, Chile, Estonia, France, Korea, Mexico, United Kingdom, Brazil and India, providing in-depth analysis of their political finance mechanisms and challenges in different institutional settings.

Many economically advanced countries are failing to fully enforce regulations on political party funding and campaign donations or are leaving loopholes that can be exploited by powerful private interest groups, according to a new OECD report.

Financing Democracy: Funding of Political Parties and Election Campaigns and the Risk of Policy Capture says that private donors frequently use loans, membership fees and third-party funding to circumvent spending limits or to conceal donations. Tightening regulation and applying sanctions more rigorously would help to restore public trust at a time when voters in advanced economies are showing disillusionment with political parties and fear that democratic processes can be captured by private interest groups.

Policy making should not be for sale to the highest bidder," said OECD Secretary-General Angel Gurría, launching the Organisation's first report on political financing at a meeting of the OECD Global Parliamentary Network, a forum for legislators from member and partner countries to compare policies and discuss best practices. "When policy is influenced by wealthy donors, the rules get bent in favour of the few and against the interests of the many. Upholding rigorous standards in political finance is a key part of our battle to reduce inequality and restore trust in democracy," he said.

Many countries struggle to define and regulate "third-party" campaigning by organisations or individuals who are not political parties or candidates, enabling election spending to be channelled through supposedly independent committees and interest groups. Only a handful of countries have regulations on third-party campaigning, and these regulations vary in strictness.

Globalisation is complicating the regulation of political party funding as multinational companies and wealthy foreign individuals are increasingly integrated with domestic business interests. Where limits and bans on foreign and corporate funding exist, disclosure of donor identity is a vital deterrent to misuse of influence. While 17 of the 34 OECD countries ban anonymous donations to political parties, 13 only ban them above certain thresholds and four allow them.

Even when donations are not anonymous, countries have differing rules about disclosing donor identity. In nine OECD countries political parties are obliged to publically disclose the identity of donors, while in the other 25 OECD countries parties do so on an ad-hoc basis.

Only 16 OECD countries have campaign spending limits for both parties and candidates. While such limits can prevent a spending race, challengers who generally need more funds to unseat an incumbent may be at a disadvantage in the other 18 countries.

Finally, a lack of independence or legal authority among some oversight institutions leaves big donors able to receive favours such as tax breaks, state subsidies, preferential access to public loans and procurement contracts.

The report recommends that:

- Countries should design sanctions against breaches of political finance regulations that are both proportionate and dissuasive.
- Countries should strike a balance between public and private political finance, bearing in mind that neither 100% private nor 100% public funding is desirable.
- Countries should aim for fuller disclosure with low thresholds, while taking privacy concerns of donors into consideration.
- Countries should focus on enforcing existing regulations, not adding new ones.
- Institutions responsible for enforcing political finance regulations should have a clear mandate, adequate legal power and the capacity to impose sanctions.
- Political finance regulations should focus on the whole cycle – the pre-campaign phase, the campaign period and the period after the elected official takes office.

"Table 1: Framework on Financing Democracy – Objectives, Policy Options, and Complications Overall Objective Policy Options and Remaining Complications Promoting a Level Playing Field Balancing direct and indirect public contributions Remaining complications include

1. Determining the eligibility threshold, and
2. Determining the allocation criteria. Framing private funding Remaining complications include preventing creative circumvention of regulations, and
3. Addressing the increasing complexities due to globalization. Applying spending limits. Remaining complications include
4. Determining the limit, and
5. Ensuring that challengers are not at a disadvantage.
6. Limiting privileged access to state resources.
7. Remaining complications include:
    i. The undetected illicit use of state resources by incumbents.
    ii. Ensuring Transparency and Accountability Requiring disclosure:
    iii. Comprehensive and timely reporting.

iv. Enabling scrutiny: timely, reliable and accessible reports.

v. Fostering a Culture of Integrity.

vi. Applying the integrity framework in the public sector: codes of conduct, disclosure provisions, and whistle-blower protection. Promoting standards of professionalism, integrity, and transparency in private donors: appropriate accounting practices, and a code of conduct. Ensuring Compliance and Review Assuring independent and efficient oversight: resources, methodologies, and authorities.

vii. Applying dissuasive and enforceable sanctions: confiscation, fines, and criminal charges. Regularly appraising the system: period review, involvement of stakeholders, identifying mitigation strategies. Supporting political parties: helping to comply with regulations, and better understand political finance. {Source: OECD Report Financing Democracy (2016); authors' analysis."

On occasional understanding basis of the methods followed by the different countries in the world on financial of elections, it could be inferred that most of them such as EU and OECD countries opted for a combinational process of financing the elections that includes public funding in various formats while some other countries including our own country are leaning heavily towards financing elections by the corporates and recognized trusts. This has acted and continue to act detrimental to the working of the democracy, as rightly pointed in the OECD report stated before, as sale policies which understanding is more scientifically and emphatically noted in the book: The book "LAW AND PUBLIC CHOICE-A Critical Introduction" authored by Daniel A. Farber and Philip P. Frickey makes critical analysis of legislative characters and public choice, some of which are reproduced below:

"The Impact of Interest Group Theory: One view of the political process is often called "pluralism." According to pluralists, legislative outcomes simply reflect private political power. Although it may be mechanical and rather disheartening, it is no new view that "the balance of …….group pressure is the existing state of society." Public law theorists who accept the empirical accuracy of this conception have two options. They may celebrate pluralism. Or, if they find pluralism empirically accurate but morally repulsive, they may favor judicial activism to protect those who lose in political power struggle. Either way, trying to promote legislative deliberation is useless, since the mechanistic process of legislation leaves no room for a thoughtful legislative response………..

……..Public choice models often treat the legislative process as a microeconomic system in which "actual political choices are determined by the efforts of individuals and groups to further their own interests, efforts that have been labelled "rent-seeking". Thus, "the basic assumption is that taxes, subsidies, regulations, and other political instruments are used to raise the welfare of more influential group." Although this assumption is obviously simplistic, its very simplicity creates the possibility of constructing powerful formal models. The similarity between pluralism and these economic models is obvious.

Several leading legal scholars have been influenced by this vision of the role of the special interests. The economic theory of legislation recounted by William Landes and Ricdhard Posner is firmly grounded in that tradition:

"In the economists' version of the interest-group theory of government, legislation is supplied to groups or coalitions that outbid rival seekers of favourable legislation. The price that the winning group bids is determined both by the value of legislative protection to the group's members and the group's ability to overcome the free-rider problems that plague coalitions. Payments take the form of campaign contributions, votes, and implicit promises of future favors, and sometime outright bribes. In short, legislation is "sold" by the legislature and "bought" by the beneficiaries of the legislation."...............

The suggested framework for the financing elections in India, having taken note of the recommendations of the Law Commission and the guidelines and codes issued by the ECI, endeavours to submit a different approach to funding of the elections within the existing available financial resources to the political parties and the candidates and without the need for the state raising additional financial resources or for incurring any additional expenditure. The recommendations of the Law Commission stated before as well as the intent of the ECI on state funding the elections in India are more leaned towards presumptive understanding that the state would need huge financial resources to meet its obligation there for. The suggested framework, on the other hand, finds the scope for the funding the elections using the same funds that are lawfully permitted to the political parties and candidates presently.

It may also be submitted that the concerns expressed the OECD 'Framework on financing of democracy' noted before have already been duly taken into consideration and incorporated in the Framework included in Part 02 of this book, the variation being that in the Framework under consideration for election financing in our country has been guided by the concept of 'pooling' of the as available financial resources for the elections financing into a 'Fund" so that it does not call for any additional financial resources to be sought from the state thereby there is no ground to look down the proposed Framework under the plea that the Framework involves any additional financial burden on state which is also one of the main reasons some of the committees and ECI hesitated state financing the elections as noted in the Law Commission Report stated before.

The entire object is to rationalize the system into a centrally created and controlled point and open up much needed playing field among the political parties. Today, it is absent because unholy nexus and quid pro quo that exists among the political fiefdom and the crony capitalism where around revolves the business interests more than the national interests. By pooling all the financial resources made available to the political parties from various sources with highest contributions by the corporates suggested in the Framework minimizes, if not eliminates, the 'interest groups' inference or influence in the policy consideration and in all other important matters of governance. This is considered practical and pragmatic from democratic interests point of view with necessary amendments to the provisions of the existing relevant laws and rules regarding election financing to the political parties such that the same financial resources are directed to be contributed to the designated National Fund, suggested in the Framework and regulating the Fund according to the eligibility criteria and governing conditions as have been proposed therein. **"Make the most of the best and the best of the worst, and keep your standards high. Never settle for anything less than you deserve or are capable of achieving. Roy T. Bennett, The Light in the heart"**

'The Representation of the People Act, 1950 and 1951{Section 123: Corrupt Practices} is attributable to the candidates contesting the election from the constituencies. While ECI has issued several guidelines, Code of Conduct and so on from time to time applicable to the party and the candidates in the election, it overlooked the need also for informing the voters the definition of corrupt practices that embrace several kinds of corrupt practices in an appropriate manner so that the voters are also aware in advance the kinds of corrupt practices the candidates are likely to resort to during the election to enable them to have basic knowledge of those practices and be watchful and sensitive to detect them and instantly bring to the notice of the election authorities at the site that would help catching the culprit red-handed. ECI also needs to ensure adequate safeguards to protect such informer in the constituency from threats to his or her life. Such a move on the part of ECI also creates psychological fear among the candidates and deters them to think twice before embarking upon corrupt and illicit acts.

The provisions in the said Act on this subject matter should be made available to the citizens {voters} in all the officially recognized languages which would go a long way to educate them. How this missed the kind attention of the ECI during all these years needs to be considered by the ECI and do the needful for the future. Earliest it is acted upon by ECI would be beneficial to the democratic functioning. This would create a new awareness among the voters and establishes a linkage between voters and the candidates as to what kind of unlawful and illegal deeds and acts are being done by the candidates. In the absence of the knowledge of the governing provisions regarding corrupt practices, the voters also become almost dumb for; they cannot open their mouth which would invite mockery from the candidates labelling them as illiterate supposed to have no knowledge of the corrupt practices.

Today, illiteracy has substantially been reduced and level playing platform exists in urban, semi-urban and rural areas. Youths are busy in acquiring newer learning process, educating themselves to a respectful level and using their knowledge to understand the corrupt practices if they are able to know them. The RPA 1951 is mainly maintained by the practising lawyers. If the voter goes to a lawyer to consult him about the corrupt practices, the voter would have to pay certain charges, there being no free services when dealing with the lawyer.

The crux of the matter in the elections is voting by the people whereas the corrupt practices stated before are considered to be relevant only for the candidates. This understanding fails to fulfil full extent of the spirit and object intended to be achieved under the provisions aforesaid unless the same are also known to the voters in the language they are used to without which it would be like beating the drum one side keeping the other side open. A simili to this is a person was crossing a road and another person driving the car sounding the horn bugle like, yet the person on the road was not aware of what was happening. The driver of the car came to the person on the road and asked why he is not moving away to which he replied I am deaf. This common sense went beyond the thoughts of the driving person. That is what we have made the voters as deaf as also blind to know what all is happening around in the election process. That should compel the ECI to also inform the voters the provisions aforesaid sections in their vernacular language which is expected to work like an automatic break of a car

The government needs to appreciate the urgency for expeditious legislation of the recommendations made by the ECI and the Law Commission pending for nearly five years. Financing of election needs to be rethought about earliest to bring fairness and transparency. Lot of reforms continued to be made in the election process, equal attention has not been paid to reforms in financing election, gradually eroding the faith reposed by the people in the governance. There has hardly been any consultation process with the political parties and the public on this so far rather there had been unilateral policies being brought up for the benefit of the political parties opening opportunities for concealing the sources of financing the elections. The state is becoming a party to this process justifying it when ECI objected to certain recent amendments {in 2016} but with no concern from the government.

The government is not supposed to supersede the ECI in matters involving sanity of elections and public interest, not even prior consultations. It reflects ignorance of the government to recognize the existence of an independent body exclusively entrusted with the duties and responsibilities on matters of elections. Question is could the government independently act by itself as it wishes to relax laws intended for transparency and fairness in the public with sole object of increasing financing sources for the political parties through unfair means? This is blindness towards fairness and transparency on a matter concerning high public interest. Does it not amount to undermining the authority of ECI by the government when the reservations expressed in writing by the ECI to the government were put aside without any valid reasons? Even if there is no express provision in the Representation of People Act, 1951on consultation process, it has to be construed as existing, ECI being the sole body for regulating the elections and all matters related thereto. The government expects ECI to consult it in accordance with the governing laws and on important policy matters as well.

According to R. Jagannathan, learned journalist and editor "Is state funding of elections affordable? The answer is a decisive yes, even if we set aside qualitative pay-offs coming in the form of better candidates and cleaner party funding. If we assume that each Lok Sabha constituency needs ₹5 crore of candidate funding, with the top three candidates sharing this booty in the ratio of their vote shares, 543 constituencies will cost ₹2,715 crore. This is an entirely acceptable level of spending for clean politics once in five years. It should even be possible to find these resources by stopping another kind of indirect distortion of the political process—the availability of₹5 crore annually for each Lok Sabha and Rajya Sabha candidate from Members of Parliament Local Area Development Scheme (MPLADS). The total cost of MPLADS funding for all MPs is nearly₹4,000 crore every year, and scrapping the scheme even for one year in an MP's five-year term will be enough to bankroll state funding of Lok Sabha candidates……….. Over the years, the scheme has acquired a momentum of its own, and has been extended not only to Rajya Sabha MPs (who have no constituencies to tend), but also many state assemblies. Put simply, this is a legalized way of allowing MPs and MLAs to shower money on their constituencies at state expense. It is not going to be easy to prise this lollipop away from the clasping hands of MPs, but it is worth a try. Even without it, however, there is no question that the time has come to experiment with state funding of elections." {Source: Mint 12 Feb, 2019}.

There seems some erroneous application of the provisions of the RBI Act, 1934 for issue Electoral Bonds. This is so because the powers assumed by the central government for issue of electoral bonds under subsection (3) of the RBI Act, 1934 do not fall within any of the central banking functions. On the other hand, Section 2 of the Government Securities Act, 2006 (The Public Debt Act, 1944 was an act of the Parliament of India which provided a legal framework for the issuance and servicing of government securities in India. It was considered outdated, and the Government Securities Act, 2006 was introduced to replace it). defines (f) "Government security" means a security created and issued by the Government for the purpose of raising a public loan or for any other purpose as may be notified by the Government in the Official Gazette and having one of the forms mentioned in section 3; Section 3 of the same Act defines Forms of Government securities. (ii) a bearer bond payable to bearer; (a) "agent" means a scheduled bank within the meaning of clause (e) of section 2 of the Reserve Bank of India Act, 1934, or any other person specified as such; "constituents' subsidiary general ledger account" means a subsidiary general ledger account opened and maintained with the Bank by an agent on behalf of the constituents of such agent.

The central government enjoyed powers to issue 'electoral bonds' under the provisions of the Government Securities Act, 2006 and it would have been appropriate if the same had been issued under that Act rather than under the RBI Act, 1934, having regard to the fact that 'electoral bond' comes within the meaning of financing election by the political parties and not within the meaning of central RBI functions specified in the said Act. The matter is subjudice; I refrain from commenting on this matter any further.

Views expressed by the various organizations and individuals noted support state funding of the elections. Damage has been done to the fabric of democracy; continuance of which would amount to willfully ignoring the credence of the constitution, why it was not done so far, there being no bar as such, is another matter for which there is no information in the public domain and therefore, only the government could be able to explain. However, absence of this made the election system to go out of control. Elections have now become synonymous with money and muscle power. The democracy in our country has been functioning within many limitations for the last seventy two years; however, prevailing financing of elections has upturned the faith and has become source of all sins.

Existing practice has been made permanent as if the state has no alternative or the state does not want to think about the same at all. As noticeable, the state seems to be more interested in promoting and encouraging the existing system; if that is so; how the society or the people of the country would be able assume elections as fair and transparent elections? Or, does the state want that the present financing system is an accepted practice, fair and transparent, citizens should not question it, the political parties employ it as a right means of financing and the governance would be conducted by the party winning the elections? What a citizen could do under these conditions? At best, go to the highest Court of Law at own cost. Why we are indifferent to ourselves when we know what we are doing about financing election cannot stand to moral and ethical test? Or, should we say moral and ethical tests are nothing to do with election financing?

It is seen from the available material that the countries opted for state funding of the election have been following different methods for funding the political parties/candidates and, as such, there is no uniform method available. The methods followed by the other countries consist of subsidies or making available of funds by the states. These methods, as noticed, might have been considered appropriate by the countries considering their size and voting population. Our country being the largest democracy in the world calls for evolving its own method for state funding to the political parties. It is a matter of concern and perplex to note here the governments which ruled this country for seventy two years never thought of the need for state funding the election with openness and transparency even being well aware of how the illegitimate money and muscle power had been prevailing and persisting the election process cutting at the very root of the democratic functioning and creating chaos.

Question that begs answer from the political parties which ruled this country until now as to why they placed and continue to place their self-serving interests above the country's interests jeopardizing the country's democracy architected by the founding fathers of our constitution? Didn't it strike to them all through these years that the country stood above the political parties; the political parties are the products under a specific Act made under the Constitution; and stabilization of the democratic system was more paramount for their own survival? Are we not aware of what has been happening even today threatening the democratic fabric warned by Dr. Ambedkar in the last speech to the Constituent Assembly that it could happen once we place self-interest before service to the country? Democracy was attained and handed over to the generations which would continue in years to come but who would build the fortress to safeguard the democracy - are we to remain asleep or wake up to the call that it is better even today than never? This is an urge from the author and not intended to be construed as criticizing or challenging for, what has been written is within the boundary of the democracy considered in the best interests of the nation and has to be preserved by the unity and united strength of the political parties, the people and the forces.

It is in the foregoing context that the author has placed in before the authorities and the general public in Part 02 – Suggested Framework for Financing the Elections in India by his own insights as a suggestion to invite respectful attention of the authorities and the public for opening up debate on the subject so that the process is given a push to establish a system for state funding of election. This also provides opportunity for others to suggest alternative methods. To facilitate such a process, the Election Commission of India may consider issuing a "Consultation Paper" in such manner as it may consider appropriate, to the political parties and place the same in the public domain so that the general public would also have opportunity to make its suggestions which would strengthen the hands of ECI to proceed with the process.

I earnestly hope the ECI would be kind enough to look into the framework and publish it with or without modifications to enable the readers to spare few minutes to have a glance on the framework, consider it in the light of the issues aforementioned and form their own opinion on the subject matter. In my personal view, seventy two years of Republic of India has been struggling to lay down a sound system on election financing, What the country, on the other hand, witnessed all these years the parties that ruled the country have created consciously more and more ill-conceived leakages on how to relax the laws, rules and regulations to facilitate the corporate and other bodies like trusts could ensure expanding the size of their donations and contributions to the political parties to keep their treasury fattening without any explanation and the accountability. This practice has assumed as the best conduit for showering wealth in the treasury of the political parties. Today the country is unable to introduce checks and balances on election financing other than guidelines issued by the ECI routinely on the eve of the elections. The enormous burden on this account is placed on the people as a result of increasing cost of food items, vegetables, fruits and other normal necessities arising due to recouping the increasing patronaging the political parties, especially the ruling party, the economic development having been shaken having come under the obligation of obliging the corporate and industry. That is the main reason why the large scale infrastructure development that has the potential to create multiplying employment opportunities to the people, more so, in rural areas has been declining in volume. Economic development condition is truly worrying rather deepening with the introduction of substituted social welfare schemes under various attractive names which works like serving half-baked food to the people, the poorest and those living in misery

I am not a democrat engrossed what lies within democratic system and how it should function but a humble citizen of the democratic country; My country's Constitution vests in me inherent power as 'one of the peoples' of the country' to bring to the kind notice of the parliament, the ruling party and the opposition parties as well as the citizens what was ought to have been done during the last seventy two years of the country becoming Republic has to be done at least now as the say goes 'Better Late than Never'. Someone in the governance system that ruled the country in the past and is now in place, owe an explanation to the nation why such important ROL or governance obligations have been overlooked and continued to be do so which act like anchor for controlling the movement of the democratic ship in right direction in the ocean of democracy.

Our negligence to do so has bruised the democratic structure with everyone talking as they like and do what they want to do disregarding the need for safeguarding the democratic functioning. Democracy will remain only in words to speak about in the absence of responsibility, accountability and discipline among all the stakeholders – the parliament, the governing system, the judiciary, political parties, religious bodies and the people. I work on the basis of Doctrine of Common Sense that I have put best in writing this book. Other books {1} "Sounds of Silences in India's Constitution – Dangers Ahead {2020} and "India'[s Futuristic Democracy – Threats Constitutional Gaps and Digital Era"{2022} authored by me also serves as a stern warning to the rulers what it could cost the country if we failed to make the political reforms soonest possible. Let us not remain unawakened when we are awake which is like inviting a whirlwind to pass over us. The damage would be enormous to reconstruct ourselves. Besides above mentioned books, I have also authored ten other books on various subject matters stated in the page "About the Author".

What is the sanctity of election laid down under the constitution and under the relevant laws and rules if we, the citizens of India, being well aware, more particularly the political leaders, of the intent and purpose of the constitution and the laws and rules; yet we consciously bye pass them to achieve one's own interests at the cost of the national interests? Are we not fooling ourselves by following unfair means and methods prohibited under those very laws and rules? Is it not insult to the entire process of election if we call the way we do is the way of our democracy? Things done in shadows and darkness in the matter of election process are disrespectful and disgraceful. Better to read again and again the last address of Dr. B.R.Ambedkar to the Constituent Assembly dealt in the latest book stated before in its last section as 'The Last Word'. Let us also remember of what we have done so far and doing today in the name of the election is driving us to what Dr. Ambedkar said 'anxiety' about the future of democracy in our country. What is paramount to us: the 'Democracy' or 'Funding Elections' in the name of Democracy? We have so far been impressed by the latter that is self-disrespecting and self-cheating. The consequences are unpredictable. A sense of anxiety will be chasing us as foretold by Dr. Ambedkar.

It is not that what the author has submitted is a steel frame but an attempt to highlight to find a way out for state financing of the election in order to induct much needed discipline and control in the field open free for all for the last sixty eight years. It is time we should stop it here and think about the alternative, the best one being the state financing that squeezes all the open space now available to the political parties and the corporate and will curtail the corrupt practices to the minimal that also becomes identifiable for questioning by the authorities.

The silence of the government to the Election Commission's letter to the Law Ministry which raised serious concerns over the Finance Bill, 2017, which introduced amendments in other laws, especially the Representation of the People Act and the Companies Act, noting that the changes would have a serious impact on ensuring transparency in funding of political parties. EC is said to have severely criticized the four amendments made to different acts of the 2017 Bill, calling them a "retrograde step". The Law Ministry is reported to have stated that the concern expressed by the Election Commission regarding proviso of 29C appears genuine (para 2) and proposed that necessary changes in section 29C of the RP Act, 1951, in consonance of Section 13A of the Income Tax Act may be made.

According to Section 29C of the Representation of People Act, 1951, all political parties must declare donations above Rs 20,000 to the Election Commission every year. However, according to the amendment made by the government, it was proposed that the contributions received through electoral bonds would be excluded from the ambit of the RP Act. "This is a retrograde step as far as transparency of donations is concerned and this proviso needs to be withdrawn," the Election Commission is stated to have said in its letter to the Law Ministry. The Finance Ministry, on the other hand, stated to have said the electoral bonds scheme would increase transparency and cleanse the system of political funding in the country. It is not said so in the case of amendments to the RP Act, 1951 and the Companies Act, 2013. This shows due process of consultations within the government had not been done before introducing the amendments in the Finance Bill, 2017 which amounts to unilateral action open for discussions in the public domain. The provisions that stand amended, on plain reading, are more of the nature of covering up the transparency and cleansing up the system of political funding in the country, the disclosure having been barred.

Further, a RTI petition stated to have sought information about the registration of trusts, financing and other communication about pay-outs made under the Electoral Trust Scheme. The CBDT is said to have rejected the information on the ground of personal privacy under Section 8(1)(j) of the RTI Act. The section holds that information may be exempted from disclosure if it is private information unless the public information officer feels that it is in larger public interest to reveal it. Section 8(1)(j) becomes an unreasonable restriction on RTI which is a fundamental right guaranteed under Article 19(1)(a) of the Constitution contended the RTI. There is public interest information related to electoral trusts being disclosed since such trusts give money to political parties and the public nature of political parties has already been well established by the CIC order.

This is the problem the country is facing when it comes to contributions to political parties whether by the companies or by electoral trusts or electoral bonds, more so, in the present case where the denying authority is the authority which notified electoral trusts rules and it was aware that the rules do not contain any such provision that empowers such authority to withhold disclosure of the details of the nature sought in the RTI query. This may be a novel idea on the part of the authority but is of disturbing nature considering its importance to the public interest, purity of functioning of political parties and piousness of the election process. One wonders why the political parties or for that matter the authorities who are when dealing with a matter of political parties are flatly reluctant to make one or other information relating to political parties public, sought even through RTI? Such concealment of information will continue to raise more questions to one answer and creates an environment of suspicion and mistrust between the political parties, the authorities concerned and the public.

Longer we believe in continuing postponement of public funding of election will, in all probability, endanger the sustainability of true democratic functioning laid down in the constitution by our founding fathers and may open up an uncertain era for the generations to come. We enjoyed democracy so far as we wished without the principles of transparency and fairness with major part of the people remaining illiterate but its continuance would invite the curse of the generations to come who would be moving ahead to acquire literacy and advancing technology with the changing times to keep themselves apace with the world. Let us not deny this legitimate right to them by plunging ourselves into more and more messy and chaotic conditions in the governance of our country.

Legislative measures must be taken to impose substantial restrictions on the use of cash in the conduct of election campaigns by candidates, election associations, and election blocs. The presence of cash as an important factor of campaign finance may block the entire system of campaign finance regulation; affect the effectiveness of the efforts made by the Central Election Commission to monitor relevant financial flows. The use in election campaigning of cash funds which are not officially accounted for is, as a rule, a manifestation of corruption in the political sphere and one of the channels through which criminal circles influence politics. Therefore, it would be most adequate to take steps to establish differentiated responsibility for these offences (including criminal responsibility for the most serious manifestations of corruption in this sphere). Of course, the effectiveness of these measures will depend on the activeness of the law-enforcement bodies.

Improvement of procedures for financial reporting of candidates, election associations and blocs, measures to ensure openness and accessibility of current information concerning the sources of funds and spending of finances of election funds will facilitate control over relevant financial operations both on the part of election commission and election participants themselves, as well as mass media. The required volume of such information and terms of its submission shall be regulated legislatively.

The elections being organized today according to the relevant laws, rules and model codes may look on the face of it are done to uphold the democratic system but, in this process, none is concerned whether the elections were or are being conducted according to democratic obligations, the main players being the candidates, the voters and financial resources, first two are clearly identifiable but the last one evades the identification and visibility process and further adds its muscle power to enhance it strength to win the elections. Should we call it democratically processed elections? We are avoiding ourselves to understand the difference that lies between the two. One is perfunctory and the other is precision, first is adhered to and the second is disregarded. There were news items and continue to be so wherein what the international community thinks of the elections in our country more with negativity than positivity. "Everything that we see is a shadow cast by that which we do not see." - Martin Luther King, Jr. The democracy that our founders and forefathers envisioned was to maintain purity and parity at the crest of democratic crown. When what would happen unpredictable but the people have the power and strength even to make impossible as possible. That is what we should look at the futuristic democracy.

The minimum conditions of democratic elections are as follows:

i. Everyone should be able to choose. This means that everyone should have one vote and every vote should have equal value.

ii. There should be something to choose from. Parties and candidates should be free to contest elections and should offer some real choice to the voters.

iii. The choice should be offered at regular intervals. Elections must be held regularly after every few years.

iv. The candidate preferred by the people should get elected.

v. Elections should be conducted in a free and fair manner where people can choose as they really wish.

National Academies Press of US notes the following {excerpts} under the Title 'Ensuring the Integrity of Elections' posted on its Website: {National Academies of Sciences, Engineering, and Medicine. 2018. Securing the Vote: Protecting American Democracy. Washington, DC: The National Academies Press. https://doi.org/10.17226/25120}

There are numerous ways in which the integrity of elections can be affected. Election results may be improperly tallied or reported. Inaccuracies may be introduced by human error or because of a lack of proper oversight. Vote counts can be affected if fraudulent voting, e.g., multiple voting, illegal voting, etc., occurs. Election tallies and reporting may also be affected by malicious actors.

Malicious actors can affect vote counts by:

- introducing inaccuracies in the recording, maintenance, and tallying of votes; and/or
- altering or destroying evidence necessary to audit and verify the correct reporting of election results.1

There are many ways to prevent the casting of votes. Voters can be physically barred or otherwise deterred (e.g., by intimidation) from accessing polling sites. Information on voting locations, voting times, and voting processes may be manipulated to mislead potential voters. Disruptions in mail or Internet service may adversely affect remote voters. Registration data may be altered to disenfranchise voters. Voting equipment failures or inadequate supplies could prevent vote collection.

After votes have been cast, physical or electronic ballots can be altered, destroyed, or lost. Counting errors may affect manual or electronic tallying methods. Tallies may be inaccurately reported because of carelessness or malicious activity.

After the primary reporting of results, evidence that enables verification of the reported results may be altered or destroyed. This evidence could include original artefacts (e.g., cast ballots) or supplemental data provided to enable external auditing and verification.

Disruptions of Electronic Systems:

Security vulnerabilities can be exploited to electronically disrupt voting or affect vote counts at polling locations or in instances of remote voting.

Denial-of-service Attacks

Denial-of-service (DoS) attacks interrupt or slow access to computer systems.2 DoS can be used to disrupt vote casting, vote tallying, or election audits by preventing access to e-poll books, electronic voting systems, or electronic auditing systems.

When employed against even a limited number of jurisdictions, DoS disruptions could lead to a loss in confidence in overall election integrity. A DoS attack targeting select jurisdictions could alter the outcome of an election.

Malware

Malware—malicious software that includes worms, spyware, viruses, Trojan horses, and ransomware—is perhaps the greatest threat to electronic voting.3 Malware can be introduced at any point in the electronic path of a vote—from the software behind the vote-casting interface to the software tabulating votes—to prevent a voter's vote from being recorded as intended.

Malware can prevent voting by compromising or disrupting e-pollbooks or by disabling vote-casting systems. It can prevent correct tallying by altering or destroying electronic records or by causing software to miscount electronic ballots or physical ballots (e.g., in instances where optical scanners are used in the vote tabulation process). Malware can also be used to disrupt auditing software.

Malware is not easily detected. It can be introduced into systems via software updates, removable media with ballot definition files, and through the exploitation of software errors in networked systems. It may also be introduced by direct physical access, e.g., by individuals operating inappropriately at points during the manufacturing of the election system or at the level of elections offices. It is difficult to comprehensively thwart the introduction of malware in all these instances.

Other Classes of Attacks

There are other avenues through which electronic systems may be disrupted. Malicious actors may obtain sensitive information such as user-names or passwords by pretending to be a trustworthy entity in an electronic communication. Servers may be breached to obtain administrator-level credentials. Individuals with site access (e.g., employees or contractors) might physically access a system.

Maintaining Voter Anonymity

If anonymity is compromised, voters may not express their true preferences. Anonymity can be compromised in many ways. Clandestine cameras at poll sites could be used to compromise voter anonymity. Latent fingerprints left on ballots might be used to link voters to their ballots. Full ballots dissociated from individual voters might be posted in the interest of ensuring transparency and/or to facilitate auditing, but it may be possible to tie particular ballots to individual voters. When voter anonymity is achieved using encryption, a failure in the encryption can lead to the disclosure of a voter's identity. With remote voting—voting outside of publicly monitored poll sites—it may not be difficult to compromise voter privacy. When voting, for example, by mail, fax, or via the Internet, individuals can be coerced or paid to vote for particular candidates outside the oversight of election administrators.

# PART 02
# SUGGESTED FRAMEWORK FOR FINANCING ELECTIOINS IN INDIA

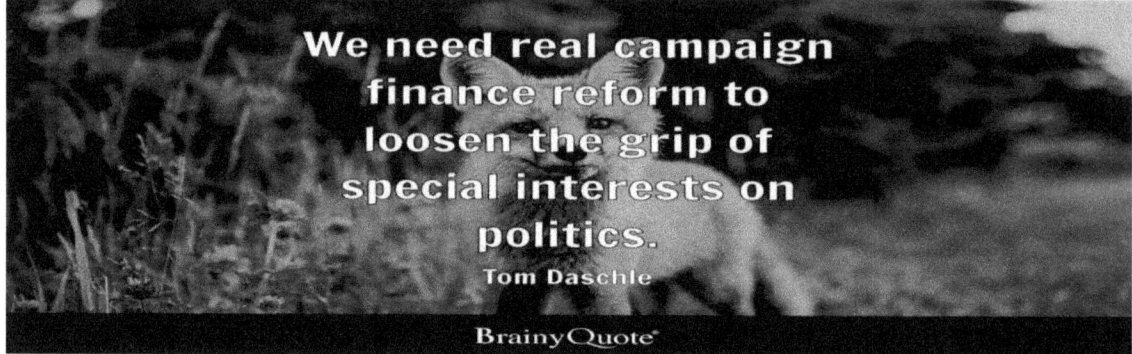

Introduction to this subject matter can well be understood reading an Article "Funding a clean polity" by Harish Khare published in "The Tribune" in its Edition of Feb 02, 2017 02:46 AM (IST) which is recapitulated below:

"Sometime in early 1959, JRD Tata, India's most respected and iconic entrepreneur, wrote to Jawaharlal Nehru that though his group, the Tatas, would continue to keep funding the Congress Party, he wanted to inform the Prime Minister that it would also be financing the newly established Swatantra Party. The Tata doyen told the Prime Minister that he found the Swatantra Party to be having a much closer appreciation of the needs of the business community; hence, he felt his group was obliged to extend whatever support it could to the Swatantra Party. Unperturbed, Nehru replied to JRD that he and his group were fully entitled to fund and finance whichever political activity they deemed worth their penny. As far as he was concerned, he had no doubt in his mind that the Swatantra Party had no future in Indian politics. Nehru was proved right: the Swatantra Party folded its tent within 15 years, though not without some spectacular successes in the 1962 and 1967 Lok Sabha elections.

What neither Nehru argued nor JRD understood was that the Indian business community did not need a party like the Swatantra Party, a political outfit that believed in plain, simple, clean capitalism, whereas the Indian businessmen had thrived only under State patronage and its louche cousin, crony capitalism. Both before and after the 1991 reforms, the so-called entrepreneurs relied on political connections for their financial prosperity. Even now, the Indian State retains a very capricious capacity to mug any business house of its happiness.

That is why the totally strange and inexplicable sight of a Ratan Tata making a pilgrimage to Nagpur to pay a 'courtesy call' on Mohan Bhagwat, the RSS boss man.

All this needs to be recalled in order to contextualise Finance Minister Arun Jaitley's attempt to cleanse the political party's dirty financial stables. Over the years, all political parties have had access to huge and, that means, really huge — funds to finance elections and political activity. And, this means a less-than-honourable juggalbandi with the dishonest businessman. This juggalbandi has been at the core of all the ills and imperfections of Indian democracy. ..........

No political party can pretend to have its hands clean, or even cleaner than the other. A handful of individual leaders may be able to claim a kind of personal honesty but none is entitled to a claim of ignorance about his/her party's ability to access dirty money. No political party can claim to be morally superior when it comes to receiving — or extorting — funds from businessmen, big or small. In recent years, AAP has sought to put in place a somewhat transparent system but, of late, it too has found itself being accused of unclean transactions.

At first glance, Mr Jaitley has taken the first step towards forcing the political parties to clean up their account books. It is a political reform whose day has come. Not a day too soon. The middle classes, who have peremptorily colonised the sites of political argumentation, can be tempted to cheer this as a transformative moment. Yet, the temptation must be resisted-for three reasons.

First, politics is an expensive business. A political party and its activities — mobilisation of support and dissent, sustenance of a large number of party activists, and, increasingly, the need for access to expensive technology of social media — cost quite a bundle. The bigger the party, the larger its establishment and larger the size of its baggage-and, the heftier its monthly bill. Second, the government — at the Centre and in the states — has not vacated its rent-seeking sites. There will always be temptation for a chief minister to use his coercive powers to generate easy money, for personal or political use. Political parties attract mostly the parasitic elements that come to the arena only to live off the taxpayer. And, third, there is no dismantling of crony capitalism. Consequently, the unclean and unethical businessman would continue to seek out the unclean and unethical politician. The businessman's greed and the politician's rapacity work in tandem.

Nonetheless, a beginning has been made. Still, it would be reassuring to know that the Finance Minister's initiative was not simply motivated by political cleverness, aimed at grounding the BJP's rivals — just as some suspect that demonetisation was primarily driven by a desire to 'pauperise' the other political parties. That calculation seems to be coming unstuck in Uttar Pradesh. The Modi government has incurred a serious trust deficit.

Political parties in India will continue to have a legitimate need for funds, both for and beyond electioneering activities. And, it is perfectly legitimate for a business house or a rich businessman to 'reward' a political party or leader on account of a platform or ideology................

Today, our politics has become so divisive and toxic that any 'reform' becomes suspect. There is no 'JRD' today who would be able to tell the Prime Minister that he would be funding his political rivals. There is no business house that does not seek a favour from the government of the day. This vulnerability induces moral timidity and financial chicanery. The unvarnished fact is that no corporate house can sanguinely acknowledge writing cheques for a political party's treasurer. No businessman can afford to earn the wrath of the ruling party and incite a visit from that ubiquitous 'ED' or the CBI who invariably end up seizing 'incriminating documents'. Even the most honest trader or contractor or entrepreneur remains vulnerable to the State's minatory inspector. ..."

Wouldn't introduction of election financing by the state act deterrent to such practice and inject a sense of confidence and acceptability of the sanctum of temple of democracy? Today, we are compulsively and sadly witnessing what had happened and continuing to happen in the country, an anxiety that is disturbing us whether we would be able to sustain the democracy considering the way the political and election systems are functioning in the country. Funding of elections by the state, as prevalent in other democratic countries, would free the democracy from the source of all sins; the present election financing system. How such an important matter remained outside the thinking of the authorities, the scholars and the people is difficult for the author to explain except stating that time has come for every one of us to introspect if we wish to uphold the values of democracy contemplated by the constitution makers.

Longest gap of time that occurred in dealing and settling this matter was beginning of the country becoming republic carrying forward the same until now. Given greatest respect to the freedom fighters and among them, those of whom formed part of the cabinet ministers, how they did not consider the need and urgency for evolving some structure for election financing presumably this was not so pressing and believed being managed within the funds available with the then political parties. This has taken a monolithic size by now whereby the political parties have almost pawned themselves in the hands of the corporate bodies and trusts.

For the convenience of the readers, the author has reproduced below the framework, formula and justification for state financing of elections for according a serious thought over that so that a beginning is made towards that end using the public, scholars and legal luminaries opinions through consultative process and the framework and formula that could be considered best could be adopted. Author is of the firm view that all the ills of democratic functioning, such as political scams, bank frauds, corruption, fake money, so called political contributions by the corporate, political overshadowing over the people and business community, the drug menace now prevailing in the country could be controlled, if not eliminated altogether, once the central government assumes the role of state financing of elections. Failing to act now would be inviting disastrous consequences to the democracy in the country in future for, it amounts to maintaining silence that is an implicit consent to the widening ills of democracy. Also, the ills mentioned above have invariably impacted the economic growth and would continue to affect if the ills are allowed to play their own games.

Compendium of Instructions on Election Expenditure Monitoring (January - 2015) of Election Commission of India. Foreword in the compendium states:

"It is true that multi-party democracy cannot function without use of money, which is essential for election campaigns, but it is also conceded at all hands that the abuse of 'Money Power' entails certain risks like uneven playing field, lack of fair competition, political exclusion of certain sectors, co-opted politicians under campaign debts and tainted governance with rule of law undermined. Keeping in view the said risks, the election expenditure monitoring mechanism was put in place by the Commission, for conduct of free and fair elections after discussions with the stakeholders like the political parties, media and civil society organizations. This Compendium of Instructions on election expenditure monitoring was issued for the first time during general election in Bihar in 2010. The said Compendium is updated before every general election, incorporating the changes made during the process of each election.

The gist of instructions and copy of all instructions relating to Election Expenditure Monitoring are given in Part-I and Part-II of this compendium. It delineates the role of political parties, candidates, Election officials and Observers and mentions the relevant case laws pertaining to the election expenditure, thus providing a ready reckoner to the Election officials, candidates and political parties. This Compendium guides the officers of various Law enforcement agencies about their role during election process.

Curbing the use of money power during election process is a very challenging job in view of its inherent complexities involved. The process is still evolving and requires tremendous efforts and cooperation from all stakeholders in order to ensure the purity of the elections. This compendium has also stood the test in the High Courts and in the Apex Court. Besides giving a perspective on the challenges faced during the elections, this compendium seeks to provide a comprehensive picture about Commission's efforts in dealing with this challenge."

The Compendium is divided in Two Parts – Part I: Introduction, Types of election expenditure, Election Expenditure Monitoring Mechanism, Functions of different teams in Expenditure Monitoring Mechanism, Procedure for Expenditure Monitoring, Maintenance of accounts by candidates, Inspection of the Election Expenditure Register, Meeting of the CEO, DEO with the political parties and Media and meeting of the RO with the candidates, Training of the election agents of the candidates on expenditure monitoring and maintaining the Registers, Expenditure by Political Parties and other persons, Scrutiny of the Statement of Accounts and the DEO's Report to the Commission, Report by the CEO, Role of the Returning Officer in Expenditure Monitoring, Role of the District Election Officer(DEO), Action at the level of the Commission Headquarters, Role of Political Parties, Training, Election Expenditure Statement of the candidate on the CEO`s Website and EEMS Software, Compilation of Seizure Reports and Ethical Voting Campaign and Part II: This Part contains various instructions on various subjects relating to the election process including reports, expenditure statement, surveillance reports, and seizure reports. The Compendium in complete is available on the website.

The Compendium is comprehensive, informative and reflective of the efforts the Election Commission has been doing for conducting the elections as fairly and transparently as possible. A cursory reading of the compendium, however, suggests the need for covering the following to the extent considered practicable:

Despite the fact that the EC has been closely and rigorously monitoring the flow of finance during the election periods to prevent corrupt practices by the candidates, invisible benefits both in kinds and money are reported to have been undertaken by the contesting candidates specially in backward and poorer class areas which give greater weight in polling and the end results. This is so because the contesting candidates seem rather assume to be wiser than the election authorities in finding out new ways and means for entering into corrupt practices including muscle power. Such incidences are well documented in one of the studies alluded herein which also pinpoints the sources active in embracing corrupt practices. Even with well built machinery in hand, it may be difficult for election authorities to reach the hidden sources encouraging corrupt practices. This is posing indirect threat to the very base of election system hindering the scope for success for deserving and devoted candidates, eventually ending up formation of parliament and legislative assemblies by the candidates elected side-lining the ethics and morality, in majority harmful to the public interests. It is time that the authorities in the government including the election authorities to think the need for state funding of the elections for developing an enduring democracy much necessary for the generations to grow in a healthy democratic system.

**Relevant provisions under Indian laws for Political party's Donations and Contribution:**

According to section 29B of Representation of People Act, every political party may accept any amount of contribution voluntarily offered to it by any person or company other than a Government company.

Section 182 of the Companies act, 2013 permits contributions to the political parties without any limit.

The donations to political parties by foreign-owned companies in India are legalized—retrospectively from 2010—considering the proviso inserted in the Foreign Contribution (Regulation) Act, 2010 (the Act/FCRA) through Finance Act, 2016.

The threshold of cash donations has been lowered to Rs 2,000, from Rs 20,000. The political parties are now allowed to get any amount of money if it comes by cheque or digitally.

Government of India has notified the Electoral Bond Scheme 2018 vide Gazette Notification No. 20 dated 2nd January 2018. As per provisions of the Scheme, Electoral Bonds may be purchased by a person, who is a citizen of India or incorporated or established in India. A person being an individual can buy Electoral Bonds, either singly or jointly with other individuals. Only the Political Parties registered under Section 29A of the Representation of the People Act, 1951 (43 of 1951) and which secured not less than one per cent of the votes polled in the last General Election to the House of the People or the Legislative Assembly of the State, shall be eligible to receive the Electoral Bonds. The Electoral Bonds shall be encashed by an eligible Political Party only through a Bank account with the Authorized Bank. An electoral bond is designed to be a bearer instrument like a Promissory Note — in effect, it will be similar to a bank note that is payable to the bearer on demand and free of interest.

As reported in the newspapers, a petition was filed in February, 2018 on the amendments to the Finance Act, 2018 that the amendments "jeopardize the very foundation of Indian democracy."

"The introduction of electoral bonds by the Finance Act by which details of donations made to political parties are not reported or recorded by the parties and whose purchasers identity remain hidden from the public realm is the creation of an obscure funding system which is unchecked by any authority," the petition contended. The petition said that the requirement of disclosure of electoral bonds, the names and addresses of their contributors in the account statement of political parties is omitted by the amendment to the Representation of the People Act of 1951. Further, the petition said the system of corporate donations has been made correspondingly "secretive by removing the requirement of disclosure of the names of political parties to whom contributions have been made by amendment to the Companies Act, 2013." "In effect, at both ends of the transaction, neither the contributor nor the recipient of the fund is required to disclose the identity of the other... Quid pro quo arrangements, not unknown to Indian polity, will only be strengthened," the petition said.

The amendment to the Companies Act results in the removal of any ceiling on the amount for donation by a company to a political party. It allows a company to be eligible as a political contributor regardless of whether the company is making profits or losses.

Challenging the passage of the amendments as a Money Bill, the petition recalls the words of the Finance Minister that the changes in laws were meant to introduce transparency and reduce the usage of black money in financing political parties. But the electoral bond scheme is "vague, arbitrary and a violation of the fundamental right to information." Instead of incentivizing political party contributors to forego black money, the scheme actually allows them to continue to bury their unaccounted wealth with political parties, the petition said."

Existing practice has been made permanent as if the state has no alternative or the state does not want to think about the same at all. As noticeable, the state seems to be more interested in promoting and encouraging the existing system; if that is so; how the society or the people of the country would be able assume elections as fair and transparent elections? Or, does the state want that the present financing system is an accepted practice, fair and transparent, citizens should not question it, the political parties employ it as a right means of financing and the governance would be conducted by the party winning the elections? What a citizen could do under these conditions? At best, go to the highest Court of Law at own cost. Why we are indifferent to ourselves when we know what we are doing about financing election cannot stand to moral and ethical test? Or, should we say moral and ethical tests are nothing to do with election financing? Curiously, we are not inclined to follow public funding of elections, adopted in many countries, though we follow many methods followed in those countries? In the view of the author, the country should move towards public funding of election. This is based on the logical suggestions made by a Hon'ble Member of the Constituent Assembly referred to before, as also considering that the present system of financing elections has created considerable rotten eggs that posing great danger to the health of the democratic functioning.

Author submits the following Framework:

1. Establishment of "NATIONAL ELECTION FUND (NEF)" under the sole control of the Election Commission of India (ECI) being a constitutional body which should be applied and administered according to the rules to be made by the ECI.

2. Registered political parties mean and include both at the national and state level duly recognized by the ECI.

3. The rules should lay down the detailed pre-requisites and procedures as have been stated illustratively under the governing conditions hereunder to provide funds for meeting election expenses to the Political Parties, one of which should be that the funds should be

provided in the ratio of the members of the Party to the total member of all the Parties both at the National and States levels. Illustratively, this may be as follows:

| Serial Number | Registered Political Party (Applicable to National/State Level) | Number of Members as per duly audited Register of Members (No) {Assumed basis} | Ratio (%) of Entitlement (Rounded Off@) to Funds in NEF |
|---|---|---|---|
| 1. | Party ABC | 50,00,000 | 20.31 |
| 2. | Party DEF | 45,00,000 | 18.29 |
| 3. | Party GHI | 35,00,000 | 14.24 |
| 4. | Party JKL | 30,00,000 | 12.22 |
| 5. | Party MNO | 25,00,000 | 10.19 |
| 6. | Party PQR | 20,00,000 | 08.17 |
| 7. | Party STU | 15,00,000 | 06.14 |
| 8. | Party VXY | 10,00,000 | 04.12 |
| 9. | Party AAA | 7,00,000 | 02.90 |
| 10. | Party BBB | 5,00,000 | 02.11 |
| 11. | Party CCC | 3,00,000 | 01.31 |
|  | Total of (1) to (11) | 2,47,00,000 | 100.00 |

@ Before rounding off, sum total works out to Rs. 99.12 based on actual ratios of each Party Numbers to the Total Numbers. Difference of 0.82 added to each Party @ 0.07 (82/7) x 0.07 x 11 = 77. Balance 0.05 added @ 0.02 to Serial Number 10 and @ 0.03 to Serial Number 11 to make up the Total to 100.00.

4. The above eligibility criteria apply to both national and state level parties provided that the registered political parties are not debarred or disqualified as per the provisions of RPA, 1951.

5. This would compel the political parties to come close to each other to seriously consider merger of their parties that enables them to claim a larger number of members and a larger share of funds allocation.

6. Independent candidates, in order to be eligible for allocation of funds from NEF, should give an unconditional undertaking that if he or she wins the election in that capacity would not join or associate with any registered political party of his or her choice {defect} failing which he or she would be considered ineligible for allocation of the funds, that would eliminate the horse trading after the election results are announced.

7. The rules to be made by ECI should provide for allocation and disbursement of funds from NEF according to the suggested entitlement criteria.

8. Total funds for electioneering that should be available to the registered political parties at their disposal should be the fees collected from their members for enrolment as party members and the funds made available from out of the NEF in accordance with the rules.

9. Eligibility threshold and the allocation criterion can be on the basis of suggested approach or any other basis as considered appropriate.

10. Funding of NEF:

a. According to section 29B of Representation of People Act, every political party may accept any amount of contribution voluntarily offered to it by any person or company other than a Government company. Such contributions should be remitted into the NEF. Necessary amendments to the existing provisions need to be made.

b. Electoral Trusts established under the Electoral Trust Scheme, 2013 are allowed to receive voluntary contributions and are authorized to distribute to any political party at least ninety five percent of the aggregate donation and the contributions so received by the Trust including the contributions received from the foreign companies and all such funds should be contributed to NEF annually on or before 31st March. Necessary amendments to the existing provisions need to be made.

c. Section 182 of the Companies act, 2013 permits contributions to the political parties without any limit. This should be contributed to NEF annually on or before 31st March which shall, in any case, not be less than 7.5% of its average net profits during the three preceding financial years as existed prior to amendment of the Act. Necessary amendments to the existing provisions need to be made.

d. All permissible cash donations and the donations made digitally or by cheque should be made to the NEF. Necessary amendments to the existing provisions need to be made.

e. The donations to political parties by foreign-owned companies in India legalized—retrospectively from 2010—considering the proviso inserted in the Foreign Contribution (Regulation) Act, 2010 (the Act/FCRA) through Finance Act, 2016 should be contributed to the NEF. Necessary amendments to the existing provisions need to be made.

f. The Confederation of Industries have suggested levying of certain percentage of Cess for elections financing as stated in Part 01 of this book. A new cess known as "Election Funding Cess" {EFC} may be introduced on all the persons whose net taxable annual income is more than Rs. 25,00,000 in the case of individuals, Rs. 25,00,00,000 in the case of sole trading and partnership firms and Rs.50,00,00,000 in the case of the companies at the rate of 0.75 percent on the net income exceeding the above limits in addition to tax recovered as per the prevailing taxable rates under the Income Tax Act, 1961.All the monies realized levying the

Election Cess should be remitted into the NEF according to the rules governing the NEF. Necessary amendments to the existing provisions need to be made.

g. Accumulated funds in NEF should be invested in such a manner as considered most beneficial to the fund; necessary provision needs to be made in the proposed rules.

h. Income derived from investment of funds accumulated in the NEF should be wholly exempt from Income Tax or any other kind of Tax; the income so derived shall be added to and shall form part of the NEF.

i. The amount of the electoral bonds gifted by a buyer to a registered political party should be treated as donation to the party and deducted from NEF on the basis of the information available with the designated bank and necessary provision to this effect may be made in the proposed rules. Necessary amendments to the existing provisions need to be made.

j. Allocation of funds made available to the political parties in the manner stated to their candidates should be sole responsibility of the political parties in accordance with their internal governing rules and procedures which should, however, be vetted by the ECI before incorporating in the internal rules of the parties so that uniformity of allocation of funds to the candidates among the political parties is ensured. This is so because the candidates contesting the election are the members of the registered political parties, the allocation of funds to them thus establishes a legal relationship between them.

k. As such, no funds from NEF should be paid to the contesting candidates of the parties direct which, if done, would not only undermines the authority of the registered political parties but also involve accounting complexities.

l. Distribution of the funds thus available in NEF to the registered political parties should be regulated in such a way that no recognized party is denied such funds subject to the proviso under the eligibility criteria.

m. Every such party should render account of the expenditure incurred by it from out of the funds made available from NEF, constituency and candidate-wise, to the Election Commission of India failing which the defaulting party should be derecognized and the party should be asked to refund the amount received from NEF, failing which, the party should be disqualified from contesting the election for a period of five years.

n. The Election Commission should render full account of receipt and distribution of funds from out of NEF to the political parties and the manner in which the funds were utilized by the political parties in its Annual Report;

o. Any political party which has received the funds from NEF for electioneering including its candidate (s) indulge in collection of funds from any other source in whatsoever manner other than membership fee should be disqualified for a period of five years if it is proved that the party has in actual collected such funds. The rules referred to above should also provide an appropriate procedure of inquiry to be conducted in such cases.

p. The above measures are expected to mobilize adequate funds in NEF and introduce most desired financial discipline on election expenditure of the political parties with transparency and accountability.

q. These measures will act as deterrent and compulsion to minimize election expenditure of the political parties as well as control corruption and generation of black money.

r. From what has been stated, it will provide much wanted level playing field among the parties and their candidates in place of prevailing money and muscle power.

s. The relevant laws and rules as existing should be suitably amended to give effect to the above suggestions for funding of NEF.

11. Above basis for allocation of funds from NEF is based on the following assumptions:

(a) Larger the number of members the greater the number of candidates in a given constituency.

(b) Election expenses will be more where the candidates number is greater and less where the candidates number is smaller.

(c) There will be total transparency of inflow and outflow of funds from NEF for electioneering expenses.

(d) Parties will be obligated to account in their books of accounts funds received and spent towards election expenses as notified by the ECI and in force or with further amendment, if so considered necessary, which will also incorporated or defined under the rules proposed and will be auditable as in the ordinary course according to the internal rules of the Party.

(e) The Internal Audit Report will be further supplemented by the special audit by the Comptroller and Auditor General of India (CAG), the funds in the NEF being public funds. The Report of the CAG should be placed in the Parliament.

(f) Return/Reports to be made to the Election Commission by the political parties as per the existing requirements or as may be further supplemented under the proposed rules will be based on the official books of accounts of the political parties maintained and audited.

(g) Election Commission will be authorized under the proposed rules to order special audit/inspection of the books of accounts of any party if there is reason to believe that the accounts rendered do not reflect the true and fair account of monies received and spent.

(h) There will be penal provisions to be incorporated in the proposed rules which may be made liable to be imposed on the Office Bearers of the Party or Parties if they are found to have indulged in misstatement or misrepresentation of the facts and figures or committed any kind of fudging or fraud as well as in cases where the Party or Parties is or have sought or secured political funds from any source other than sources available from the membership fees and the funds made available from NEF including their candidates.

(i) This will impulsively compel the existing multiple parties to engage them towards merger of small parties as they are likely to find it difficult to manage their affairs and also inbuilt constraints in spending large sums on electioneering, which should be the object aimed at achieving political discipline for a decent and democratic functioning.

12. In deference to what the learned member of CAD stated before, I have attempted a Framework for election financing, the compulsion, sources for financing by the state, the governing conditions and so on, a self-explanatory document that is contained above.

13. The framework submitted is a measure to create a central pooling of funds available from the same existing sources for election financing. Formula and criteria as well as the governing conditions are incorporated in the framework according to which, the distribution of funds in the central pool, named as National Election Fund {NEF} will be in the ratio in proportionate to the number of members of the parties recognized by the ECI to the total number of the members all the recognized parties together. It is neither intended nor to be understood that the suggested election financing method would entail additional expenditure on the part of the centre and the states. The process is intended to systematize and centralize the collection and distribution of available funds in the NEF in a scientific and logical manner with full accountability on the part of the eligible political parties. Needless to state that the observations made by the honourable Member of the Constituent Assembly noted above are fully justifiable based on his conclusion in the circumstances stated therein.

14. The Framework is a suggestive self-contained framework based on the views I could find from the articles on the website and according to my own understanding. The essence is not to suggest I have done something to solve the problem of election financing but to bring home to all the stakeholders that the present method{s} practised for election financing are illogical viewed from any angle, the same being of concealing nature open for enormous misuse in the process of elections as if the funds used by the parties and the candidates though are said to be according to permitted laws and rules, in reality they are not to so for two reasons; one that there is no mechanism to assess the funds applied or used for elections are within the total funds available at the disposal of the parties according to the their declarations and second that thereby the political parties and the candidates have their own

inbuilt channels invisible to anyone to route the illegally held funds in the election process, an open field for both the political parties and their candidates.

15. I have exhaustively justified the need and urgency of state financing of the elections with logic and reasoning along with the Formula and the Framework of the Rules for that purpose and have prepared a self-documented instrument. It deals every aspect and intricacies of election including basis for allocation of funds and the A to Z governing conditions. This is suggestive one begging for government and public attention. If the readers and the government want to move towards this end, this is the only time that they can do for; we would have lost the fertility of soil if we think we could wait for the future. It is the present that makes the future, would we be there to see the future? We will only be forcing the futuristic generation to continue to yoke the burden of present system, not being sure, when it becomes seriously detrimental to the interests of democracy so far followed. This will dissuade the present practice of election financing which is insidious and impossible to detect and connect how and wherefrom the huge funds have been flowing in the hands of the political parties and politicians that is opening access to politicians to associate with the criminals and criminal activities. I have also submitted justifiable urgency for acting on major constitutional gaps listed in this Part. We need to act upon them with high priority if the country and we the people want to uphold the democratic functioning in the futuristic India. Action Is Hope and inaction is Despair that may put the Futuristic Democracy in Jeopardy.

16. From what has been submitted in the proposed Framework for Election Financing in India, it would be seen that the Representation of the People Act 1951 an independent body created thereunder as Election Commission of India {ECI} placed the body in a weakest position on the several matters including the procedure and practice of appointment of Chief Election Commissioner and the Election Commissioners and dealing with election financing though it enjoys adequate powers in the matter of conduct of elections.

17. Article 324 in The Constitution Of India 1949 -Superintendence, direction and control of elections to be vested in an Election Commission (1) The superintendence, direction and control of the preparation of the electoral rolls for, and the conduct of, all elections to Parliament and to the Legislature of every State and of elections to the offices of President and Vice President held under this Constitution shall be vested in a Commission (referred to in this Constitution as the Election Commission), (2) The Election Commission shall consist of the Chief Election Commissioner and such number of other Election Commissioners, if any, as the President may from time to time fix and the appointment of the Chief Election Commissioner and other Election Commissioners shall, subject to the provisions of any law made in that behalf by Parliament, be made by the President (3) When any other Election

Commissioner is so appointed the Chief Election Commissioner shall act as the Chairman of the Election Commission

18. The matter regarding appointment of Chief Election Commissioner and Election Commissioners of the Election Commission of India {ECI} is presently being heard in the Hon'ble Supreme Court of India. With due respect and without prejudice the matter being heard mentioned above, I have refrained myself from any comments in respect thereof.

19. IAS Parliament Website in an Article "Issues with Appointment of Election Commissioner" dated November 24, 2022 posted on its Website notes as follows:

"The ongoing hearing before the Supreme Court on the need to have a neutral mechanism for appointment of Election Commissioners raises questions on the body's functional independence.

What is the structure of Election Commission of India (ECI)?

- **Establishment** - The ECI is an **autonomous permanent constitutional authority** established in 1950 for administering election processes in India.

- The Election Commission operates under **Article 324 (Part XV of the Constitution)** and the subsequently enacted Representation of the People Act.

- **Elections** - The body administers elections to the
  - Lok Sabha
  - Rajya Sabha
  - State Legislative Assemblies
  - Office of the President
  - Office of the Vice President

- **Composition** - Originally the commission had only a Chief Election Commissioner (CEC).

- Since 1993, it has become a multi-member commission with Chief Election Commissioner and two Election Commissioners (ECs).

- Article 324(2) empowers the President of India to fix from time to time the number of Election Commissioners other than the CEC.

- If the CEC and other ECs differ in opinion on any matter, such matter shall be decided by according to the opinion of the majority.

- **Appointment** - The President appoints Chief Election Commissioner and Election Commissioners.

- **Tenure** - They have tenure of 6 years, or up to the age of 65 years, whichever is earlier.
- They enjoy the same status and receive salary and perks as available to Judges of the Supreme Court of India.
- **Removal** - The Chief Election Commissioner can be removed from office only through impeachment by Parliament.
- **State level** - At the state level, the election work is supervised, subject to overall superintendence, direction and control of the Commission, by the Chief Electoral Officer of the State.

What are the major functions of the ECI?

**Political parties** - Election Commission is responsible for conducting free and fair elections across the country.

The ECI is involved in the registration of political parties and ensures inner party democracy.

The registered political parties are granted recognition at the State and National levels by the ECI according to criteria prescribed by it.

The ECI ensures a level playing field for the political parties through strict observance by them of a Model Code of Conduct.

**Advisory jurisdiction** - The Commission has advisory jurisdiction in the matter of post-election disqualification of sitting members of Parliament and State Legislatures.

The cases of persons found guilty of corrupt practices at elections which come before the Supreme Court and High Courts are referred to the ECI for its opinion.

The opinion of the Commission in all such matters is **binding** on the President or the Governor to whom such opinion is tendered.

**Quasi-judicial functions** - The Commission settles disputes between the splinter groups of recognised parties.

The Commission has the power to disqualify a candidate who has failed to lodge an account of his election expenses within the time and in the manner prescribed by law.

The Commission has also the power for removing or reducing the period of such disqualification as also other disqualification under the law.

What are the provisions available for ECI's independence?

**Removal** - The Chief Election Commissioner can be removed from office only through impeachment by Parliament.

The procedure is similar to the process of removal of Supreme Court judge.

Election Commissioners cannot be removed from office except upon the recommendation of the CEC.

**Service conditions** – The service conditions of CEC cannot be varied to their disadvantage after the appointment.

What is the current issue with appointments?

**Appointments-** At present, the CEC and ECs are appointed by the president on the advice of the Cabinet under Transaction of Business Rules, 1961 of the Union cabinet.

The current convention is to appoint ECs, and elevate them as CEC on the basis of seniority.

The issue is related to the

likelihood of bias in the appointments

possibility of biased conduct by CEC and ECs in the future

scope for personal whimsy in appointments of EC

Given the Court's vocal concern about the ECI's independence, the question is whether the Commissioners should be appointed on the recommendation of a high-powered committee independent body.

**Tenure** – The Court has questioned the practice of appointing CECs close to the age of 65 so that they have only a brief tenure.

Equal tenure security for CEC and Election Commissioners will boost their independence.

The ECs must also be provided with security of tenure as they can be removed from office on the CEC's recommendation.

20. My submissions, however, are as under:

(a) It will be seen from the above constitutional provision that The Election Commission shall consist of the Chief Election Commissioner and such number of other Election Commissioners, if any, as the President may from time to time fix and the appointment of the Chief Election Commissioner and other Election Commissioners shall, subject to the provisions of any law made in that behalf by Parliament, be made by the President

(b) The parliament did make law known as The Representation of People Act, 1950 further amended by the Act in 1951. The Act as amended further from time to time thereafter continues to be in force. The appointments of Chief Election Commissioner and other Election Commissioners were appointed right from the time the Act came into force were made by the President with the aid and advice of the Council of

Ministers presumably there was no other law, if any made by the parliament in that behalf as stated therein.

(c) With due respect and without prejudice to the Hon'ble Supreme Court of India which is hearing the subject matter presently, I wish to respectfully submit that the word "shall" and the words "if any" used in Article 324 of the Constitution of India do not provide any option to the parliament to make or not to make such law, the reason being the words 'if any' lose their significance once the word 'shall' is preceding them. In my personal view, it was expected of the parliament to have made the law on the subject matter rather than considering it as an option. Also, in my personal opinion, the absence of such understanding left no choice to the President to appoint the Chief Election Commissioner and Election Commissioners with the aid and advice of the Council of Ministers. This is where, according to me, Article 324 lost its constitutional direction.

(d) Election Commission of India (ECI): The Constitution made the ECI as an independent constitutional body bringing it into force from November 26th, 1949. To provide a legal framework for the conduct of elections, Parliament passed the Representation of the People Act, 1950, Representation of the People Act, 1951 and Delimitation Commission Act of 2002. What is an independent constitutional body? Wikipedia states 'In India, a **Constitutional body** is a body or institute established by the Constitution of India. They can only be created or changed by passing a constitutional amendment bill, rather than an Act of Parliament. The members of Constituent Assembly of India recognised the need for independent institutions which can regulate sectors of national importance without any executive interference. As such, they introduced constitutional provisions, paving the way for creation of Constitutional bodies. A classic example of a constitutional body is the Election Commission of India, which is created to conduct and regulate the national and state elections in India.'

(e) The EC can direct, control, and conduct the election of the Parliament and State legislatures and the offices of the President and Vice-President of India under article 324. Powers of ECI include:

(f) Registering eligible voters and preparing electoral rolls.

(g) Deciding the date of elections.

(h) Scrutinising nominations.

(i) Setting a code of conduct for the parties participating in the polls.

(j) Appointing officers to manage disputes of electoral arrangements.

(k) Cancelling voting polls in case of a breach, violence, and other issues.

(l) Ensuring free and fair elections.

(m) Section 2 (b) "appropriate authority" means, in relation to an election to the House of the People or the Council of States 2 * * *, the Central Government, and in relation to an election to the Legislative Assembly or the Legislative Council of a State, the State Government; (g) "prescribed" means prescribed by rules made under this Act;

(n) 29B. Political parties entitled to accept contribution.—Subject to the provisions of the Companies Act, 1956 (1 of 1956), every political party may accept any amount of contribution voluntarily offered to it by any person or company other than a Government company: Provided that no political party shall be eligible to accept any contribution from any foreign source defined under clause (e) of section 2 of the Foreign Contribution (Regulation) Act, 1976 (49 of 1976). Explanation.—For the purposes of this section and section

(o) 29C,— (a) "company" means a company as defined in section 3; (b) "Government company" means a company within the meaning of section 617; (c) "contribution" has the meaning assigned to it under section 293A, of the Companies Act, 1956 (1 of 1956) and includes any donation or subscription offered by any person to a political party; and (d) "person" has the meaning assigned to it under clause (31) of section 2 of the Income-tax Act, 1961 (43 of 1961), but does not include Government company, local authority and every artificial juridical person wholly or partially funded by the Government. 169. Power to make rules.—(1) The Central Government may, after consulting the Election Commission, by notification in the Official Gazette, make rules for carrying out the purposes of this Act. It is seen that the rules specified in the said section do not include any rule with respect to contributions to the political parties.

(p) Interesting to note here is that the statutory bodies created under various laws made by the parliament e.g. Electricity Act, 2003 empowers the bodies created thereunder – Central Electricity Authority [CEA}, Central Electricity Regulatory Commission [CERC} to make rules and regulations thereunder but in the case of independent Constitutional Bodies, the powers to make rules are reserved to the central government. ECI being an independent Constitutional body stands at a much higher pedestal than the statutory bodies such as those mentioned before but has no powers to make rules under the Act, more so, when the entire responsibility of conducting the elections is placed upon it. By reserving the rules making powers to itself, the central government and also the powers to appoint the CEC and ECs has the effect of overshadowing influence on the functioning of the ECI.

(q) The only provision in this regard is what is contained in section 29B stated before, that is, 'Political parties entitled to accept contribution.—Subject to the provisions of the Companies Act, 1956 (1 of 1956), every political party may accept any amount of contribution voluntarily offered to it by any person or company other than a Government company: Provided that no political party shall be eligible to accept any contribution from any foreign source defined under clause (e) of section 2 of the Foreign Contribution (Regulation) Act, 1976 (49 of 1976'. The other sources of funding the political parties for election financing, as notified by the central government from time to time are:

  i. Electoral Trusts established under the Electoral Trust Scheme, 2013 are allowed to receive voluntary contributions and are authorized to distribute to any political party at least ninety five percent of the aggregate donation and the contributions so received by the Trust including the contributions received from the foreign companies.

  ii. Section 182 of the Companies act, 2013 permits contributions to the political parties without any limit.

  iii. All permissible cash donations and the donations made digitally or by cheque.

  iv. The donations to political parties by foreign-owned companies in India legalized—retrospectively from 2010—considering the proviso inserted in the Foreign Contribution (Regulation) Act, 2010 (the Act/FCRA) through Finance Act, 2016.

  v. The threshold of cash donations has been lowered to Rs 2,000, from Rs 20,000. The political parties are now allowed to get any amount of money if it comes by cheque or digitally.

  vi. Government of India has notified the Electoral Bond Scheme 2018 vide Gazette Notification No. 20 dated 2nd January 2018. As per provisions of the Scheme, Electoral Bonds may be purchased by a person, who is a citizen of India or incorporated or established in India. A person being an individual can buy Electoral Bonds, either singly or jointly with other individuals. Only the Political Parties registered under Section 29A of the Representation of the People Act, 1951 (43 of 1951) and which secured not less than one per cent of the votes polled in the last General Election to the House of the People or the Legislative Assembly of the State, shall be eligible to receive the Electoral Bonds. The Electoral Bonds shall be encashed by an eligible Political Party only through a Bank account with the Authorized Bank. An electoral bond is designed to be a bearer instrument like a Promissory Note — in effect, it will be similar to a bank note that is payable to the bearer on demand and free of interest.

(r) There is no other law other than section 29B of the RPA 1951 that deals with contributions to the political parties. The sole source provided therein for contributions is from the companies other than the government companies and the foreign sources under FEMA. Section 29B is the controlling section as regards to the contributions to the political parties. The original jurisdictional powers on contributions to the political parties lie solely under section 29B. The powers to make rules conferred upon the central government under the said Act do not include powers with respect to contributions to the political parties. The other sources opened up by the central government from time to time as part of the budgetary process {which was also questionable in the light of the observations made by the Hon'ble Speaker of the House} lack the original jurisdictional authority. In particular, permitting of the foreign sources under FEMA for contributions to the political parties is in direct conflict with the provisions of the said section. Except item {ii}, all other items mentioned above suffer from sanctity of jurisdictional authority and, unless, they are brought within the purview of said section 29B, their operational effectiveness remains questionable.

(s) I wish to reiterate that the provisions of section 29B are the single and sole source to deal with contributions to the political parties or entitling the political parties to accept the contributions from any other source other than specified under that section. All the new avenues in this regard considered necessary by the central government must originate under the provisions through amendments to the relevant provisions in the said Act. **""The care of human life and happiness, and not their destruction, is the first and only object of good government." "They that give up essential liberty to purchase a little temporary safety deserve neither liberty nor safety." "That government is best which governs least."** {Source: Online}

(t) There is thus a disjoint between primary power vested in said Act and the powers exercised by the central under various other laws which, as noted before, cannot become operative unless and until all the powers so exercised by the central government in that respect are placed within the ambit of the RPA 1951 through appropriate rules by amendment of that Act. My understanding may be wrong; if so, where does the central government derive the powers to make amendments to various laws expanding the scope for contributions to the political parties, other than section 12B of RPA 1951? All other laws relied upon by the central government in that respect is in exercise of secondary power, the primary power being vested in the said section. Can we make white color into black color? We can but that can be done only through coating various colours thereon, the white colour continues to retain its original colour, that is, whiteness. All other colours are offshoots. So also, the basic character of the contributions to the political parties specified in section 12B cannot be altered and, accordingly, additions of the contributions through amendments of other laws are the offshoots of section 12B, the original source of contributions which cannot be ignored while amending the other laws in that respect and all such amendments form integral part of section 12B and, therefore, are to be so made in order to make them operationally effective. Otherwise, they are amendments but remain outside the purview of the said section 12B thereby operationally not effective. Such course of action adopted by the central government is not in consistent with the governing law?

(u) The amendments proposed by the ECI based on the recommendations of the Law Commission in 2016 are still to receive the attention of the central government. All the matters in connection with the elections, other than making rules,[which is also in isolation from the spirit and intent of the RPA 1951] deemed to vest with the ECI overlooking which amounts to undermining the authority of the ECI.

(v) What happens in the case of other Acts? Can the central government introduce some benefit to the political parties through schemes etc. outside the provisions of the governing Acts such as the Companies Act, 2013 or the Income Tax Act, 1961? It cannot without necessary amendments thereto specifically incorporated under the RPA 1951.

(w) Lot of reforms continued to be made in the election process, equal attention has not been paid to reforms in financing election, gradually eroding the Faith reposed by the people in the governance.

(x) There seems to be lack of consultation process among ECI, the central government, the political parties and the public on this so far rather there had been unilateral policies being brought up by the central government for the benefit of the political parties opening opportunities for concealing the sources of financing the elections.

(y) The state seems becoming a party to this process justifying it when ECI objected to certain recent amendments but with no concern from the government. The government is not supposed to supersede the ECI in matters involving sanity of elections and public interest, not even prior consultations. It reflects hesitancy of the government to recognize the existence of an independent constitutional body exclusively entrusted with the duties and responsibilities on matters of elections. There is no such provision in the RPA 1951 that accords superior powers to the central governments in the matters related to elections which is the sole domain of the ECI except regarding making rules on matters specified therein.

(z) This is blindness towards fairness and transparency on a matter concerning high public interest. Does it not amount to undermining the authority of ECI by the government when the reservations expressed in writing by the ECI to the government were put aside without any valid reasons? Unheard. It is a different matter ECI did not approach the highest court of law as a matter of respect to the central government.

(aa) Even if there is no express provision in the Representation of People Act, 1951 on consultation process, it has to be construed as existing, there being no express bar, ECI being the sole constitutional body for regulating the elections and all matters related thereto and such consultation process having been followed on code of conduct of political parties during election. Also, it is time to make specific provision in this regard in the said Act.

21. The Supreme Court of India has provided express authority for the ECI's approach to interpreting and augmenting India's electoral law. In the case of Mohinder Singh Gill & Anr. v. The Chief Election Commissioner, the Court commented, "the framers of the Constitution took care to leaving scope for exercise of residuary power by the Commission, in its own right, as a creature of the Constitution, in the infinite variety of situations that may emerge from time to time in such a large democracy as ours." And, further, "Once the appointment is made by the President, the Election Commission remains insulated from extraneous influences, and that cannot be achieved unless it has an amplitude of powers in the conduct of elections – of course in accordance with the existing laws. But where these are absent, and yet a situation has to be tackled, the Chief Election Commissioner has not to fold his hands and pray to God for divine inspiration to enable him to exercise his functions and to perform his duties or to look to any external authority for the grant of powers to deal with the situation."(Mohinder Singh Gill & Anr. v. The Chief Election Commissioner, December 2, 1977.).

22. In certain matters under the provisions of the Representation of Peoples' Act,1950 and 1951, it is mandatory for the EC to consult the central government for implementation of decisions while that is not so, where the central government is issuing schemes, to consult EC. Example of this kind is stated before.

23. Lack of provisions in the constitution as well as in the Representation of the People Act as to the procedures, checks and balances regarding political contributions or funding the parties seems to have led the political parties to have their own ways to collect contributions and funds for funding election. Certain sources are influenced to meet the expenses of the political parties for their various purposes through discreet methods.

24. A candidate who spends crores on his election is in a hurry to recover his investment by hook or crook. This creates an unholy politician-bureaucrat nexus. Once the two most powerful instruments of governance come to such an arrangement, people would have no alternative but to pray GOD to save the democracy.

25. The second issue is transparency in financing parties. Parties raise funds mainly through donations. People suspect some big corporate houses run governments by proxy — influencing key decisions, getting ministers of their choice appointed. It is not political parties alone who do not want to disclose sources of income, Corporate houses also seem to prefer secrecy. They would not like competing parties to know what they gave their rivals and would not want the quid pro quo exposed.

26. In both the cases, the political parties and the corporates are undermining the sanctity of the public cause and irreverence to the people {voters} who are supreme in terms of the Preamble of the Constitution but not able to react or respond for want of growth of a matured civil society. The existing civil society organizations should consider this in all its seriousness to evolve and ensure respect to the voters and upholding their basic rights under the Constitution. The Preamble of the Constitution otherwise remains in a dormant status and at the mercy of the governance.

27. Corruption has resulted in incalculable damage to the nation in terms of economic and social development. The abysmally high level of graft in India has resulted into what many experts call a 'revolving door' electoral democracy. The lack of transparency and accountability has also slowed the process of building up strong institutions of democracy. Thus, it emerges that just holding free and fair elections in a peaceful manner does not mean all is well with our democracy.

28. The intent and purpose of the proposed framework on financing elections to size up the evil monetary sources flying all over the country and in foreign countries and if necessary, the government should not hesitate to prune their wings.

29. The real issue is how we tackle the underlying problem of political finance – the source of all sins. Funding of political parties and elections is an important function in a democracy. What is needed is sufficient amount of funds that comes from clear channels without any strings attached. But over the decades, the influence of money has grown so significantly that it has disturbed the level playing field for political players and alienated masses from political participation. Hyperbolic growth in campaign expenditure has rightly created a perception that electoral politics only belongs to those who have money power, lung power and muscle power.

30. The silence of the government to the Election Commission's letter to the Law Ministry which raised serious concerns over the Finance Bill, 2017, which introduced amendments in other laws, especially the Representation of the People Act, the RBI Act and the Companies Act, noting that the changes would have a serious impact on ensuring transparency in funding of political parties. EC is said to have severely criticized the four amendments made to different Acts of the 2017 Bill, calling them a "retrograde step". The Law Ministry is reported to have stated that the concern expressed by the Election Commission regarding

proviso of 29C appears genuine (para 2) and proposed that necessary changes in section 29C of the RP Act, 1951, in consonance of Section 13A of the Income Tax Act may be made. According to Section 29C of the Representation of People Act, 1951, all political parties must declare donations above Rs 20,000 to the Election Commission every year. However, according to the amendment made by the government, it was proposed that the contributions received through electoral bonds would be excluded from the ambit of the RP Act. "This is a retrograde step as far as transparency of donations is concerned and this proviso needs to be withdrawn," the Election Commission is stated to have said in its letter to the Law Ministry. Can the central government issue an instrument on contributions to the political parties which itself falls within the ambit of the said Act, and declare that the limits and compliances specified therein will not apply to such instrument [s]? This at best is considered as obduracy and disregard to the governing law.

31. The Finance Ministry, on the other hand, stated to have said the electoral bonds scheme would increase transparency and cleanse the system of political funding in the country. It is not said so in the case of amendments to the RP Act, 1951 and the Companies Act, 2013. This shows due process of consultations within the government had not been done before introducing the amendments in the Finance Bill, 2017 which amounts to unilateral action open for discussions in the public domain. The provisions that stand amended, on plain reading, are more of the nature of covering up the transparency and cleansing up the system of political funding in the country, the disclosure having been barred. Also, it is surprising to note that the government itself not only encouraging but also justifying an act which on the face of it seems injurious to the health of the democratic system.

32. Further, a RTI petition stated to have sought information about the registration of trusts, financing and other communication about pay-outs made under the Electoral Trust Scheme. The CBDT is said to have rejected the information on the ground of personal privacy under Section 8(1)(j) of the RTI Act. The section holds that information may be exempted from disclosure if it is private information unless the public information officer feels that it is in larger public interest to reveal it. Section 8(1)(j) becomes an unreasonable restriction on RTI which is a fundamental right guaranteed under Article 19(1)(a) of the Constitution contended the RTI. There is public interest information related to electoral trusts being disclosed since such trusts give money to political parties and the public nature of political parties has already been well established by the CIC order.

33. Mutual reciprocation, respect, regard and participation that we expect from the society must first originate and visible within and without the governance that reflects upon the people as good governance and the people in the society will also adhere to such attitudes. Rule of Law is meant for citizens who are Very Ordinary Persons [VOPs] and not for public leaders, Legislators, VVIPs and VIPs [that is what is in practice today] that is causing

increasing tension not only in the governance but also in the society. God has given to humans goodness and badness and left to humans to think over according to their wisdom what is good and what is bad. Democracy has only one standard, dividing it in sub-standards results in rupture of governing system, thereby the democratic system. Exceptions, if any, are those which are specified under the relevant laws and rules. These have now become most common than those specified. Who are we? Citizens created under the constitution and the laws and rules made thereunder. Governance has therefore to be based on equality laid down under the Fundamental Rights. We have already crossed the decent limits set by our forefathers who made the Constitution hurting their best efforts and sentiments they left behind.

# PART 03
# FREEBIES AND WELFARE

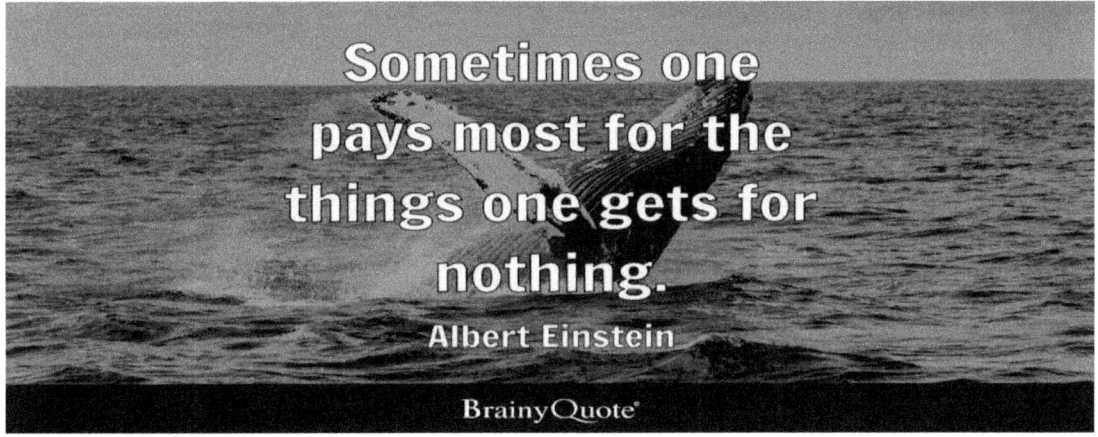

[*What the above quote means "you pay the most in the sense that an obligation you feel, but can't put a value or price, can cause you to keep paying more than what any reasonable valuation might have been.*]

Creativity alone has the capacity to create wealth of the nation for the welfare of the people and the interests of the country. Its absence is bereft of development and the development looks like a colourful Glasshouse.

Freebies are like pouring water in a bottomless bucket. Welfare is like keeping a person begging all through his or her life whereas the essence of welfare is to convert his or her thoughts, deeds and actions into productive purposes providing facilities and economic opportunities that helps him or her to self-earn and live with self-dignity.

The meanings of freebie and welfare can be better understood by reading the following Article that clarifies in clear cut terms welfare is achievable through providing facilities and economic opportunities by the State to the people, the underlying dictum of the Preamble and the Directive Principles of State Policy:

**Social and Economic Justice under Constitution of India: A Critical Analysis Mahantesh G. S. Principal and Coordinator, ABBS School of Law, Bangalore Karnataka, India published in ©2018 IJLMH | Volume 2, Issue 1 | ISSN: 2581-5369 {Excerpts}:**

"I. INTRODUCTION

A society, which protects the rights and liberties of people and provides all the economic and social advantages to the greatest benefit of the least advantaged sections in the society, could be considered Just 1. The Constitution of India was adopted on November 26; 1949.The Indian Constitution is unique in its contents and spirit. Though borrowed from almost every Constitution of the world, the Constitution of India has several salient features that distinguish it from the Constitutions of other countries The Preamble of Constitution of India is designed to realize socio-economic justice to all the people in India…………………………….

III. SOCIAL AND ECONOMIC JUSTICE

Social justice broadly incorporates economic justice also. The socio economic justice as visualized by the Indian Constitution is found mostly in the Directive Principles of State Policy – Part IV of the Constitution of India and to a little extent in the Chapter on Fundamental Rights and certain other provisions of the Constitution. Social justice denotes the equal treatment of all citizens without any social distinction based on caste, colour, race, religion, sex and so on. It means absence of privileges being extended to any particular section of the society, and improvement in the conditions of backward classes (SCs, STs, and OBCs) and women. Social Justice is the foundation stone of Indian Constitution.

Social Justice is the recognition or greater good to a larger number without deprivation or accrual of legal rights. The concept of social justice is central and integral to the Constitution and it is assumed to be to be a basic structure of the Constitution which cannot be whittled down, altered or done away with in view of the Doctrine of Basic Structure propounded in Kesavananda Bharati case2.

Simply put, Social Justice is the comprehensive form to remove social imbalance by law harmonizing the rival claims or the interest of different groups and/or section in the social structure or individuals by means of which alone it would be possible to build up welfare State3.

For prevention of social wrongs and injustice there must be efficient administration of justice according to predeclared principles of law and this can be done through the machinery of courts and legal process.

The concept of social justice is a revolutionary concept which provides meaning and significance to life and makes the rule of law dynamic. When Indian society seeks to meet the challenge of socio-economic inequality by its legislation and with the assistance of the rule of law, it seeks to achieve economic justice without any violent conflict. That is the significance and importance of the concept of social justice in the Indian context of today. Social justice is attained only through the harmonious co-operative effort of the citizens.

The term „Social Justice" is not capable of any precise definition. It has neither any specific content nor does it have any definite contours. It changes with the times, with the culture, with the state of economy and with the people.

'Economic Justice' means the banishment of poverty, not by expropriation of those who have but by the multiplication of the national wealth and resources and an equitable distribution thereof amongst all who contribute towards its production, is the aim of the state envisaged by the directive principles. Economic democracy will be installed in our sub-continent to the extent that this goal is reached. In short, economic justice aims at establishing economic democracy and a „welfare state'.

The right to economic justice to the scheduled castes, scheduled tribes and other weaker sections is a fundamental right to secure equality of status, opportunity and liberty. Economic justice is a facet of liberty without which equality of status and dignity of person is teasing illusions[4] .The ideal of economic justice is to make equality of status meaningful and life worth living at its best removing inequality of opportunity and of status-social, economic and political[5]. …………………………………………………

Distributive justice is a course that Social Justice adopts. In other words, the term Social Justice implies offering economic opportunity, economic equality and removal of social disabilities. It implies in the Indian context, programmes aimed at equality before law, equal opportunity, alleviation of poverty, bridging of the gap between the have and the have-not, re-distribution of material resources, betterment of conditions of labour and removal of caste disabilities etc. In India the idea of welfare state is that the claims of social justice must be treated as cardinal and paramount. Thus The Constitution of India in the preamble resolved to secure to all its citizens;

Justice: social, economic and political.

Therefore, concept of social justice is not foreign to legal order. Social justice is the primary objective of the State as envisaged in our Constitution. Social Justice implies that all citizens are treated equally irrespective of their status in society as a result of the accident birth, race, caste, religion, sex, title etc[7].

## IV. CONSTITUTIONAL EMPHASIS ON SOCIAL AND ECONOMIC JUSTICE

The constitutional concern of social and economic justice as an elastic continuous process is to accord justice to all section of the society by providing facilities and opportunities to remove handicaps and disabilities with which the poor etc. are languishing and secure dignity of their person[8].

Social Justice is the principles that go into the formation of a welfare state. Themes and principles of socio economic justice are amply reflected in the Preamble to the Constitution, in Part III Fundamental Rights and in Part IV the Directive Principles of the Constitution. It has been held that the validity of any law enacted by the legislature would be tested against the touchstones of the Preamble, Fundamental Rights and Directive Principles………………………….."

The Article written by the learned author stated before should open the eyes of the administrators of governance of democracy in our country. The Article is frank and forthright leaving no room for scope for different interpretation of what welfare to be ensured by the State to the people, especially weaker sections of the society. Means for achieving this object do not lie in freebies or welfare schemes as the governance understands as a self-suited programs or schemes but in providing facilities and economic opportunities using the same public funds that are used for freebies and welfare, the Consolidated Fund does not admit freebies; it admits expenditure on welfare schemes coupled with the Directive Principles of State Policy which are emphatic on economic capacity which, in other words means, the affordability by the State of the available public funds in the Consolidated Fund. If this is not understood then, one can say one is reckless in spending the public funds.

## "A BODY OF MEN HOLDING THEMSELVES ACCOUNTABLE TO NOBODY OUGHT NOT TO BE TRUSTED BY ANYBODY." — THOMAS PAINE

The public fund is the public's financial resource that the state manages as a custodian. The impact of how governments manage public funds on economic growth and citizen well-being is referred to as public fund management. Managing public resources entails determining how the government makes money (revenue) and how it spends money (expenditure).

• Taxes, money earned by state enterprises (PSUs), foreign aid, and other sources of revenue are all considered as revenue of the government.

• Expenditures include government salaries, purchases of goods and services, infrastructure and public service spending.

• Public resources should be used to the greatest extent possible for the benefit of the general public. As a result, when managing public resources, public entities (Government) should follow certain principles.

**The following principles should be demonstrated by public entities when using public funds:**

1. **Legality-** Government bodies must follow the law and fulfil their legal obligations. After receiving approval from a competent authority, the public fund must be used. Unauthorized spending will inevitably lead to excess and overspending. Furthermore, funds must be used only for the purpose for which they were approved.

1. **Accountability–** Government bodies should be held accountable for the use of public funds and should be able to provide complete and accurate accounts of their activities, as well as have appropriate governance and management arrangements in place to address any issues.

   • **Accountability is ensured in India through institutions and instruments such as:**

   a. Legislative Executive Judicial Civil Society

   b. Budget

   c. In house accountability mechanisms

   d. Judicial review

   e. Parliamentary committees

   f. CAG

   g. Suit against government and officials

   h. Social Audit, Citizen Charter

   i. Debates, discussion, question hour etc.

   j. Lokpal and Lokayukta, CVC, CBI etc.

   k. Judicial activism etc.

   l. Media etc.

3. **Transparency and openness are dependent on high reporting and disclosure standards. This has two advantages:**

a. It demonstrates that a public resource is being used appropriately, fairly, and effectively for the greatest public good.

b. It boosts public confidence in the government.

• Transparency ensures that authorities acted legally and in accordance with the law. Transparency also ensures that the authority followed the overall principles of equity and fairness and provided the best value for money to the end user.

• Some government agencies operate in less-than-ideal circumstances, such as when there is no market for providers or when those that are available lack the necessary capability or capacity.

• These conditions give government entities disproportionate discretion and power. In such situations, transparency is required to ensure that actions are taken in good faith.

4. **Value for money** – Public funds must be used effectively and efficiently, with no waste, and in a way that maximises public benefit. All public expenditure must pass one fundamental test, namely, Maximum Social Advantage.

• That is, by balancing social benefits and social costs, the government should discover and maintain an optimal level of public expenditure. Every rupee spent by a government must have the goal of maximising the welfare of society as a whole.

• It is essential to ensure that public funds are not used to benefit a specific group or segment of society. The goal is for everyone to be happy.

## THE VALUE-FOR-MONEY PRINCIPLE INVOLVES SEVERAL ASPECTS, SUCH AS:

1. Striking a balance between effectiveness and efficiency

2. Keeping the funding arrangement in place (where this is desirable)

3. Demonstrating the public entity's competence.

4. Sustainability of the funding relationship– When using public funds, a public entity should consider the long-term effects of its funding decisions as well as future funding needs.

5. Government bodies should ensure a fair and reasonable flow of funds for a cause while not jeopardising long-term service delivery expectations. Consider the case of India's fertiliser subsidy. A subsidy is given to each fertiliser manufacturer in order to ensure their financial viability. This means that the most inefficient gets rewarded for it. Such funding arrangements are not long-term sustainable, but they are strategic for the country. This creates a quandary in terms of public spending.

6. **Fairness**– Because of the public's trust in government, it has a fundamental obligation to always act fairly and reasonably when using public funds. The actions of a public entity should be transparent and unbiased. To be fair and reasonable, it is also necessary to respect the nation's diversity while avoiding discrimination on the basis of caste, community, religion, gender, or class, and to adequately protect the interests of the poor, underprivileged, and weaker sections.

7. **Integrity**– Anyone in charge of public resources should do so with the highest level of honesty. A government should have policies and procedures in place to support the highest levels of integrity, such as a code of conduct, an ethics code, and a public service code. Public servants should declare any personal interests that may affect, or appear to affect, their impartiality in any aspect of their work when using public funds ethically

## REASONS FOR INEFFICIENT USE OF PUBLIC FUNDS:

**Inefficient use of public funds can be attributed to a variety of socio-political and administrative factors.**

### 1. POLITICAL REASONS

a. **Political rivalry:** Political rivalry can sometimes devolve into vendettas, undermining the cooperation and collective efforts required for development.

b. **Irrational freebie distribution:** Irrational freebie distribution and loan signing off for electoral popularity puts a strain on the budgetary balance.

c. **Politicized protests:** Repeated ill-intentioned protests and bandhs by any political faction raise the costs incurred as a result of delays in public works projects.

### 2. ADMINISTRATIVE REASONS

a. **Policy paralysis:** One of the main causes of inefficiency in the use of public funds is the government's or its various departments and agencies' delays, inaction, and inability to make policy decisions.

b. **Bureaucratic attitude:** Officials' despotic and obstructionist attitudes, particularly in higher echelons of the bureaucracy, can obstruct the implementation of developmental activities.

c. **Inadequate political will:** The Members of Parliament Local Area Development Scheme (MPLADS) was recently suspended for two financial years due to inefficiency and underutilization of funds.

d. **Red tape:** Excessive regulation and the practise of requiring excessive paperwork and time-consuming procedures prior to official action obstructs the implementation of schemes and projects, thereby obstructing the effective use of public funds.

e. **Lack of public participation:** Due to a high level of illiteracy and ignorance about government policies and schemes, many citizens (particularly the poor) were unable to demand payment from the government for their legitimate financial obligations.

f. **Public watchdogs lack autonomy:** For example, the Central Vigilance Commission lacks the authority to make decisions because it is merely an advisory body with no authority to file criminal charges against government officials. Similarly, the CAG's limited jurisdiction and CIC's lack of autonomy harmed the ability to report and check accountability for public finance irregularities.

g. **Citizen charter non-implementation:** Many public institutions have yet to adopt a citizen charter, a tool of good governance that enables citizens to receive public services as rights in a timely manner. Failure to adopt a citizen charter is a barrier to effective use of public funds.

## 3. SOCIAL REASONS

a. **Corruption-**related social apathy: In India, many people accept corruption as the norm, so even those with ill-gotten wealth have the same status as the honest wealthy. This is in contrast to some societies, such as Japan, where social boycotts of corrupted people have been observed.

b. **Ineffective educational system:** The educational system has failed to instil the moral values of honesty and integrity in its citizens.

c. **Inequality:** In Indian society, social and economic equality encourage people to amass as much wealth as possible when given the chance. Corruption can be seen in the use of public funds at the community level, such as in Panchayats.

d. **Lack of institutionalised social accounting:** In the MNREGA scheme, the process of communicating the social and environmental effects of government actions and inactions to specific interest groups within society is not institutionalised.

Let me now cite the related provisions to understand their significance and relevance in the present context:

Introduction

Background: The source of the concept of Directive Principles of State Policy (DPSP) is the Spanish Constitution from which it came in the Irish Constitution. The concept of DPSP emerged from Article 45 of the Irish Constitution. Constitutional Provisions: Part IV of the Constitution of India (Article 36–51) contains the Directive Principles of State Policy (DPSP). Article 37 of the Indian Constitution states about the application of the Directive Principles. These principles aim at ensuring socioeconomic justice to the people and establishing India as a Welfare State.

Fundamental Rights Vs DPSP:

Unlike the Fundamental Rights (FRs), the scope of DPSP is limitless and it protects the rights of a citizen and work at a macro level. DPSP consists of all the ideals which the State should follow and keep in mind while formulating policies and enacting laws for the country. Directive Principles are affirmative directions on the other hand; Fundamental Rights are negative or prohibitive in nature because they put limitations on the State. The DPSP is not enforceable by law; it is non-justiciable. It is important to note that DPSP and FRs go hand in hand. DPSP is not subordinate to FRs. Classification of Principles: The Directive Principles are classified on the basis of their ideological source and objectives.

Amendments in DPSP: 42nd Constitutional Amendment, 1976: It introduced certain changes in the Part-IV of the Constitution by adding new directives:

Article 39A: To provide free legal aid to the poor.

Article 43A: Participation of workers in management of Industries.

Article 48A: To protect and improve the environment.

44th Constitutional Amendment, 1978: It inserted Section-2 to Article 38 which declares that; "The State in particular shall strive to minimise economic inequalities in income and eliminate inequalities in status, facilities and opportunities not amongst individuals but also amongst groups".

It also eliminated the Right to Property from the list of Fundamental Rights.

86th Amendment Act of 2002: It changed the subject-matter of Article 45 and made elementary education a fundamental right under Article 21 A.

Conflicts between Fundamental Rights and DPSP: Associated Cases

Champakam Dorairajan v the State of Madras (1951): In this case, the Supreme Court ruled that in case of any conflict between the Fundamental Rights and the Directive Principles, the former would prevail.

It declared that the Directive Principles have to conform to and run as subsidiary to the Fundamental Rights.

It also held that the Fundamental Rights could be amended by the Parliament by enacting constitutional amendment acts.

Golaknath v the State of Punjab (1967): In this case, the Supreme Court declared that Fundamental Rights could not be amended by the Parliament even for implementation of Directive Principles.

It was contradictory to its own judgement in the 'Shankari Parsad case'.

Kesavananda Bharati v the State of Kerala (1973): In this case, the Supreme Court overruled its Golak Nath (1967) verdict and declared that Parliament can amend any part of the Constitution but it cannot alter its "Basic Structure"

Thus, the Right to Property (Article 31) was eliminated from the list of Fundamental Rights.

Minerva Mills v the Union of India (1980): In this case, the Supreme Court reiterated that Parliament can amend any part of the Constitution but it cannot change the "Basic Structure" of the Constitution.

Implementation of Directive Principles of State Policy: Associated Acts and Amendments
Land Reforms: Almost all the states have passed land reform laws to bring changes in the agrarian society and to improve the conditions of the rural masses. These measures include:

Abolition of intermediaries like zamindars, jagirdars, inamdars, etc.

Tenancy reforms like security of tenure, fair rents, etc.

Imposition of ceilings on land holdings

Distribution of surplus land among the landless labourers

Cooperative farming

Labour Reforms: The following acts were enacted to protect the interests of the Labour section of the society.

The Minimum Wages Act (1948), Code on Wages, 2020

The Contract Labour Regulation and Abolition Act (1970)

The Child Labour Prohibition and Regulation Act (1986)

Renamed as the Child and Adolescent Labour Prohibition and Regulation Act, 1986 in 2016.

The Bonded Labour System Abolition Act (1976)

The Mines and Minerals (Development and Regulation) Act, 1957

The Maternity Benefit Act (1961) and the Equal Remuneration Act (1976) have been made to protect the interests of women workers.

Panchayati Raj System: Through 73rd Constitutional Amendment Act, 1992, government fulfilled constitutional obligation stated in Article 40.

Three tier 'Panchayati Raj System' was introduced at the Village, Block and District level in almost all parts of the country.

Cottage Industries: To promote cottage industries as per Article 43, the government has established several Boards such as Village Industries Board, Khadi and Village Industries Commission, All India Handicraft Board, Silk Board, Coir Board, etc., which provide essential help to cottage industries in finance and marketing.

Education: Government has implemented provisions related to free and compulsory education as provided in Article 45. Introduced by the 86th Constitutional Amendment and subsequently passed the Rights to Education Act 2009, Elementary Education has been accepted as Fundamental Right of each child between the 6 to 14 years of age.

Rural Area Development: Programmes such as the Community Development Programme (1952), Integrated Rural Development Programme (1978-79) and Mahatma Gandhi National Rural Employment Guarantee Act (MGNREGA-2006) were launched to raise the standard of living particularly in rural areas, as stated in the Article 47 of the Constitution.

Health: Central Government sponsored schemes like Pradhan Mantri Gram Swasthya Yojana (PMGSY) and National Rural Health Mission (NRHM) are being implemented to fulfil the social sector responsibility of the Indian State.

Environment: The Wildlife (Protection) Act, 1972, the Forest (Conservation) Act, 1980 and the Environment (Protection) Act, 1986 have been enacted to safeguard the wildlife and the forests respectively.

The Water and Air Pollution Control Acts have provided for the establishment of the Central Pollution Control Board.

Heritage Preservation: The Ancient and Historical Monument and Archaeological Sites and Remains Act (1958) have been enacted to protect the monuments, places and objects of national importance. {Source: https://www.drishtiias.com/to-the-points/Paper2/directive-principles-of-state-policy-dpsp}

**)Pleaders Website posted an Article "Directive Principles of State Policy – August 9, 2019 written by Richa Singh of Faculty of Law, Aligarh Muslim University {Excerpts}:**

The concept behind the DPSP is to create a '*Welfare State*'. In other words, the motive behind the inclusion of DPSP is not establishing political democracy rather; it's about establishing social and economic democracy in the state. These are some basic principles or instructions or guidelines for the government while formulating laws/policies of the country and in executing them.

According to Dr B R Ambedkar, these principles are 'novel features' of the Constitution. DPSP acts as a guideline for the state and should be taken into consideration while coming up with some new policy or any law. But no one can compel the State to consider and follow all that which is mentioned in DPSP, as DPSP is not justiciable.

Part 4 of the Indian Constitution consists of all the DPSP (Directive Principles of State Policy). It covers the Articles from 36 to 51.

Article 36 of Part IV defines the term "**State**" as the one, who has to keep in mind all the DPSP before formulating any policy or law for the country. The definition of "State" in the part IV will be the same as that of Part III, unless the context otherwise requires a change in it. In Article 37 the nature of DPSP has been defined. DPSPs are non-justiciable.

Article 38 to 51 contains all the different DPSP's: History

- The source of the concept of DPSP is the Spanish Constitution from which it came in the Irish Constitution. The makers of the Indian Constitution were very much influenced by the Irish nationalist movement and borrowed this concept of DPSP from the Irish Constitution in 1937.

- The Government of India Act also had some instructions related to this concept which became an important source of DPSP at that time.

- The Directive Principles of the Constitution of India have been greatly influenced by the Directive Principles of Social Policy.

- The Indians who were fighting for the independence of India from the British rule were greatly influenced by the movements and independence struggles of Ireland at that time, to free themselves from the British rule and move towards the development of their constitution.

- DPSP become an inspiration for independent India's government to tackle social, economic and various other challenges across a diverse nation like India.

- DPSP and fundamental rights have a common origin. The Nehru Report of 1928 contained the Swaraj Constitution of India which contained some of the fundamental rights and some other rights such as the right to education which were not enforceable at that time.

- Some Instruments of Instructions, which also became the immediate source of DPSP, have been taken from the Government of India Act, 1935.

- Sapru Report of 1945 divided fundamental rights into justifiable and non-justifiable rights.

- **Justifiable rights**, the one which was enforceable in a court of law and included in Part III of the Constitution. On the other hand, **Non-justifiable rights** were listed as directive principles, which are just there to guide the state to work on the lines for making India a welfare state. They were included in part IV of the Constitution of India as Directive Principles of State Policy.

- The Constituent Assembly was given the task of making a constitution for India. The assembly composed of elected representatives and Dr. Rajendra Prasad was elected as its President.

- Both the Fundamental Rights and the DPSP were enlisted in all the drafts of the constitution (I, II and III) prepared by the Drafting Committee whose chairman was Dr. B.R. Ambedkar.

Features

- DPSP are not enforceable in a court of law.

- They were made non-justifiable considering that the State may not have enough resources to implement all of them or it may even come up with some better and progressive laws.

- It consists of all the ideals which the State should follow and keep in mind while formulating policies and enacting laws for the country.

- The DPSPs are like a collection of instructions and directions, which were issued under the Government of India Act, 1935, to the Governors of the colonies of India.

- It constitutes a very comprehensive economic, social and political guidelines or principles and tips for a modern democratic State that aimed towards inculcating the ideals of justice, liberty, equality and fraternity as given in the preamble. The Preamble consists of all the objectives that need to be achieved through the Constitution.

- Adding DPSP was all about creating a "welfare state" which works for the individuals of the country which was absent during the colonial era."

## 2. About Welfare

**'WHENEVER THERE ARE SIX ECONOMISTS, THERE ARE SEVEN OPINIONS! - MRS. BARBARA WOOTTON**

Before we start, let us recall what Pandit Jawaharlal Nehru said "There will be no complete freedom as long as there is starvation, hunger, lack of clothing, lack of necessaries of life and lack of opportunity of growth for every single human being, man, woman and child in the country." Nehru said in the Constituent Assembly on 22nd July, 1947 (On 22 July 1947, in the Constituent Assembly.

Economic Development of a country does not lie only between the government and the monetary regulator revolving around the corporate through incentives, policy rate cuts and rushing the liquidity; the need for these arises only when the economic infrastructure of the country stands on sound foundation; consultation process for revitalizing the economic development has reached out to all the stakeholders such as various national sector-wise associations and federations as well as the people's bodies (rural, semi urban and urban) whose contribution is much more than the corporate(except in the case of contributions to the political parties as part of funding election financing). Active involvement of acknowledged experts from all the major fields of economy is more important than merely the bureaucracy for evolving policies and programs for making the country economically self-reliant. Such bodies and experts are the depository of practical knowledge and experience; their association would add to confidence and enhance the meaning and value of real economic development. It may look impossible but, we should also know that, possibility exists within the impossibility if one is honest to search for it. It is only the democratic system that permits evolvement of such bodies and experts with openness. This we seem to have overlooked for the last three decades that widened the gaps of basic economic development evolution.

Lack of appreciation of the above in the years that followed created a new class of economists and experts who believed it would be wiser to spend huge expenditure for short term aimed at welfare schemes in order to accelerate the economic development. They seem to have failed to understand using such path for speedier economic development is like building a house without pillars.

These short-term welfare measures are, no doubt, alluring for the COMMON PEOPLE and the politicians not knowing that short term measures by their very nature and meaning live for short time, burning the long-term development approach, the only one that has the capacity and capabilities to sustain the economic growth. Whereas, long term economic development measures in vogue prior to the eighties encompassed all kinds of short-term welfare measures and the past course of economic development adopted is self-evident. Institutional sanctity of schemes and programs for speeding up economic development started being substituted by the individualized or personalized schemes and programs from late seventies. When the funds applied for the economic development entirely comes from the public funds, institutionalized funding must prevail otherwise, it shows use of the public funds for enhancing the importance of individualization and personalization. A constitutional democracy does not permit individualization or personalization character that are followed in Authoritarian democracy; it permits only the collective effort, spirit and upholding of institutionalized instruments, systems and procedures. The institutionalized instruments, systems and procedures ensure sanctity of the public funds and their sanitized utilization for the economic development of the country. If we have to sustain and succeed enjoying constitutional democracy, we need to stop undermining the institutions, systems and procedures that stand as fortress from attacks and adventurism.

As stated in Kautilya's Arthashastra, Kings in the past were more concerned with the people's needs and their economic dispensation was aimed at that having based on the prevailing reality on the ground level. They never sought to be done for their own sake or in their names that is the way they followed to keep the people socially and economically happy.

Elementary essence of economic development is to start with infrastructure development, education including skill development and make people hale and healthy capable to sustain growing weight for speedy economic development. Despite best efforts from the start of the Five Year Plans up to the 12th Five Year Plan in making overall visible economic development, the basic question remained unanswered is the reason for side-lining the crucial need for the simultaneous development of above sectors. Electricity, the lifeline for economic development, though maintained its marked growth until the seventh five-year plan, utterly failed to sustain it from eighth plan onwards. Targets continued to increase while achievements continued to decrease. Turned into a continuing chronic problem not knowing when it would be able to come up to the expectations of economic development. What one reads in print media or listens to speeches are only signs of assurances but no signs of action or achievements that one could say would give impetus to the economic development.

That shows we have no concern whatsoever for real development and believe more in rhetoric development not realizing the seriousness of the consequences lying underneath. Every developmental period has its time frame that continues to assure the people and once that assurance turns out distrustful, the development takes a different course visible in different parts of the country. The development of whatever nature is a sincere effort to embrace the confronting situation; calls for reaching up to the people, honest understanding of their problems, build trust and create mutual confidence. Once that starts, the development starts of its own. Threats or pressures do not last long because the people affected are born in those places and have to live there whereas the force gets exhausted to serve its purpose for long time. Enmity, if any, is born out of injustice and perpetual persecution. Because, we think this is the only best course to keep the people at their place and under control. This is a misconceived idea. Look back to our ancestral periods which kept their step pace to pace with the people; achieved real development. This missed the course especially after twenty-five years of the country becoming republic, solely because of increasing personalization and discarding the people's zeal and the need for developing the institutional robustness according sanctity to their purpose. There was no system of origination for ascertaining what the COMMON PEOPLE wanted and to assimilate their reactions to what the governing system wanted to impose upon them. Gram Panchayats and Zillah Parishad are there in every state which are in constant touch with ground realities and whose words and views should have been given due weightage. Gandhian Economics that the economic development should start from the root did not find its place rather what emerged was from top to bottom.

Advent of so-called poverty reduction measures through social schemes since last three decades has predominated huge state expenditure from the treasury without establishing a rigorous mechanism for implementation to ensure reaching the benefits to the intended beneficiaries. The governments believed in spending as if that is in itself the end of the objective. There were no physical or compensatory benefits to the society in general and the government. The resultant widening gap between expenditure and revenue went almost beyond control of the government. This led to inventing new measures on how to make the gap as much as possible. The counter effects on economic and financial sectors received meagre attention throwing open free for all market prices of essential commodities including vegetables and fruits, the COMMON PEOPLE survive with.

The revenue shortfall started staring at with untold impacts on all fronts. These measures are good for announcement for populism while the same acted against the basic concept and principle of economic development which creates social welfare that is, social and economic justice. Food production was stated to be increasing year after year with food wastage also stated to be reaching almost 40% of the food produced in government silos; denying food to those who were direly in need of food; in some cases, died due to hunger. The government and its experts seemed to have overlooked the basic fact that the hunger dies only through providing economic activity to the poor and not by distributing cash or cereals. Every economic activity recreates something compensatory to the expenditure in physical or revenue. Reverse economic policies and programs only saw expenditure with no compensatory accruals. There is a strong thinking to provide cash under Universal Basic Income (UBI) scheme by introducing which many of the countries have burnt their fingers.

It is hard to overstate the degree of gloom we find in policy and business circles in India right now, at least behind closed doors. There was a time, not long ago, when 7 per cent or even 8 per cent growth was considered India's birth right, the floor below which GDP growth would not drop unless there was a global crisis. Today, we're staring instead at a 7 per cent ceiling -- a ceiling that, most of the time, may loom out of reach." The government, the RBI, the media, Rating Agencies and multinational funding agencies are struggling to maintain that ceiling as is evident from the statements appearing in the print and electronic media of the day to day likely variations they are talking about the same ceiling. None is sure to stand up and confirm, that is the uncertainty of the course of economic development and what the central government holds in hand at last is the official one.

Economic development depends upon two factors or series of factors. These are (1) its geographical situation, that is, how rich its land is in food products, minerals, forest, power, and favourable climate, situation for trade and transport, means of communication, availability and readiness of infrastructure, capital, the credit system, security, marketing structure to absorb demand and supply, free trade and protection; and (2) its people, that is, how energetic and wise they are in using the natural resources and acquiring technical skill for the purpose. The former is more or less fixed for a nation, and can be altered by man only to a very limited extent, while the latter is changeable. Therefore, in economics the latter is more important than the former. In making use of both of the above factors the habit of economizing is also important whereon the prosperity of the nation depends. Public finance deals with expenditure and income of the public authorities of the state as also with financial administration and control. The main concerns of the public finance are public expenditure, public income, public debts and assets and financial administration.

Basic assumption of economic development is the optimal exploitation of items (1) and (2) mentioned above which address comprehensively all the social aspects including education, employment, social welfare, self-earning capacity, improved standard of living and much desired dignity of life both in the rural and urban areas, the metros being an independent class in themselves with inbuilt system of self-development. The parameters referred to are inclusive with the factors in (1) and (2), thus suggesting the need that was necessary to accord highest priority for development of those factors. This is what the economic development means and understood all over the world until the time the process of their splintering started somewhere towards end of the seventies. Successive efforts of economic development displaced the above originality concept with accentuation towards so called measures for poverty reduction, social welfare, social wellbeing, calls for education for all, urban rural sanitation, Twenty Point Programme, food security, personalized health and welfare schemes, Electricity for All by 2012 which continued to increase both in number and budget provision year after year. This had two implications on the economic development of the country. First, fragmentation of infrastructure components into individualized (personalized) schemes and second, dividing the integrated financial resources for development into piecemeal application, both the implications having the effect of separation of integrated or economic infrastructure development both in rural and urban areas involving increasing burden on the execution system and scope for more and more leakages. Later assessment of the achievements was found to be the achievements being far below the envisaged targeted benefits.

Given the above background, let us read the Articles in Part IV – Directive Principles of State Policy and to make an analysis which of them have relationship and bearing on the two counts: One, Welfare and Two, Freebie.

Welfare Scheme:

The debates and discussions on the subject matter confined to exchange of political language vocabulary among the political parties, media debates, scholars writings in the print media. What however, one could find was there was no reference to or reflections of the Constitution on the point of discussions and debates. 'Creativity' cannot be substituted for the 'beneficiary' for; the creativity is inborn in every human to understand and act upon economic opportunities created by the governance under the Directive Principles as also confer right to citizens under the Fundamental Rights that convey the realistic meaning of what welfare and equality fundamentals are enshrined therein. That is beneficial to any one; more so, to the poor which confers as a birth right to learn, earn and live with self-dignity. Such welfare measures envisaged under the Constitution of the country do not empower the ruling political party converting them into welfare schemes as self-defined by them. Doing so, amounts to overshadowing the obligations of fulfilling aspirations of the citizens for their self-sustenance, also as application of the public funds on selective basis and purposes that cut the **umbilical cord** of equality guaranteed under the Fundamental Rights. The silence of the provisions of the Directive Principles of State Policy to spell out in broad terms what welfare policies and programs mean on the lines as well stated therein free legal aid, the only permissible freebie, emboldened the governing system to draw their own definitions or conclusions about those two critical words, the umbrella of the weaker sections of society and further different political parties understood them in their own way but not in the same way as contemplated under the Principles.

Every rupee spent from the Public Funds even for the poorest of the people must of be regenerative with enablement of such people with supportive measures such as providing them tools and tackles or reviving their traditional skills and crafts injecting in them a sense of self-generation of earnings to meet their day to day needs, a lifelong sustainable step utilizing the same funds applied otherwise under one or the other welfare scheme. These are in other words are the same as brought out in the first Article stated before, that is, facilities and economic opportunities.. Welfare, according to me, means utilizing the earmarked public funds to generate or regenerate the skill inborn in every individual, to achieve which, extend the economic opportunities, facilities, tools and tackles, knowledge upgradation on a continual basis to ensure the individuals who possess one or the other rural skilfulness traditional handed down to them or survey the areas and explore the potential opportunities available around the areas and exploit them for the benefit of the rural and semi-urban population.

This is one time effort with upgradation now and then according to the advancing technologies. This is the foundation of welfare that self-constructs the future growth of the area. Dispersal of public funds to keep the people breathing is short-lived for; the system and mechanism remain open for leakage of public funds adding more physical and financial weight of the political leaders, bureaucrats and the administering authorities. The people in such areas don't have the changing technology in tools and tackles and providing public funds for such purposes would build them physically, financially and mentally stronger, a power that confers self-earning for self-living with self-dignity. Social orderliness is the backbone. This is the sense and essence of the welfare enshrined under the constitution. That is how the civilizations born, sustained and continue to survive in futuristic democracy if the right path is paved by the preceding generations.

## List of important Schemes launched by the Government of India

| S.No. | Scheme | Ministry | Author's Analysis |
|---|---|---|---|
| 1 | 2 | 3 | 4 |
| **Skill Development, Employment and Entrepreneurship** | | | |
| 1 | Make in India | Ministry of Commerce and Industry | Self –reliance. The political parties that ruled the country fifty years back |

|   |   |   | supposed to have done this. Import was considered more suited than indigenous creation and production. This was the period when there was line-up of commission agents. Country would have saved huge expenditure from the imports. Capabilities exist within the country but their exploitation and promotion was greater than mere existence. We remained on the alms of the advanced countries. Better done late than never. This spirit needs to be given whole hearted support irrespective of the fact whether self-reliance is pursued through government or private organizations. Sole object is country's interests. This is regenerative and reproductive economic effort. |
|---|---|---|---|
| 2 | Startup India, Standup India | Government of India | Much needed move has taken shape and come into reality. Greater pushing up through policies and finance will wake up the sleeping citizens opening up increasing opportunities for self-development and newer employment opportunities. This is regenerative and reproductive economic effort. |
| 3 | Skill India | Ministry of Skill Development and Entrepreneurs | Initial years of democracy in the country witnessed least consideration on this subject. Illiteracy was preferred more beneficial than literacy and skill development for other considerations such elections, that was the reason the annual budget allocations were the lowest on those accounts. |
| 4 | Digital India | Ministry of Electronics and Information Technology | Before the last four decades, we considered we are not capable to induct digital sense and essence and waited watching what the advanced countries are doing. We were habituated with such thinking not because of want of our capabilities but because of the darkness surrounded us for want governance guidance and policies framework. Now, we are catching up rather advancing in the area. This is regenerative and reproductive economic effort. |
| 5 | Pradhan Mantri Kaushal Vikas | Ministry of Skill Development and | Same as stated above. |

| | | Yojana | Entrepreneurs | |
|---|---|---|---|---|
| | 6 | Startup India seed fund scheme | Department for Promotion of Industry and Internal Trade | Same stated above. |
| | 7 | NIRVIK Scheme (Niryat Rin Vikas Yojana) | Export Credit Guarantee Corporation of India (ECGC) | This was introduced well in time in the past and has been greatly helpful for export efforts. This is regenerative and reproductive economic effort. |
| | 8 | Pradhan Mantri 'YUVA' Yojana | Ministry of Skill Development and Entrepreneurs | Same as stated above. |
| | 9 | National Technical Textiles Mission (NTTM) | The ministry of Textiles | There is a greater recognition accorded to this now compared in the past. This has highly potential growth prospects with increasing attraction and earning larger foreign exchange. This needs to be further spurred up in the rural and semi-urban areas which had ancestral and traditional gifted skills which were taken away during the colonial rules and now need to be regenerated and renovated with changing technology. This is regenerative and reproductive economic effort. |
| **Schemes & Initiatives through NSDC** | | | | |
| | 1 | Rozgar Mela | Ministry of Skill Development and Entrepreneurs | This needs to be done as part and parcel of the normal process in the democratic environment rather than identifying it differently as has been named. This suggests in negative thinking because any Mela means business consideration. Let it be known as Rozgar Yojana to be structured as a part of the government system through institutional support. .This is part of employment opportunities efforts but lacks regenerative and reproductive economic spirit which a creative economics calls for. |
| | 2 | Pradhan Mantri Kaushal Kendras (PMKK) | | Same as stated above. |
| | 3 | Capacity Building Scheme | | Same as stated above. |
| | 4 | Udaan | | Economic generative and reproductive effort. |
| | 5 | School Initiatives and Higher Education | | This needs to be part of the existing institutional growth rather than making focus specific. End objects and means |

| | | | need to assure potential for regenerative and reproductive economic efforts. |
|---|---|---|---|
| 6 | India International Skill Centres (IISCs) | | Same as stated above. |
| 7 | Pre Departure Orientation Training (PDOT) | | Same as stated above. |
| **Schemes & Initiatives through Directorate of General Training** | | | |
| 1 | Craftsmen Training Scheme (CTS) | Ministry of Skill Development and Entrepreneurs | Same as stated above. Ultimate aim needs to create regenerative and reproductive economic effort. |
| 2 | Crafts Instructor Training Scheme (CITS) | | |
| 3 | Apprenticeship Training under the Apprentices Act, 1961 | | |
| 4 | Advanced Vocational Training Scheme (AVTS) | | |
| 5 | Vocational Training Programme For Women | | |
| 6 | Upskill India | | |
| 7 | Flexi MoUs | | |
| 8 | STRIVE | | |
| 9 | Initiatives in the North East and LWE Regions | | |
| 11 | Dual System of Training (DST) | | |
| 12 | Polytechnics | | |
| **Schemes related to Health and Sanitation** | | | |
| 1 | Swachh Bharat Abhiyan | Ministry of Housing and Urban Affairs | Awareness promotional effort. |
| 2 | Namani Gange | Ministry of Water Resources | |
| 3 | National Bal Swachhta | Ministry of Women and Child Development | |
| 4 | Pradhan Mantri Bhartiya Janaushadhi Pariyojana' (PMBJP) | Ministry of Chemicals and Fertilisers | |
| **Health** | | Ministry of Health and Family Welfare | |
| 5 | National health | | Towards fulfillment of the State |

| | | | |
|---|---|---|---|
| | mission | | obligations under the Directive Principles of State Policy. |
| 6 | National Digital health mission | | |
| 7 | Pradhan Mantri Swasthya Suraksha Yojana | | |
| 8 | Rashtriya Swasthya Bima Yojana | | |
| 9 | PM- Ayushman Bharat Health Infrastructure Mission(PM-ABHIM) | | |
| | Universal Immunisation programme | | |
| | Pulse Polio programme | | |
| **Schemes related to Education** | | | |
| 1 | New Education Policy 2020 | Central Government | Towards fulfillment of the State obligations under the Directive Principles of State Policy as supplementary to main objects. |
| 2 | Sarva Shiksha Abhiyan | Ministry of human resource development | |
| 3 | Mid-Day Meal | Ministry of human resource development | |
| 4 | Mahila Samakhya | Ministry of Women and Child Development. | |
| 5 | Strengthening for providing quality Education in Madrassas ( SPQEM) | Ministry of Education | |
| 6 | Rashtriya Madhyamik Shiksha Abhiyan | Ministry of human resource development | |
| 7 | National Initiative for School Heads' and Teachers' Holistic Advancements (NISHTHA) | Part of NEP | |
| 8 | Scheme for Higher Education Youth in Apprenticeship and Skills (SHREYAS) | Ministry of Human Resource Development (MHRD), Ministry of Labour & Employment, Ministry of Skill Development & Entrepreneurship | |
| 9 | National Educational | Ministry of Education | |

| | | | |
|---|---|---|---|
| | Alliance for Technology (NEAT) | | |
| 10 | IMPRESS scheme | Ministry of human resource development | |
| 11 | The Scheme for Promotion of Academic and Research Collaboration (SPARC) | Ministry of human resource development | |
| 12 | Global Initiative of Academic Networks (GIAN) | Ministry of human resource development | |
| 13 | PM POSHAN Scheme | Ministry of Education | |
| 14 | National Initiative for Proficiency in Reading with Understanding and Numeracy (NIPUN BHARAT) | Part of NEP | |
| 15 | PM e-VIDYA | Ministry of Education | |
| 16 | Strengthening Teaching-Learning and Results for States (STARS) | Ministry of Education | |
| **Other initiatives** | | | |
| 1. | Pradhan Mantri SVANidhi Scheme | | Towards fulfillment of the State obligations under the Directive Principles of State Policy as supplementary to main objects. |
| 2. | Samarth Scheme | | |
| 3. | Rashtriya Gokul Mission | | |
| 4. | Production Linked Incentive (PLI) Scheme | | |
| 5. | PM FME – Formalisation of Micro Food Processing Enterprises Scheme | | |
| 6. | Kapila Kalam Program | | |
| 7. | Pradhan Mantri Matsya Sampada Yojana | | |
| 8. | Solar Charkha Mission | | |
| 9. | SVAMITVA Scheme | | |
| 10. | Samarth Scheme | | |
| 11. | Sahakar Pragya Initiative | | |
| 12. | Integrated Processing Development Scheme | | |
| 13. | Housing for All Scheme | | |
| 14. | Fame India Scheme | | |
| 15. | KUSUM Scheme | | |
| 16. | Nai Roshni Scheme | | |
| 17. | Swadesh Darshan Scheme | | |
| 18. | National Water Mission | | |

| | | |
|---|---|---|
| 19. | National Nutrition Mission | |
| 20. | Operation Greens Scheme | |
| 21. | PM-KISAN (Pradhan Mantri Kisan Samman Nidhi) Scheme | |
| 22. | Pradhan Mantri Kisan Maan Dhan Yojana | |
| 23. | PM Garib Kalyan Yojana (PMGKY) | |
| 24. | Pradhan Mantri Shram Yogi Maan-Dhan | |
| 25. | New Jal Shakti Ministry | |
| 26. | Jan Dhan Yojana | |
| 27. | Make in India | |
| 28. | Sansad Adarsh Gram Yojana | |
| 29. | Sukanya Samriddhi Scheme – Beti Bachao Beti Padhao | |
| 30. | HRIDAY Scheme | |
| 31. | PM Mudra Yojna | |
| 32. | Ujala Yojna | |
| 33. | Atal Pension Yojana | |
| 34. | Prime Minister Jeevan Jyoti Bima Yojana | |
| 35. | Pradhan Mantri Suraksha Bima Yojana | |
| 36. | AMRUT Plan | |
| 37. | Digital India Mission | |
| 38. | Prime Minister Ujjwala Plan | |
| 39. | Atal Bhujal Yojana (ABY) | |
| 40. | Prime Minister's Citizen Assistance and Relief in Emergency Situation (PM CARES) | |
| 41. | Aarogya Setu | |
| 42. | Ayushman Bharat | |
| 43. | UMANG – Unified Mobile Application for New-age Governance | |
| 44. | Saansad Adarsh Gram Yojana (SAGY) | |
| 45. | Shramev Jayate Yojana | |
| 46. | Smart Cities Mission | |
| 47. | Pradhan Mantri Gram Sadak Yojana (PMGSY) | |
| 48. | Mission for Integrated Development of Horticulture (MIDH) | |
| 49. | National Beekeeping & Honey Mission (NBHM) | |
| 50. | Deen Dayal Upadhyaya Grameen Kaushalya Yojana (DDU-GKY) | |
| 51. | Unique Land Parcel Identification Number (ULPIN) Scheme | |
| **52.** | UDID Project | |

[Source: **response net**. Details of each Scheme – are available at https://www.india.gov.in/my-government/schemes [also for updated schemes and programs]

Above analysis shows that there is only one Freebie obligation placed upon the State. So for as the Schemes as have been shown above can be classified into State Obligatory and Supplementary to Obligatory Schemes to be fulfilled by the State under the Directive Principles of the State Policy. Within the Schemes, there are Schemes in respect of which the entire expenditure is to be met by the State from the Consolidated Fund. These schemes being mainly welfare oriented are not reproductive economic efforts. Few Schemes as noted in the Analysis in the above Table are of regenerative and reproductive economic efforts. There does not appear any Scheme that enables, with one time financial aid by the State to the poorer and poorest class of people in the rural areas and urban areas become capable of self-exerting their traditional skills, crafts and so on handed over to them by their ancestors, creating self-earning capacity, self-sustenance and living with the self-dignity. This is the crux and cream of the objects of the Directive Principles of the State Policy. Mere expenditure on such people by the State unsure of the same being reaching the hands of the intended beneficiaries is not the intent and spirit of the Directive Principles of State Policy but inculcate in such expenditure imbibing of the economic creation culture, the ultimate direction to ensure that such people become self-reliant also in course of time. Among the names of the Schemes submitted in the Table above, barring some of them as having a close relationship towards fulfillment of the Directive Principles of State Policy, most of them are in the nature of recurring expenditure whether in terms of distribution of food grains or transfer of money including through digital means. This is the main cause why the fiscal deficit has been widening and accumulating with multifarious economic consequences. This is anti-thesis of creation of economic efforts, self-reliance and revenue to the State. Let us look back how our country developed based on Five-year Plans conceived and adopted till the end of the Twelfth Five Year Plan {2012}.

After the Second World War, many developing countries turned to economic planning. These plans, typically five years, would analyse the state of the economy and include investment and expenditure plans for almost every area, from transport and energy to agriculture and industry. The Indian economy was in shambles when it attained freedom. The Indian economy was hamstrung by British rule; therefore, the fathers of development created a 5-year plan to develop it. The Planning Commission of India, draughts oversees and evaluates the five-year plan in India. The planning ideology sustained the Indian economy from 1947 to 2017. The Planning Commission (1951–2014) and the NITI Aayog created, carried out, and supervised this through the Five-Year Plans (2015-2017). The new government abolished the Planning Commission, headed by Narendra Modi. He was elected in 2014 and replaced with the NITI Aayog (an acronym for National Institution for Transforming India).

**Focus of Five-Year Plans:**

- Economic development is the primary focus of Indian planning. India's economic development is measured by its rising Gross Domestic Product (GDP) and per capita income.

- **Increment of number in Employment:** A key goal for economic planning in India is to increase employment to utilize the nation's human resources better.

- Planning in India has always emphasized social justice, which is connected to all other set targets. It attempts to decrease the number of poor individuals and give them access to social services and work.

- Raising the quality of life through increased per capita income and equitable income distribution is one of India's primary economic expected outcomes.

- **Social Welfare and the Provision of Efficient Social Services:** Increasing labor welfare and social welfare for all socioeconomic sectors is one of the goals of all five-year plans and programs recommended by the NITI Aayog. Planning in India has included developing social services like healthcare, education, and emergency services.

- **Reducing Economic Inequality**: Since independence, India's economic planning has placed a strong emphasis on measures that will reduce inequality through progressive taxation, job creation, and job reservation.

- Through careful economic planning, India wants to grow exports and achieve self-sufficiency in key commodities. During the third five-year plan, from 1961 to 1966, the Indian economy reached the take-off stage of development.

- **Economic Stability:** In addition to the country's overall economic growth, India's economic planning also attempts to maintain stable market conditions. This entails preventing price deflation but simultaneously maintaining a modest level of inflation. Economic planning seeks to prevent structural flaws in the system from being caused by extremely high or extremely low wholesale price index increases.

- **Comprehensive and Sustainable Development:** One of the main goals of economic planning is the development of all economic sectors, including agriculture, industry, and services.

- **Regional Development:** India's economic planning tries to lessen development gaps between regions. For instance, whereas states like Uttar Pradesh, Bihar, Assam, Orissa, and Nagaland are economically underdeveloped, others like Punjab, Haryana, Maharashtra, Gujarat, and Tamil Nadu have more advanced economies. Others, including Karnataka and Andhra Pradesh, have had unequal development, with world-class economic hubs in their cities and a hinterland that has seen less growth. Planning in India seeks to understand these gaps and offer solutions.

Achievements of the Five-Year Plans:

Significant achievements of the Five-Year Plans include:

1. **Increase in National Income:** India's national income grew by 0.5% annually before planning. India's average yearly growth rate has been around 5% during the planning period.

2. **The rise in per capita income during the planning period:** The annual per capita income growth rate was 2.9%.

3. **Institutional and technical advancements** in agricultural planning have significantly contributed to the growth of agriculture in our nation. The average annual growth rate of agricultural output was 2.8% during the planning period.

4. **Industry expansion and diversification:** During the planned period, the growth rate of industrial production was roughly 7% annually. Industries producing capital and essential goods have expanded significantly. The nation is now independent in the consumer products sector. The industrial sector has evolved and been modernized.

5. **Economic and social infrastructure:** During the planning phase, financial and insurance infrastructure, as well as transportation and communication infrastructure, irrigation, and power infrastructure, has grown significantly. Facilities for health and education have seen a tremendous increase.

6. **Increased job prospects** have been the focus of targeted efforts throughout the plan period. The government set a goal of 58 million employees in the eleventh five-year plan.

7. **Foreign trade:** India's trading abroad has also expanded astronomically. The value of international commerce in 1948–1949 was Rs. 792 crores. It was Rs. 38, 11,422 crores in 2011–2012.

8. Therefore, we may conclude that during the plan period, our economy made significant improvement.

Failures of the Five-Year Plans:

Almost every strategy had poverty alleviation as its primary goal. But upon closer inspection, we find that it has not been adequately treated. With spiralling unemployment, inflation rates were at an all-time high. The equitable sharing of social and economic gains was the planning's ethical objective. But the gap between classes continues to grow. Yet to be received were the desired findings to address inequities. People were becoming more vulnerable and excluded due to infrastructure issues.

NITI Aayog:

Since the Planning Commission was disbanded, no official plans for the economy have been developed anymore, but five-year defense plans are being created. 2017 through 2022 would have been the most recent. There isn't a thirteenth five-year plan, though.

- A political think tank called the NITI Aayog was established to advise the government. Establishing a plan created from the standpoint of the Centre will not be a part of the NITI Aayog. Instead, it attempts to involve all states in creating systematic policies unique to each state.
- The NITI Aayog's mission is to improve the effectiveness and cooperation of our country's federal system by implementing the sustainable development goals (SDGs) that are developed in international fora………………..

Conclusion:

After India gained its independence in 1950, economic planning was implemented since it was seen as crucial to expanding and developing the nation's economy. The Planning Commission (1951–2014) and the NITI Aayog's Five-Year Plans, which were created, put into action, and monitored, served as the vehicles for carrying this out (2015-2017)

[Source: https://www.geeksforgeeks.org/importance-of-five-year-plan-in-india/#:~:text=Objectives%20of%20Five%2DYear%20Plans,Economic%20self%2Dreliance

The differences between NITI Aayog and Planning Commission are:

| Niti Aayog | Planning Commission |
|---|---|
| NITI Aayog has not been given the mandate or powers to impose policies on States. NITI Aayog is basically a think-tank or an advisory body. | The Planning Commission had the power to impose policies on States and for the projects approved by the Planning Commission. |
| The powers for the allocation of funds have not been given to the NITI Aayog. The powers are with the Finance Ministry. | The Planning Commission had the power to allocate funds to the State Governments and various Central Government Ministries for various programmes and projects at the National and State Levels. |
| In NITI Aayog, State Governments have to play a more proactive role. | State Governments did not have much role to play apart from taking part in the meetings. The State Government's role was confined to the National Development Council. |
| Based on the requirements, there are part-time members appointed in NITI Aayog. | The Planning Commission did not have any provisions for the appointment of part-time members. |
| The Governing Council of NITI Aayog has Lieutenant Governors of Union Territories | The National Development Council had Lieutenant Governors and State Chief Ministers. Planning |

| | |
|---|---|
| and State Chief Ministers. | Commission had to report to the National Development Commission |
| The CEO of NITI Aayog is appointed by the Prime Minister. Secretaries are known as CEO. | Planning Commission secretaries were appointed through the usual process. |
| The number of full-time members in NITI Aayog could be lesser than the numbers that the Planning Commission had. | The last Planning Commission had eight full-time members. |
| Under the NITI Aayog organisation structure, new posts were created – CEO, Vice-Chairperson. CEO has the rank of a Secretary. Four Cabinet members would serve as ex-officio members. NITI Aayog has two-part time members and five full-time members. | The Planning Commission's organisational structure consisted of full-time members, a member secretary and a Deputy Chairperson. |
| In NITI Aayog, the final policy would bear fruit after due consultations are held with State Governments in the policy formulation stage. | The Planning Commission first formulated policies, and then State Governments were consulted regarding the allocation of funds for the programmes or projects. |
| NITI Aayog is also an Executive Body as it is not mentioned in the Constitution of India, and it was not established by an Act of Parliament. However, if needed, it can be converted into a Statutory Body by passing a law in Parliament; an example is UIDAI. | The now-defunct Planning Commission was an Executive Body. |

[Source:https://byjus.com/free-ias-prep/difference-between-niti-aayog-and-planning-commission/]

| PLAN | FOCUS |
|---|---|
| First Plan (1951 - 56)<br>Target Growth : 2.1 %<br>Actual Growth: 3.6 % | • It was based on **Harrod-Domar Model**.<br>• Influx of refugees, severe food shortage & mounting inflation confronted the country at the onset of the first five year Plan.<br>• The Plan Focussed on **agriculture**, price stability, power and transport<br>• It was a **successful** plan primarily because of good harvests in the last two years of the plan. Objectives of rehabilitation of refugees, food self-sufficiency & control of prices were more or less achieved. |
| Second Plan<br>(1956 - 61)<br>Target Growth: 4.5%<br>Actual Growth: 4.3% | • Simple aggregative Harrod Domar Growth Model was again used for overall projections and the strategy of resource allocation to broad sectors as agriculture & Industry was based on two & four sector Model prepared by Prof. P C Mahalanobis. (Plan is also called **Mahalanobis Plan).**<br>• Second plan was conceived in an atmosphere of economic stability.<br>• It was felt agriculture could be accorded lower priority.<br>The Plan Focussed on **rapid industrialization- heavy & basic**<br>• **Industries.** Advocated huge imports through foreign loans.<br>• The Industrial Policy 1956 was based on establishment of a **Socialistic pattern of society** as the goal of economic policy. |

|  |  |
|---|---|
|  | • Acute shortage of forex led to pruning of development targets, price rise was also seen (about 30%) vis a vis decline in the earlier Plan & the 2nd FYP was only **moderately successful**. |
| Third Plan (1961 - 66) \|Target Growth: 5.6% Actual Growth: 2.8% | • At its conception, it was felt that Indian economy has entered a "**takeoff stage**". Therefore, its aim was to make India a **'self-reliant'** and **'self-generating'** economy.<br>• Based on the experience of first two plans (agricultural production was seen as limiting factor in India's economic development), agriculture was given top priority to support the exports and industry.<br>• The Plan was **thorough failure** in reaching the targets due to unforeseen events - Chinese aggression (1962), Indo-Pak war (1965), severe drought 1965-66. Due to conflicts the approach during the later phase was shifted from development to **defence & development.** |
| Three Annual Plans (1966-69) euphemistically described as Plan holiday. | • Failure of Third Plan that of the devaluation of rupee (to boost exports) along with inflationary recession led to postponement of Fourth FYP. Three Annual Plans were introduced instead. Prevailing crisis in agriculture and serious food shortage necessitated the emphasis on agriculture during the Annual Plans.<br>• During these plans a whole new agricultural strategy was Implemented. It involving wide-spread distribution of high-yielding varieties of seeds, extensive use of fertilizers, exploitation of irrigation potential and soil conservation. |
|  | • During the Annual Plans, the economy absorbed the shocks generated during the Third Plan<br>• It paved the path for the planned growth ahead. |
| Fourth Plan (1969 - 74) Target Growth: 5.7% Actual Growth: 3.3% | • Refusal of supply of essential equipments and raw materials from the allies during Indo Pak war resulted in twin objectives of " **growth with stability** " and "**progressive achievement of self-reliance** " for the Fourth Plan.<br>• Main emphasis was on growth rate of agriculture to enable other sectors to move forward. First two years of the plan saw record production. The last three years did not measure up due to poor monsoon. Implementation of **Family Planning Programmes** was amongst major targets of the Plan.<br>• Influx of Bangladeshi refugees before and after 1971 Indo-Pak war was an important issue along with price situation deteriorating to crisis proportions and the plan is considered as **big failure**. |
| Fifth Plan (1974-79) Target Growth: 4.4% Actual Growth: 4.8% | • The final Draft of fifth plan was prepared and launched by D.P. Dhar in the backdrop of economic crisis arising out of run-away inflation fuelled by hike in oil prices and failure of the Govt. takeover of the wholesale trade in wheat.<br>• It proposed to achieve two main objectives: 'removal of poverty' **(Garibi Hatao)** and **'attainment of self-reliance'**<br>• Promotion of high rate of growth, better distribution of income and significant growth in the domestic rate of savings were seen as key instruments.<br>• Due to high inflation, cost calculations for the Plan proved to be |

| | |
|---|---|
| | completely wrong and the original public sector outlay had to be revised upwards. After promulgation of emergency in 1975, the emphasis shifted to the implementation of Prime Ministers 20 Point Programme. FYP was relegated to the background and when Janta Party came to power in 1978, the Plan was terminated. |
| Rolling Plan (1978 - 80) | There were 2 Sixth Plans. Janta Govt. put forward a plan for 1978-1983 emphasising on **employment**, in contrast to **Nehru Model** which the Govt criticised for concentration of power, widening inequality & for mounting poverty. However, the government lasted for only 2 years. Congress Govt. returned to power in 1980 and launched a different plan aimed at directly attacking on the problem of poverty by creating conditions of an expanding economy. |
| Sixth Plan (1980 - 85) Target Growth: 5.2% Actual Growth: 5.7% | The Plan focussed on Increase in national income, modernization of technology, ensuring continuous decrease in poverty and unemployment through schemes for transferring skills(TRYSEM) and (IRDP) and providing slack season employment (NREP),controlling population explosion etc. Broadly , the sixth Plan could be taken as a **success** as most of the target were realised even though during the last year (1984-85) many parts of the country faced severe famine conditions and agricultural output was less than the record output of previous year. |
| Seventh Plan (1985 - 90) Target Growth: 5.0% Actual Growth: 6.0% | • The Plan aimed at accelerating food grain production, increasing employment opportunities & raising productivity with focus **on 'food, work & productivity'**.<br>• The plan was **very successful** as the economy recorded 6% growth rate against the targeted 5% with the decade of 80's struggling out of the' **Hindu Rate of Growth'**. |
| Eighth Plan (1992 - 97) Target Growth 5.6 % Actual Growth 6.8% | • The eighth plan was postponed by two years because of political uncertainty at the Centre.<br>• **Worsening Balance of Payment** position, rising debt burden, widening budget deficits, recession in industry and inflation were the key issues during the launch of the plan.<br>• The plan undertook drastic policy measures to combat the bad economic situation and to undertake an annual average growth of 5.6% through introduction of **fiscal & economic reforms including liberalisation** under the Prime Minister ship of Shri P V Narasimha Rao.<br>• Some of the main economic outcomes during eighth plan period were rapid economic growth (highest annual growth rate so far – 6.8 %), high growth of agriculture and allied sector, and manufacturing sector, growth in exports and imports, improvement in trade and current account deficit. High growth rate was achieved even though the **share of public sector in total investment had declined** considerably to about 34 %. |
| Ninth Plan (1997- 2002) Target Growth:6.5% Actual Growth: 5.4% | The Plan prepared under United Front Government focussed on "**Growth With Social Justice & Equality** " Ninth Plan aimed to depend predominantly on the private sector – Indian as well as foreign (FDI) & State was envisaged to increasingly play the role of facilitator & increasingly involve itself with social sector viz education , health etc and infrastructure where private sector participation was likely to be limited. It assigned priority to agriculture & rural development with a view to generate |

| | |
|---|---|
| | adequate productive employment and eradicate poverty |
| *Tenth Plan (2002 - 2007)* <br> *Target Growth 8 %* <br> *Actual Growth 7.6 %* | Recognising that economic growth can't be the only objective of national plan, Tenth Plan had set **'monitorable targets'** for few **key indicators (11) of development** besides 8 % growth target. The targets included reduction in gender gaps in literacy and wage rate, reduction in Infant & maternal mortality rates, improvement in literacy, access to potable drinking water cleaning of major polluted rivers, etc. Governance was considered as factor of development & <br> Agriculture was declared as prime moving force of the economy. States role in planning was to be increased with greater involvement of Panchayati Raj Institutions. State wise break up of targets for growth and social development sought to achieve balanced development of all states. |
| *Eleventh Plan (2007 - 2012)* <br> *Target Growth 9 %* <br> *Actual Growth 8%* | • Eleventh Plan was aimed "**Towards Faster & More Inclusive Growth** "after UPA rode back to power on the plank of helping Aam Aadmi (common man). <br> • India had emerged as one of the fastest growing economy by the end of the Tenth Plan. The savings and investment rates had increased, industrial sector had responded well to face competition in the global economy and foreign investors were keen to invest in India. But the growth was not perceived as sufficiently inclusive for many groups , specially SCs , STs & minorities as borne out by data on several dimensions like poverty, malnutrition, mortality, current daily employment etc . <br> • The broad vision for 11th Plan included several inter related components like rapid growth reducing poverty & creating employment opportunities , access to essential services in health & education, specially for the poor, extension if employment opportunities using National Rural Employment Guarantee Programme , environmental sustainability, reduction of gender inequality etc. Accordingly various targets were laid down like reduction in unemployment( to less than 5 % among educated youth ) & headcount ratio of poverty ( by 10 %), reduction in dropout rates , gender gap in literacy , infant mortality , total fertility , malnutrition in age group of 0-3 ( to half its present level), improvement in sex ratio, forest & tree cover, air quality in major cities, , ensuring electricity <br> connection to all villages & BPL households (by 2009) & reliable power by end of 11th Plan , all weather road connection to habitations with population 1000& above (500 in hilly areas) by 2009, connecting every village by telephone & providing broad band connectivity to all villages by 2012, <br> • The Eleventh Plan started well with the first year achieving a growth rate of 9.3 per cent, however the growth decelerated to 6.7 per cent rate in 2008-09 following the global financial crisis. The economy recovered substantially to register growth rates of 8.6 per cent and 9.3 per cent in 2009-10 and 2010-11 respectively. However, the second bout of global slowdown in 2011 due to the sovereign debt crisis in Europe coupled with domestic factors such as tight monetary policy and supply side bottlenecks, resulted in deceleration of growth to 6.2 per cent in 2011-12. Consequently, the average annual growth rate of Gross Domestic Product (GDP) achieved during the Eleventh Plan was 8 per cent, which was lower than the target |

| | |
|---|---|
| | but better than the Tenth Plan achievement. Since the period saw two global crises - one in 2008 and another in 2011 – the 8 per cent growth may be termed as satisfactory. The realised GDP growth rate for the agriculture, industry and services sector during the 11th Plan period is estimated at 3.7 per cent, 7.2 per cent and 9.7 per cent against the growth target of 4 per cent, 10-11 per cent and 9-11 per cent respectively.<br>• The Eleventh Plan set a target of 34.8 per cent for domestic savings and 36.7 per cent for investment after experiencing a rising level of domestic savings as well as investment and especially after emergence of structural break during the Tenth Plan period. However, the domestic savings and investment averaged 33.5 per cent and 36.1 per cent of GDP at market prices respectively in the Eleventh Plan which is below the target but not very far.<br>• Based on the latest estimates of poverty released by the Planning Commission, **poverty** in the country has declined by 1.5 percentage points per year between 2004-05 and 2009-10.The rate of decline during the period 2004-05 to 2009-10 is twice the rate of decline witnessed during the period 1993-94 to 2004-05. Though the new poverty count based on **Tendulkar Formula** has been subject of controversy, it is believed by the Committee that whether we use the old method or the new, the decline in percentage of population below poverty line is almost same.<br>• On the **fiscal front,** the expansionary measures taken by the government to counter the effect fo global slowdown led to increase in key indicators through 2009-10 with some moderation thereafter.<br>• The issue of **Price Stability** remained resonating for more than half of the Plan period. Inability to pass on burden on costlier imported oil prices might have constrained the supply of investible funds in the government's hand causing the 11th Plan to perform at the levels below its target. |
| | ***The growth targets for the first three Plans were set with respect to National Income. In the Fourth Plan it was Net Domestic Product. In all the Plans thereafter, Gross Domestic Product has been used*** |
| Twelfth Five Year Plan (2012-17) | • The Twelfth Plan commenced at a time when the global economy was going through a second financial crisis, precipitated by the sovereign debt problems of the Eurozone which erupted in the last year of the Eleventh Plan. The crisis affected all countries including India. Our growth slowed down to 6.2 percent in 2011-12 and the deceleration continued into the first year of the Twelfth Plan, when the economy is estimated to have grown by only 5 percent. The Twelfth Plan therefore emphasizes that our first priority must be to bring the economy back to rapid growth while ensuring that the growth is both inclusive and sustainable. The broad vision and aspirations which the Twelfth Plan seeks to fulfil are reflected in the **subtitle**: **'Faster, Sustainable, and More Inclusive Growth'**. Inclusiveness is to be achieved through poverty reduction, promoting group equality and regional balance, reducing inequality, empowering people etc. whereas sustainability includes ensuring environmental sustainability, development of human capital through improved health, education, skill development, nutrition, information technology etc. and development of institutional capabilities , infrastructure like power telecommunication, roads, transport etc. |

- Apart from the global slowdown, the domestic economy has also run up against several internal constraints. Macro-economic imbalances have surfaced following the fiscal expansion undertaken after 2008 to give a fiscal stimulus to the economy. Inflationary pressures have built up. Major investment projects in energy and transport have slowed down because of a variety of implementation problems. Some changes in tax treatment in the 2012–13 have caused uncertainty among investors. These developments have produced a reduction in the rate of investment, and a slowing down of economic growth.
- The policy challenge in the Twelfth Plan is, therefore, two-fold. The immediate challenge is to reverse the observed deceleration in growth by reviving investment as quickly as possible. This calls for urgent action to tackle implementation constraints in infrastructure which are holding up large projects, combined with action to deal with tax related issues which have created uncertainty in the investment climate. From a longer term perspective, the Plan must put in place policies that can leverage the many strengths of the economy to bring it back to its real Growth potential.
- Immediate priority is to revive the investor sentiment along with next short term action of removing the impediments to implementation of projects in infrastructure, especially in the area of energy which would require addressing the issue of fuel supply to power stations, financial problems of discoms and clarity in terms of New Exploration Licensing Policy (NELP).
- Although planning should cover both the activities of the government and those of the private sector, a great deal of the public debate on planning in India takes place around the size of the public sector plan. The Twelfth Plan lays out an ambitious set of Government programmes, which will help to achieve the objective of rapid and inclusive growth. In view of the scarcity of resources, it is essential to take bold steps to improve the efficiency of public expenditure through plan programmes. Need for fiscal correction viz tax reforms like GST, reduction of subsidies as per cent of GDP while still allowing for targeted subsidies that advance the cause of inclusiveness etc and managing the current account deficit would be another chief concerns.
- Achieving sustained growth would require long term increase in investment and savings rate. Bringing the economy back to 9 per cent growth by the end of the Twelfth Plan requires fixed investment rate to rise to 35 per cent of GDP by the end of the Plan period. This will require action to revive private investment, including private corporate investment, and also action to stimulate public investment, especially in key areas of infrastructure especially, energy, transport, water supply and water resource management. Reversal of the combined deterioration in government and corporate savings has to be a key element in the strategy.

A key component of the Nehruvian socialism—the economic approach adopted by India's first Prime Minister Jawaharlal Nehru—the Five-Year Plans have been laid to rest by the Narendra Modi-led NDA government. The 12th Plan, the last of the Five-Year Plans, is coming to an end on March 31, though it has been given an extension of six months to allow ministries to complete their appraisals. The decades-old Five-Year Plans made way for a three-year action plan, which formed part of a seven-year strategy paper and a 15- year vision document.

## 26 important schemes launched by Narendra Modi government

PM-KISAN (Pradhan Mantri Kisan Samman Nidhi) Scheme

Main purpose: This scheme promises to pay all poor farmers (small and marginal farmers having lands up to 2 hectares) Rs 6,000 each every year in 3 installments through Direct Bank Transfer. It would reportedly benefit around 14.5 crore farmers all over India.

Pradhan Mantri Kisan Pension Yojana:

Main purpose: To address the problems of farm sector distress, the Modi 2.0 Cabinet has approved a proposal to provide small and marginal farmers with a minimum Rs 3,000 per month fixed pension, costing Rs 10,774.5 crore per annum to the exchequer.

The eligible farmers in the 18-40 years age group can participate in this voluntary and contributory pension scheme.

Once the beneficiary of the pension dies, the spouse will be entitled to receive 50% of the original beneficiary's pension amount.

Mega Pension Scheme

Main purpose: A Mega Pension Scheme has been approved for the traders, shopkeepers, and self-employed persons (whose GST turnover is less than Rs 1.5 crore).

The scheme guarantees a minimum assured pension of Rs 3,000 per month for around 3 crore small traders, self-employed persons, and shopkeepers, once they attain 60 years of age.

New Jal Shakti Ministry

Main purpose: It aims at providing piped water connection to every Indian household by the year 2024. Reports say that the ministry will now be able to formulate plans to address the issue of water management.

Jan Dhan Yojana

Main purpose: Pradhan Mantri Jan Dhan Yojana is a National Mission on Financial Inclusion which has an integrated approach to bring about comprehensive financial inclusion and provide banking services to all households in the country. The scheme ensures access to a range of financial services like availability of basic savings bank account, access to need based credit, remittances facility, insurance and pension.

Skill India Mission

Main purpose: The Mission has been developed to create convergence across sectors and States in terms of skill training activities. Further, to achieve the vision of 'Skilled India', the National Skill Development Mission would not only consolidate and coordinate skilling efforts, but also expedite decision making across sectors to achieve skilling at scale with speed and standards.

Make in India

Main purpose: PM Narendra Modi launched the 'Make in India' campaign to facilitate investment, foster innovation, enhance skill development, protect intellectual property & build best in class manufacturing infrastructure.

'Make in India' has identified 25 sectors in manufacturing, infrastructure and service activities and detailed information is being shared through interactive web-portal and professionally developed brochures. FDI has been opened up in Defence Production, Construction and Railway infrastructure in a big way.

Swachh Bharat Mission

Main purpose: On 2nd October 2014, Swachh Bharat Mission was launched throughout length and breadth of the country as a national movement. The campaign aims to achieve the vision of a 'Clean India' by 2nd October 2019.

The Swachh Bharat Abhiyan is the most significant cleanliness campaign by the Government of India.

Sansad Adarsh Gram Yojana

Main purpose: It is a rural development programme broadly focusing upon the development in the villages which includes social development, cultural development and spread motivation among the people on social mobilization of the village community.

Pradhan Mantri Shram Yogi Maan-dhan (PM-SYM)

Main purpose: It is a voluntary and contributory pension scheme, under which the subscriber would receive the following benefits:

(i) Minimum Assured Pension: Each subscriber under the PM-SYM, shall receive minimum assured pension of Rs 3000/- per month after attaining the age of 60 years.

(ii) Family Pension: During the receipt of pension, if the subscriber dies, the spouse of the beneficiary shall be entitled to receive 50% of the pension received by the beneficiary as family pension. Family pension is applicable only to spouse.

(iii) If a beneficiary has given regular contribution and died due to any cause (before age of 60 years), his/her spouse will be entitled to join and continue the scheme subsequently by payment of regular contribution or exit the scheme as per provisions of exit and withdrawal.

Beti Bachao Beti Padhao

Main purpose: The goal of this scheme is to make girls socially and financially self-reliant through education.

Hridaya Plan

Main purpose: To take care of world heritage sites and to make these sites economically viable.

PM Mudra Yojna

Main purpose: Pradhan Mantri MUDRA Yojana (PMMY) is a scheme launched by the Hon'ble Prime Minister on April 8, 2015 for providing loans up to 10 lakh to the non-corporate, non-farm small/micro enterprises.

To create an inclusive, sustainable and value based entrepreneurial culture, in collaboration with our partner institutions in achieving economic success and financial security.

Jala Yojna

Main purpose: State run Energy Efficiency Services Ltd (EESL) has distributed over 30 crore light emitting diode (LED) bulbs across country under zero-subsidy Unnat Jyoti by Affordable LEDs for All (UJALA) scheme.

Atal Pension Yojana

Main purpose: Atal Pension Yojana is a pension scheme mainly aimed at the unorganized sector such as maids, gardeners, delivery boys, etc. This scheme replaced the previous Swavalamban Yojana which wasn't accepted well by the people.

Prime Minister Jeevan Jyoti Bima Yojana

Main purpose: Pradhan Mantri Jeevan Jyoti Bima Yojana is a government-backed Life insurance scheme in India. Pradhan Mantri Jeevan Jyoti Bima Yojana is available to people between 18 and 50 years of age with bank accounts.

Pradhan Mantri Suraksha Bima Yojana

Main purpose: Pradhan Mantri Suraksha Bima Yojana is a government-backed accident insurance scheme in India. As of May 2016, only 20% of India's population has any kind of insurance, this scheme aims to increase the number.

AMRUT Plan

Main purpose: Providing basic services (e.g. water supply, sewerage, urban transport) to households and build amenities in cities which will improve the quality of life for all, especially the poor and the disadvantaged is a national priority.

The purpose of Atal Mission for Rejuvenation and Urban Transformation (AMRUT) is to:

- Ensure that every household has access to a tap with the assured supply of water and a sewerage connection.
- Increase the amenity value of cities by developing greenery and well maintained open spaces (e.g. parks) and
- Reduce pollution by switching to public transport or constructing facilities for non-motorized transport (e.g. walking and cycling). All these outcomes are valued by citizens, particularly women, and indicators and standards have been prescribed by the Ministry of Housing and Urban Affairs (MoHUA) in the form of Service Level Benchmarks (SLBs).

Digital India Mission

Main purpose: The Digital India programme is a flagship programme of the Government of India with a vision to transform India into a digitally empowered society and knowledge economy.

Gold Monetization Scheme

Main purpose: Gold Monetization Scheme was launched by Government of India in 2015, under this scheme one can deposit their gold in any form in a GMS account to earn interest as the price of the gold metal goes up.

UDAY

Main purpose: Ministry of Power, GoI launched Ujwal DISCOM Assurance Yojana (UDAY) which was approved by Union Cabinet on 5th November, 2015.

The scheme envisages:

- Financial Turnaround
- Operational improvement
- Reduction of cost of generation of power
- Development of Renewable Energy

- Energy efficiency & conservation Start-up India
- Main purpose: Startup India is a flagship initiative of the Government of India, intended to catalyze startup culture and build a strong and inclusive ecosystem for innovation and entrepreneurship in India.

Setu Bhartam Yojana Main purpose: This Yojana aims to make all national highways free of railway crossings by 2019.

Main purpose: Stand-Up India Scheme Facilitates bank loans between 10 lakh and 1 Crore to at least one Scheduled Caste (SC) or Scheduled Tribe (ST) borrower and at least one woman borrower per bank branch for setting up a greenfield enterprise.

Prime Minister Ujjwala Plan

Main purpose: Pradhan Mantri Ujjwala Yojana (PMUY) was launched by Prime Minister of India Narendra Modi on May 1, 2016 to distribute 50 million LPG connections to women of BPL families.

Namami Gange Yojana

Main purpose: The Government launched an integrated Ganga conservation mission called 'Namami Gange' to arrest the pollution of Ganga River and revive the river.

The Development Monitoring and Evaluation Office (DMEO) is an attached office of NITI Aayog. As the apex monitoring and evaluation (M&E) office in the country, DMEO supports the Government achieve the national development agenda through M&E of government policies and programs. Since its inception in 2015, the office aims to support rigorous, data-driven, citizen-centric, and outcomes-driven program management and policymaking.

According to the Cabinet Note that constitutes NITI Aayog, DMEO's mandate currently involves; (i) monitoring progress and efficacy of strategic and long-term policy and program frameworks and initiatives to help innovative improvements, including necessary mid-course corrections; and (ii) actively monitoring and evaluating the implementation of programs and initiatives, including the identification of the needed resources so as to strengthen the probability of success and scope of delivery. Its mandate also expands to technical advisory to States, under NITI Aayog's mandate of cooperative and competitive federalism. DMEO's institutional positioning gives the organization convening power to create a platform for M&E advancement in the country.

DMEO was established by the Government of India on 18th September, 2015 as an attached office of the NITI Aayog by merging the erstwhile Program Evaluation Office and Independent Evaluation Office. To ensure that DMEO is able to function independently, it has been given separate budgetary allocations and manpower in addition to complete functional autonomy. The Programme Evaluation Organization (PEO) was established by the Government of India in October, 1952 with a specific task of evaluating the community development programmes and other intensive area development schemes which were being funded by the Government of India. It worked as a Division of erstwhile Planning Commission and was headed by an Adviser (PEO) who reported to the Member, Planning Commission. PEO had 15 field units (7 Regional Evaluation Offices + 8 Project Evaluation Offices) located across the country. In an effort to accord more functional autonomy to the programme evaluation mechanism in the country, the Government of India established the Independent Evaluation Office (IEO) in November, 2010. The IEO was headed by a Director General, equivalent to a Union Minister of State in rank and status.

DMEO has been mandated to actively monitor and evaluate the implementation of Government of India (GoI) programmes and initiatives so as to strengthen their implementation and scope of delivery on an ongoing basis. Additionally, DMEO undertakes evaluation of selected programmes/schemes, suo-moto or on the request of the Prime Minister's Office (PMO) or programme implementing Ministries/ Departments of the Government of India. Broadly, DMEO functions can be categorized into i) Monitoring, ii) Evaluation, and iii) Strategic Initiatives encompassing partnerships and capacity building.

| |
|---|
| 1. Output Outcome Monitoring Framework for 67 M/Ds |
| 2. Data Governance Quality Index for all M/Ds |
| 3. Sector Reviews of 13 infrastructure and 4 social sectors |
| 4. Monitoring 30 Global Indices for Reform & Growth |

**Fifteenth Finance Commission Report for FY 2021-26 - Volume-I Main Report October 2020 - Chapter 13 Fiscal Architecture for Twenty-First Century India: Fiscal Rules, Financial Management and Institutions [Excerpts]:**

13.2 Raising the quality and efficiency of public spending is a critical challenge for India, given overall resource constraints. The strain on public finances from the Covid-19 crisis, especially the need for reprioritising expenditures and financing the health and infrastructure response, accentuates the importance of ensuring that public financial management policies, processes and systems adopt best practices. There is considerable evidence of the high costs of inefficiencies in fiscal management, especially for key health and education outcomes. Studies highlight that with improved efficiency, States could, on average, raise their output indicators by 2 30 per cent with the same level of inputs. There is also clear correlation with higher capacity and better governance stemming from improved public financial management practices. Thus, the 3 quality of public financial management has direct implications for the delivery of public services and sustaining economic growth.

13.3 International experience confirms that a public financial management system with strong budget institutions is critical to the delivery of effective fiscal outcomes and the overall path to 4 fiscal consolidation. Thus, improving public financial management would raise intended programme outcomes and the quality of service delivery, release public and private resources for productive sectors and catalyse sustainable growth. In particular, reprioritising public expenditure during the current Covid crisis becomes essential as government resources are constrained. At the same time, international experience also confirms that financial crises have frequently been triggered by the realisation of risks stemming from ineffective surveillance at all levels of government, especially from sub-national governments and extra budgetary borrowing of the 'public sector'.

13.4 These factors have special implications for all levels of the government. Many of the key economic, social and environmental challenges are in the purview of the States and local governments. The costs of inefficiencies in fiscal and financial management are becoming more important as the volume of untied resources available to the States have risen and these have highlighted the need for intensifying public financial management reforms to raise the quality of development expenditure and overall public investment management. With States accounting for roughly half of India's general government fiscal deficit, the strength of States' fiscal rules legislations and their consistency with the amended Fiscal Responsibility and Budget Management (FRBM) Act, 2003 of the Union Government are also important to ensure the sustainability of public finances and macro-economic stability.

13.5 This will mean strengthening budgetary institutions at all levels of government to better anchor the framework for inter-governmental reform, meet policy priorities as efficiently as possible and deliver better development outcomes. Building India's fiscal architecture towards these ends is central to the future of India's fiscal federalism.

India's Fiscal Rule: Challenges in Implementation

13.11 Compared with other emerging market countries, India was relatively early in its adoption of fiscal rules through the enactment of the FRBM Act in 2003, mirrored by the 5 successive adoption of fiscal responsibility legislation by all the States. Since then, through a number of amendments, the Union has updated the FRBM Act, adopted multiple fiscal indicators as target indicators, added direct rules on the Union and the General Government debt ceilings, clarified the escape clauses, made the Medium Term Expenditure Framework (MTEF) statement mandatory for the Union, and tried to bring India into the second generation of fiscal rules (changes to the FRBM Act in 2018 are contained in Box 13.1).

13.12 However, challenges in implementing these fiscal rules remain, as the underlying public financial management system meets only a fraction of best practice standards. The majority of the practices affecting budget formulation, execution and reporting are still without sufficient legislative strength; they are, instead, governed by a multiplicity of constitutional provisions, executive rules, orders and manuals. These have been replicated at the State level, but without consistency in framework and practices across levels of government, resulting in marked differences in the extent to which the Union and the States have progressed (Annex 13.1).

---

Box 13.1: Recent Amendments to FRBM Act, 2003

The major amendments made through the Finance Act 2018 in the FRBM Act are;

• Government debt became the primary anchor, with the fiscal deficit as the key operational target. The fiscal deficit was to be reduced to 3 per cent of gross domestic product (GDP) by the end of financial year 2020-21.

• Achieving the General Government debt target of 60 per cent of GDP and Central Government debt target of 40 per cent by the end of financial year 2024-25.

• The scope of 'Central Government Debt' has been expanded to include the total outstanding liabilities on the security of the Consolidated Fund of India and Public Accounts plus financial liabilities of any body, corporate, or other entity owned or controlled by the Central Government, which the Government is to repay or service from the Annual Financial Statement.

• Widening of grounds (escape clauses) on which the Union Government is allowed to breach the deficit targets, including national security, act of war, national calamity, collapse of agriculture, structural reforms and decline in real output growth. However, any deviation from the fiscal deficit target shall not exceed one-half per cent of GDP.

• In case of an increase in real output growth of a quarter by at least 3 percentage points above its average of the previous four quarters, reduce the fiscal deficit by at least one quarter per cent of GDP in a year.

---

13.13 As a result, there are significant inconsistencies and gaps in the public financial management framework that affect the consistency, comprehensiveness and reliability of fiscal 6 statistics across all levels of government. In addition, the fiscal deficit defined in the revised FRBM Act (as the balance of operations incurring into the Consolidated Fund of India) falls short of the new debt ceiling that covers a broader definition of accounts and implementing agencies that deliver public services on behalf of the government. In practice, this has led to the fiscal rules being effectively circumvented, in particular by the use of public sector entities for off-budget fiscal operations, inconsistent budget classification and accounting practices (and the misclassification of revenues and expenditures) and the use of the public accounts for budgetary purposes.

13.14 The absence of an independent fiscal institution to assess and evaluate the fiscal plan as well as performance and forecasts published by governments (as is now the reality in many advanced and emerging market countries) has also further diminished the capacity to monitor compliance. Thus, target dates have been periodically shifted, escape clauses have been modified and compliance to the FRBM Act continues to reflect the discretion of the government. Most States have not legislated their outstanding debt targets and their MTEFs have not been developed consistently to reflect their strategic budgeting and planning. As a result, after early improvement in fiscal consolidation following the enactment of fiscal rules, the deficits of many States have recently been on a rising trajectory (Figure 13.1).[Not reproducible]

13.15 Recent reports of the Comptroller and Auditor General (CAG) on the Union Government's compliance with the FRBM Act list many of the mismatches between the Act's provisions and reported outcomes. These involve the use of one-off measures to enable 7 compliance, such as deferring payments, raising off-budget financing , and the transfer of funds from the Consolidated Fund to the Public Accounts in case of some states which risk distorting the assessment of fiscal activity. Similar observations have also been made in the CAG's reports on State Finances published every year for all the States.

13.16 More fundamentally, the challenge remains of strengthening budget institutions as a whole, and the underlying public finance and accountability architecture. This involves updating the coverage and availability of critical fiscal data across levels of government to be commensurate with the FRBM rules. As we discuss later in this Chapter, this is essential also to build market discipline which will supplement the role of fiscal rules in strengthening fiscal discipline.

13.17 Principal among the challenges is that India does not compile or monitor consistent 8 general government fiscal aggregates on a timely basis. Against this, the number of countries 9 providing general government data has nearly doubled in past decade. This reflects the reality that India's fiscal reporting systems at the Union and the State levels are not aligned with international practice, despite the last four Finance Commissions making specific recommendations on the implementation of public financial management reforms (Annex 13.3).[Not reproduced].

13.18 From the recommendations of previous Finance Commissions, three themes stand out: (a) strengthening the budgetary process and the performance orientation of budgets; (b) moving towards the adoption of accrual accounting; and (c) standardising and consolidating key fiscal and financial information across Union and State Governments and local bodies, including all "other liabilities" such as from off-budget borrowing and accumulated losses from State-owned enterprises. This last point is particularly important given the difficulties in assembling a comprehensive, coherent set of fiscal data for the States and the third tier of government that allows for in-depth analysis of policy options.

13.56 We recommend the establishment of an independent Fiscal Council with powers to access records as required from the Union as well as the States. The fiscal council would have only an advisory role clearly separated from enforcement, which is the prerogative of the other organs of the government.

13.57 Based on international experience, some indicative functions of the proposed fiscal council can be:

(i) providing multi-year macro-economic and fiscal forecasts;

(ii) evaluating fiscal performance vis-à-vis targets across levels of government;

(iii) assessing the appropriateness and consistency of fiscal targets in the States;

(iv) carrying out an independent assessment of long-term fiscal sustainability;

(v) assessing fiscal policy statements by governments under fiscal responsibility legislations;

(vi) advising on the conditions for using escape clauses under fiscal responsibility legislations;

(vii) policy costing of new measures with significant fiscal implications;

(viii) providing analytical support to the Finance Commissions, including at the State levels; and (ix) publication of all their reports and underlying methodologies.

13.58 The mandate of a fiscal council could be broadened to cover not only the production of macroeconomic and fiscal forecasts to inform the budget, but also to advise on setting and recalibrating fiscal targets and rules at national and sub-national levels, as well as monitoring compliance with such targets and rules. The fiscal council can also work towards improving the quality of fiscal statistics at all levels of government.

Moving Ahead

13.59 The real challenge in establishing these pillars of the fiscal architecture lies in motivating, launching and sustaining such coordinated institutional reforms. Toward this end, the Ministry of Finance could launch the process of stakeholder consultations and prepare a time-bound plan for the implementation of comprehensive public financial management reforms at all levels of government. Such consultation could bring together all the relevant stakeholders like the Finance departments of States, CAG of India (and subordinate field offices of Accountant General in States), Controller General of Accounts, Reserve Bank of India and technical research bodies working in the area of public financial management systems. Such a process could also become part of the discussion agenda of existing forums of Union State consultations, such as the Inter-State Council or the governing council of NITI Aayog.

13.60 The objective would be to put in place a consultative process to promote deliberation and awareness of the reform agenda with the publication of regular reports on implementation. Publication of information on the progress of reforms and benchmarking of progress across States will facilitate third-party review and scrutiny from interested non-governmental organisations, thereby exercising pressure to sustain reform.

13.61 International experience suggests that major reforms such as these may typically take several years for completion of all of its elements. Regular monitoring will help decision-makers keep track of reforms over time. It will also help track progress and performance across States. Hence, there is need of an institutional mechanism driving budgetary and public financial management reforms in a coordinated, transparent and inclusive way across levels of government to deliver consistency, transparency and accountability.

Freebies

Most disquieting growth in the elections campaigning is about the political parties promising freebies to entice the voters. This, in other words, amounts to official corrupt practices of the campaigning political parties; by doing so, they want to jump the corrupt practices recognized and defined in the RPA, 1951. The ruling of the Hon'ble Supreme Court of India is that inclusion of freebies in the manifesto does not come within the corrupt practices. With due respects to this ruling, what also needs to be considered is the promised freebies are to be fulfilled by the party that promised and got elected, forms government by majority or with coalition. This is the critical stage to apply the golden test where would the party get financial resources to feed the freebies other than public funds at its disposal; none other than the public funds. Once the incidence of defraying the public funds for freebies occurs, the promise that contained in the manifesto, though then not amounted to corrupt practice, converts itself into corrupt practices, the fact being that the party was well aware while making the promise that it had to lean upon the public funds to fulfil the promise if elected to form the government. Public funds thus defrayed for freebies to select class of people amounted to discrimination and placed additional financial burden upon those who stood outside the ambit of the freebies. This I have dealt further in the succeeding paragraphs. It is suffice to submit here the distinction of freebies as viewed in the manifesto and as actually implemented using the public funds has not been appreciated in the ruling stated before.

Relevant Articles under the Constitution are:

282. Expenditure defrayable by the Union or a State out of its revenues.—The Union or a State may make any grants for any public purpose, notwithstanding that the purpose is not one with respect to which Parliament or the Legislature of the State, as the case may be, may make laws.

283. Custody, etc., of Consolidated Funds, Contingency Funds and moneys credited to the public accounts.—(1) The custody of the Consolidated Fund of India and the Contingency Fund of India, the payment of moneys into such Funds, the withdrawal of moneys therefrom,

the custody of public moneys other than those credited to such Funds received by or on behalf of the Government of India, their payment into the public account of India and the withdrawal of moneys from such account and all other matters connected with or ancillary to matters aforesaid shall be regulated by law made by Parliament, and, until provision in that behalf is so made, shall be regulated by rules made by the President. (2) The custody of the Consolidated Fund of a State and the Contingency Fund of a State, the payment of moneys into such Funds, the withdrawal of moneys therefrom, the custody of public moneys other than those credited to such Funds received by or on behalf of the Government of the State, their payment into the public account of the State and the withdrawal of moneys from such account and all other matters connected with or ancillary to matters aforesaid shall be regulated by law made by the Legislature of the State, and, until provision in that behalf is so made, shall be regulated by rules made by the Governor 1*** of the State.

Word 'defray' or 'defrayable' used in Article 282 is not defined under any law or rule of the Central Government. Free Online Dictionary defines these words as follows:

'Defray' {tr, v}: To undertake the payment of (costs or expenses); pay.

'Defrayable': {Adjective of 'Defray'}.

Oxford LEXICO defines Freebie as under:

**Freebie**

Pronunciation /ˈfriːbi/: NOUN informal- A thing that is provided or given free of charge.

Origin: 1920s (originally US): an arbitrary formation from free.

Does the word "freebie" come within the meaning of word "defray". In my personal view, it doesn't. For, words 'defray' underlines an element of expenditure or payment of (costs or expenses); pay whereas word 'freebie' is a thing that is provided or given free of charge. Question for kind consideration is, as submitted before, the funds in the Consolidated Fund of India are explicitly for defrayal and other than grants, not for free of charge. As also submitted before, the political party which comes into power which had promised freebie (s) necessarily meets the promise of the freebies from the Consolidated Fund of India, a public fund from any angle, does not come within the meaning of the word 'defray'. The restriction on use of funds out of the said Fund is absolute and mandatory in the manner and for the purposes specified therein.

Article 39A which reads as under:

"[39A. Equal justice and free legal aid.—The State shall secure that the operation of the legal system promotes justice, on a basis of equal opportunity, and shall, in particular, provide free legal aid, by suitable legislation or schemes or in any other way, to ensure that opportunities for securing justice are not denied to any citizen by reason of economic or other disabilities" is the lone Article which uses the word 'free' for legal aid. There is no such word in any other part of the PART IV DIRECTIVE PRINCIPLES OF STATE POLICY. Any defrayal from the said Fund has to be within the ambit prescribed therein. As noted before, word 'freebie' does not come within the purview of the word defrayal.

This raises an important Constitutional interpretational dispute as to whether the political party that promised freebies in its manifesto and, to perform that, meets the funds from the said Fund, is permitted to do so of its own thus exceeding exercise of its authority in that respect when the Constitution specifies the defrayal of the funds from the said Fund for specific purposes and specific manner which do not include 'freebie'? Any political party elected into power and thus forms the government cannot commit itself to do or not to do something which the Constitution expressly excludes such something from its purview other than free legal aid. Such commitment, in my opinion, is inconsistent within the Constitutional purview.

**"Explained: What are 'freebies' and how they may burden state finances" - TIMESOFINDIA.COM / Updated: Aug 3, 2022, 15:25 IST [Excerpts]:**

"........................**What are freebies in the first place?**

"While there is no precise definition of freebies, it is necessary to distinguish them from public/merit goods, expenditure on which brings economic benefits, such as the public distribution system, employment guarantee schemes, states' support for education and health (Singh, 2022). On the other hand, provision of free electricity, free water, free public transportation, waiver of pending utility bills and farm loan waivers are often regarded as freebies, which potentially undermine credit culture, distort prices through cross-subsidisation eroding incentives for private investment, and disincentivise work at the current wage rate leading to a drop in labour force participation," explained the RBI report.

As per estimates, expenditure on freebies range from 0.1 - 2.7 per cent of gross state domestic product (SDP) for different states. Freebies announced by the State Governments:

| State | As % of GSDP | As % of revenue receipts | As % of own tax revenue |
|---|---|---|---|
| Andhra Pradesh | 2.1% | 14.1% | 30.30% |
| Bihar | 0.1% | 0.6% | 2.70% |
| Haryana | 0.1% | 0.6% | 0.90% |
| Jharkhand | 1.7% | 8.0% | 26.70% |
| Kerala | 0.0% | 0.0% | 0.10% |
| Madhya Pradesh | 1.6% | 10.8% | 28.80% |
| Punjab | 2.7% | 17.8% | 45.40% |
| Rajasthan | 0.6% | 3.9% | 8.60% |
| West Bengal | 1.1% | 9.5% | 23.80% |

Source: Budget documents of the state government.

Andhra Pradesh, Madhya Pradesh and Punjab incur a very high subsidy bill by doling out freebies that go over and above 10% of their total revenue receipts. The three states respectively give away freebies worth 14.1%, 10.8% and 17.8% of their revenue income.

Gujarat and Chhattisgarh also spend over 10% of their revenue on giving away subsidies. "The Centre's GST compensation pay-out will come to an end in June 2022, further reducing the headroom available for social sector expenditure. In such a situation, a multitude of social welfare schemes in the form of freebies will not only put a heavy burden on the exchequer but will also exert upward pressures on yields if they are financed through market borrowing. It will be important, therefore, for the state governments to reprioritise their expenditure to achieve optimum long-term welfare advantages by ensuring that the beneficiaries get empowered permanently and forego such benefits," noted the research paper

**Too much debt**

And going by the debt to GSDP ratio, Punjab, Rajasthan, Kerala, West Bengal, Bihar, Andhra Pradesh, Jharkhand, Madhya Pradesh, Uttar Pradesh and Haryana alone account for half of the total expenditure the state governments incurred. Their gross fiscal deficit (GFD):GSDP ratio was equal to or more than 3% in 2021-22.

**State debt to GDP ratio in 2021-2022**

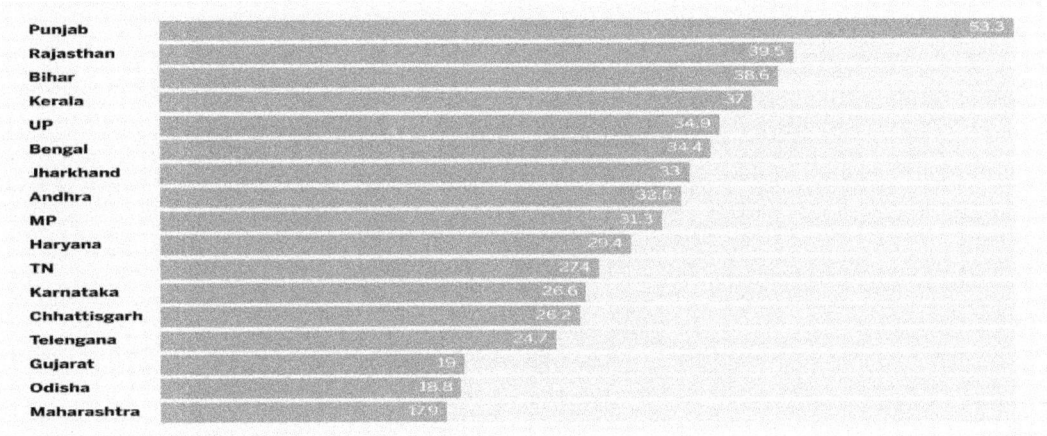

Moreover for eight of these ten states, the interest payments to revenue receipts ratio (IP-RR), a measure of the debt servicing burden on the state's finances, was more than 10%.

**Freebies and Welfare in the Articles in the Directive Principles of State Policy {DPSP}:**

| Article | Heading | Provision | Freebie/Welfare |
|---|---|---|---|
| 1 | 2 | 3 | 4 |
| Article 36 | Definition | In this Part, unless the context otherwise requires, "the State" has the same meaning as in Part III. | Definition. |
| Article 37 | Application of the principles contained in this Part | The provisions contained in this Part shall not be enforceable by any court, but the principles therein laid down are nevertheless fundamental in the governance of the country and it shall be the duty of the State to apply these principles in making laws. | Scope of application. |
| Article 38 | State to secure a social order for the promotion of welfare of the people. | [(1)] The State shall strive to promote the welfare of the people by securing and protecting as effectively as it may a social order in which justice, social, economic and political, shall inform all the institutions of the national life.<br>[(2) The State shall, in particular, strive to minimise the inequalities in income, and endeavour to eliminate inequalities in status, facilities and opportunities, not only amongst individuals but also amongst groups of people residing in different areas or engaged in different vocations.] | Welfare and Equality. |
| Article 39 | Certain principles of policy to be followed by the State. | The State shall, in particular, direct its policy towards securing—<br>(a) that the citizens, men and women equally, have the right to an adequate means of livelihood; | Welfare and Equality. |

| | | | |
|---|---|---|---|
| | | (b) that the ownership and control of the material resources of the community are so distributed as best to subserve the common good; (c) that the operation of the economic system does not result in the concentration of wealth and means of production to the common detriment; (d) that there is equal pay for equal work for both men and women; (e) that the health and strength of workers, men and women, and the tender age of children are not abused and that citizens are not forced by economic necessity to enter avocations unsuited to their age or strength; [(f) that children are given opportunities and facilities to develop in a healthy manner and in conditions of freedom and dignity and that childhood and youth are protected against exploitation and against moral and material abandonment.] | |
| Article 39A | Equal justice and free legal aid. | The State shall secure that the operation of the legal system promotes justice, on a basis of equal opportunity, and shall, in particular, provide free legal aid, by suitable legislation or schemes or in any other way, to ensure that opportunities for securing justice are not denied to any citizen by reason of economic or other disabilities.] | Freebie. |
| Article 40 | Organisation of village Panchayats. | The State shall take steps to organise village Panchayats and endow them with such powers and authority as may be necessary to enable them to function as units of self-government. | Promotion of village growth and justice through Panchayats. |
| Article 41 | Right to work, to education and to public assistance in certain cases. | The State shall, within the limits of its economic capacity and development, make effective provision for securing the right to work, to education and to public assistance in cases of unemployment, old age, sickness and disablement, and in other cases of undeserved want. | Welfare. |
| Article 42 | Provision for just and humane conditions of work and maternity relief | The State shall make provision for securing just and humane conditions of work and for maternity relief. | Welfare. |
| Article 43 | Living wage, etc., for workers. | The State shall endeavour to secure, by suitable legislation or economic organisation or in any other way, to all workers, agricultural, industrial or otherwise, work, a living wage, conditions of | Welfare and Equality. |

|  |  | work ensuring a decent standard of life and full enjoyment of leisure and social and cultural opportunities and, in particular, the State shall endeavour to promote cottage industries on an individual or co-operative basis in rural areas. |  |
|---|---|---|---|
| Article 43 A | Participation of workers in management of industries | The State shall take steps, by suitable legislation or in any other way, to secure the participation of workers in the management of undertakings, establishments or other organisations engaged in any industry. | Participation of Workers. |
| Article 43 B | Promotion of co-operative societies | The State shall endeavour to promote voluntary formation, autonomous functioning, democratic control and professional management of co-operative societies. | Promotion of cooperative societies. |
| Article 44 | Uniform civil code for the citizens. | The State shall endeavour to secure for the citizens a uniform civil code throughout the territory of India. | Uniform Civil Code. |
| Article 45 | Provision for early childhood care and education to children below the age of six years. | The State shall endeavour to provide early childhood care and education for all children until they complete the age of six years. | Child Care. |
| Article 46 | Promotion of educational and economic interests of Scheduled Castes, Scheduled Tribes and other weaker sections | The State shall promote with special care the educational and economic interests of the weaker sections of the people, and, in particular, of the Scheduled Castes and the Scheduled Tribes, and shall protect them from social injustice and all forms of exploitation. | Welfare measures for SC/ST and social justice. |
| Article 47 | Duty of the State to raise the level of nutrition and the standard of living and to improve public health. | The State shall regard the raising of the level of nutrition and the standard of living of its people and the improvement of public health as among its primary duties and, in particular, the State shall endeavour to bring about prohibition of the consumption except for medicinal purposes of intoxicating drinks and of drugs which are injurious to health. | Welfare. |
| Article 48 | Organisation of agriculture and animal husbandry | The State shall endeavour to organise agriculture and animal husbandry on modern and scientific lines and shall, in particular, take steps for preserving and improving the breeds, and prohibiting the slaughter, of cows and calves and other milch and draught cattle. | Continued Upgradation of agriculture and animal husbandry. |
| Article 48 A | Protection and improvement of environment and safeguarding of forests and wild life. | The State shall endeavour to protect and improve the environment and to safeguard the forests and wild life of the country. | Safeguarding the forests, environment and welfare of wild life. |
| Article | Protection of | It shall be the obligation of the State to protect | Protection of |

| 49 | monuments and places and objects of national importance. | every monument or place or object of artistic or historic interest, 2 [declared by or under law made by Parliament] to be of national importance, from spoliation, disfigurement, destruction, removal, disposal or export, as the case may be. | Heritage and historical monuments. |
|---|---|---|---|
| Article 50 | Separation of judiciary from executive. | The State shall take steps to separate the judiciary from the executive in the public services of the State. | Separation of judiciary from executive. |
| Article 51 | Promotion of international peace and security. | The State shall endeavour to—<br>(a) promote international peace and security;<br>(b) maintain just and honourable relations between nations;<br>(c) foster respect for international law and treaty obligations in the dealings of organized peoples with one another; and<br>(d) encourage settlement of international disputes by arbitration. | Promotion foreign policy suited best and conducive to the country. |

**News Item "God save EC if it can't stop poll freebies: SC_India News by Utkarsh Anand published in Hindustan Times - Updated on Jul 27, 2022 12:51 AM IST** reads as follows:

" May God save the Election Commission of India (ECI) if it can only wring its hands when electorates are sought to be bribed through freebies, the Supreme Court observed on Tuesday, as it sought to know from the Finance Commission if revenue allocation to states can take into account unnecessary expenditures on hand outs.

The top court found itself constrained to seek the help of the Finance Commission after ECI said that it cannot regulate promises of freebies even as the Union government assigned the responsibility to ECI for taking all possible steps under the existing legal regime.

Terming unrealistic poll promises and freebies a "serious" problem, a bench, headed by Chief Justice of India NV Ramana, said that the contentious practice has to be controlled and that the court will, therefore, seek the views of the Finance Commission if something can be done in this regard.

"God save the Election Commission of India if it's saying that we can't do anything when the electorates are sought to be bribed through freebies...We are suggesting that this (freebies) has to be controlled. How it is going to be done needs to be examined," said the bench, which also included justices Krishna Murari and Hima Kohli.

The court's remarks on ECI came after the statutory body took the position that it cannot regulate distribution of freebies and that it is for the voters to decide whether they should elect leaders even if such hand-outs could harm the economic health of a state.

ECI's affidavit was submitted in April in response to public interest litigation by advocate Ashwini Kumar Upadhyay, who sought a direction for issuance of stringent guidelines to deregister errant political parties and seize their election symbols for offering "irrational freebies" ahead of polls.

On July 16, {2022} while speaking at an event in Uttar Pradesh, Prime Minister Narendra Modi hit out at the culture of freebies.

"The 'revadi culture' is very dangerous for the development of the country," Modi said, calling on people to not fall for this culture.

The Prime Minister used the term 'revadi', a popular north Indian sweet often distributed during festivals, as a metaphor for freebies being promised by various parties to grab power.

"Those behind this 'revadi culture' do not believe in building expressways, airports and defence corridors. Together we have to defeat this thinking and remove this culture from politics," he added.

Earlier this week, in response to the PM's comments, his Bharatiya Janata Party asked state unite to refrain from offering freebies during elections.

In April, {2022} a team of senior bureaucrats warned PM Modi during a review that the culture of freebies could bankrupt state exchequers.

When Upadhyay's PIL was taken up on Tuesday, advocate Amit Sharma, appearing for ECI, informed the bench that their affidavit has culled out relevant regulations and cases on issuance of manifestos by the political parties and various advisories have also been issued. At the same time, Sharma said that there is not much that EC can do to control distribution of freebies by a winning party nor can it seize election symbols under the existing laws.

At this point, the bench expressed its dismay at ECI's stand and proceeded to enquire from the Union government about the latter's views.

Additional solicitor general KM Nataraj, representing the Centre, said the onus was on ECI. "There cannot be a general direction in matters like these. This will have to be done on a case-by-case basis and the Election Commission will have to decide it," argued the law officer.

Irked that the central government has not submitted any formal reply to convey its stand on the issue although the notice was issued in January this year, the bench told Nataraj: "Why have you not said this on an affidavit if this is your stand? Should we record your stand that you don't have any problem if the Election Commission does this? Why don't you take a stand? First of all, tell us whether it's a serious issue or not."

Responding, the ASG admitted that it is a serious issue. "Then why don't you take a categorical stand and then we can decide whether freebies can continue or not," replied the bench.

Upadhyay, on his part, argued that ECI can insert an additional condition in the electoral laws and rules that a party may lose its registration and election symbol for making irrational promises of freebies.

But the bench told the lawyer-petitioner that it may not be possible to stop political parties from making poll promises and that the issue of what is a reasonable promise and what is not would also crop up in such cases.

Drawing a parallel with Sri Lanka which is in the middle of a severe political and economic crisis, Upadhyay added that India could be soon on its way to becoming Sri Lanka if freebies were not controlled.

To this, the bench said: "How? The government of India will control it here. It's not that any state can take loan without prior approvals of RBI and the government of India. There are limits on allocations of loans. Don't worry!"

The bench, at this juncture, spotted senior advocate and Rajya Sabha MP Kapil Sibal present in the court, and decided to elicit his views on a possible solution.

Sibal said: "It's a serious matter. The solution is very difficult but the problem is very serious. You cannot expect the government of India to issue direction because that will create political issues. One way to explore a possible solution is to involve the Finance Commission. The Finance Commission, when it makes its allocation to the states from the total taxes, can take into account whether such allocations can take into account the money spent on unnecessary freebies."

Accepting Sibal's suggestion, the bench asked ASG Nataraj to enquire from the Finance Commission if a discussion on the subject and possible modalities can be initiated and revert in a week. Fixing the hearing on Wednesday next week, the court directed the Centre to come back with clear instructions on the issue.

On January 25, the bench asked for explanations from the Centre and ECI on steps taken by them since the court's 2013 judgment to regulate electoral promises and distribution of freebies by political parties using public funds.

"This is no doubt a serious issue. Budget for freebies is going above the regular budget. As the Supreme Court said before, this disturbs the level playing field," the bench observed then.

The 2013 judgment of the Supreme Court in S Subramaniam Balaji vs Government of Tamil Nadu & Ors delved on the issues of election manifestos and freebies. In this judgment, the top court said that distribution of freebies of any kind, undoubtedly, influences all people.

"It shakes the root of free and fair elections to a large degree. The Election Commission through its counsel also conveyed the same feeling both in the affidavit and in the argument that the promise of such freebies at government cost disturbs the level playing field and vitiates the electoral process and thereby expressed willingness to implement any directions or decision of this Court in this regard," the 2013 judgment held.

In response to the court's move, ECI filed its affidavit in April, expressing its inability to impose restrictions on electoral promises and freebies. ECI said that it can neither stop the political parties from making promises of freebies nor act against them in absence of a law to de-register political parties for making any unreasonable promises to the voters.

**Freebie politics is eroding fiscal federalism: NK Singh" by Roshan Kishore published in HT in its Edition of April 20, 2022**:

"The growing political culture of providing freebies to garner political gains raises the question whether India should contemplate adopting the concept of sub-national bankruptcies, said NK Singh, chairman of the Fifteenth Finance Commission. Singh made these remarks in his chief guest's address at the annual day of Delhi School of Economics, of which he is also an alumnus.

"The strength of the Centre lies in the strength of the states. Therefore, the macroeconomic stability of the Union is contingent on the macroeconomic stability of both the Centre and states", Singh said, drawing attention to the perils of "replicating the culture of competitive freebie politics".

"These are illustrations because governments across the political spectrum are now being increasingly attracted to this new slogan of freebie politics," Singh said while referring to Punjab and Rajasthan.

……….. "We must consider separate Constitutional provisions in addition to Article 282 in cases of sub-national bankruptcy."

The threat to state's fiscal situation due to the growing culture of freebies has become more pronounced after the roll-out of Goods and Services Tax (GST), as states have very little freedom in raising their own revenues, Singh said.

He gave six more reasons why the freebie culture hurts India's fiscal federalism framework: it undermines the basic framework of macroeconomic stability, distorts expenditure priorities, creates the issue of inter-generational equality, pushes governments to move away from environmentally sustainable practices (especially in agriculture); and has a debilitating effect on manufacturing.

To be sure, Singh made a case for differentiating between freebies and what he described as the concept of "merit goods and public goods" such as the public distribution system, employment guarantee schemes and outlays for education and health "on which unexceptionally, expenditure outlays has overall benefits".

Recognising the delicate interplay between politics and economics Singh underlined the fact that "what matters is political economy and not economics per se" and "one is the flipside of the other".

Singh's latest arguments for revisiting Constitutional provisions to safeguard the fiscal federalism framework come in the backdrop of his argument for revisiting the Seventh Schedule in the Constitution. "The Seventh Schedule decided to classify between the three categories... what would be in the exclusive category of the Union, exclusive domain of the states, and what would be in the concurrent list…Over a period of time, you have really transgressed from one end to the other. Most of the centrally sponsored schemes are subjects which are classic subjects in the domain of the states, such as employment, food, education…So the Seventh Schedule requires a revisit. So does the entry under Article 282 of the Constitution which has been used and misused for having all the centrally sponsored schemes", he had said in an interview to HT on February 5, 2021."

The views expressed by the Chairman of the Finance Commission at a particular occasion stated before are candid and, therefore, there does not seem to be any need to 'to enquire from the Finance Commission if a discussion on the subject and possible modalities can be initiated and revert in a week. Fixing the hearing on Wednesday next week, the court directed the Centre to come back with clear instructions on the issue' observed by the Hon'ble Court stated before based on the newspaper report..

A person of high stature when making critical observations on freebies and transgression by the centre into states territory specified under the Seventh Schedule, the entire concept and thinking on that Schedule assumes urgent intervention to restore the credibility of that Schedule. Saddening is that even when such great men are making critical observations on freebies and central sponsored welfare schemes, who should tell whom not to indulge in such anti-ethical measures not authorized under the Constitution as stated before. Above Article brings some light in the prevailing conflicts in the laws made by the Parliament and the State Legislature.

Such schemes should open up newer and newer opportunities continually to the people in the fields of education, skill development, health and sanitation, infrastructure development that has great potential to absorb the human capital and also open up industries, services and commerce in order that the obligation of creativeness if generated among the people, their living aspiration, that help them to learn and earn themselves contributing to the wealth of the nation as well as to make themselves self-sustaining. This is the sense and essence of welfare schemes and not free distribution of cash that attracts and addicts them towards beggary snatching away their life spirit, inspiration and aspirations for their self-growth, the Mother Earth offers through Nature she has created for the benefit of every Living Being including the humans. That is what the God's desire to be fulfilled by the rulers of the countries..

How? Article 282 of the Constitution of India only permits defraying of funds from the Consolidated Fund of the State for "public purpose"; (II) Freebies are violative of Article 14 since there is no reasonable classification; the monies out of the Consolidated Fund of India or the Consolidated Fund of the State can only be appropriated in accordance with law and for the purposes and in the manner provided by the Constitution. The word 'secure' used in Article 38 can at best be said to protect providing opportunities for sustained development.

What is envisaged in the Constitution is to provide tools and tackles to the people to self-involve and evolve and make them creative to generate wealth for self and for the nation, as part of the economic development process. The inventions that have been in vogue since mid-seventies and continued to be improved with the changing times which the political parties are attempting as most tempting to the people making them to believe what they have done or doing is for utilization of the public funds for the benefit of the people replacing the genuine process that involves hard thinking, planning and implementation that works as reality and a permanent benefit to the people for all the time to come that is what our Constitution yearns for.

Though the election manifestos make promises for freebies, it remains as a promise and its legality and validity is tested only when it is actually performed after assuming office after the election and based on that, as submitted before, the only conclusion could be that such expenditure does not come within the provisions of Article 38 and 282, more so, there is no concrete legal opinion or the interpretation by any highest courts of law as the freebies have to be construed as within the provisions of the aforesaid Articles. The practice followed so far and continued to be followed is not consistent with the provisions of the Constitution and, therefore, the ruling political parties that have undertaken such practice become accountable to the parliament and the people. It is highly disturbing to note the ruling political parties of the times did not follow established due consultation process within whether or not such practice was Constitutional or unconstitutional.

Tendency to give color to the words and actions to the concept and essence of 'economic development' has been growing; knowing that colours won't long last being bound to blur by the Nature. The new institutions that are functioning today are part of coating such colours, the best way to attract the attention of the people. What we assume today in our plans and projections are becoming not feasible tomorrow and, as we know, memory of the people is short; so, we find it convenient to assume newer ones. Time passes in this process but what is envisaged under the projections and plans remain where there were. The gap continues to widen day by day that assumes over the time increasing inequality in the society. We would have realized by now those essential elements of life engraved in the Directive Principles of our Constitution but for our overzealousness to show promises have more weightage than the performance that happened when the country was ruled a by single political party on its own strength or in coalition for the longest period.

A person who talks about such subjects is supposed to have seen, if not experienced, what is poverty, distress, hunger and the agony. It is something saying the sweet is very tasty and enchanting without tasting it. This is widening between the rhetoric and reality. The solutions offered in all such cases seem unsustainable because those are not based on the strength of validation. Freebies create more beggars than sustainably surviving over the poverty. There are beggars standing at every Red Light on the roads and the temples, mosques etc. What is the difference what they beg from the people for survival and those who receive freebies from the State as honourable beneficiaries? Some of the states have by now created institutions and avenues for making the beggars to learn, earn and survive with dignity. Why this principle should not apply to the so called beneficiaries? Or why the beggars should not be included by the state as regular beneficiaries and distribute the freebies? In judicial system, the 'doctrines' and 'dictums' are given due regard and consideration in interpretation of law and pronouncement of justice. That does not happen in politics. Because, the politics is not accustomed to respecting the truth but pose the false as truth. That is the reason for the people to depend more upon judicial pronouncements than the political announcements.

**OpIndia posted the following Article 'ECI comes down heavily on freebie culture, proposes proforma for political parties to explain how they will fulfil poll promises' dated 4 October, 2022 on its Website:**

"On October 4, the Election Commission of India (ECI) came down heavily on political parties over freebie culture. In a letter written to the officials of political parties, ECI not only criticised the political parties for offering freebies without explanation over how they would fulfil them but also proposed a proforma to fill where the parties have been asked to explain the roadmap which they would use to raise funds for the freebies offered in the manifesto.

Termed as 'standardised disclosure proforma', it contains sections that political parties will have to fill to explain the financial implications of the promises made and provide possible ways to fulfil them. The ECI has asked the political parties and candidates to reply with their views by October 19. In case no reply is received, ECI will assume that the parties or candidates do not have anything specific to say on the proposed amendments in the Model Code of Conduct (MCC).

In its letter, ECI said that it is the right of eligible voters to exercise their vote with ease and have authentic and adequate information at each electoral stage. ECI said, "The choice to cast the vote, i.e. the most precious gift of democracy is directly and intricately linked to access to timely and reliable information. It is in this background that timely availability of data points to assess the financial viability of the promises made to voters in the election manifestos assumes criticality."

Furthermore, ECI said that though it recognises the right of the political parties to make promises in the manifesto, "it cannot overlook the undesirable impact of some of the promises and offers on the conduct of free and fair elections and maintaining a level playing field for all political parties and candidates".

Based on the directions given by the Supreme Court in the Subramaniam Balaji Case and Article 324 of the Constitution that mandates the Election Commission to conduct elections inter alia to the Parliament and the State Legislatures, the ECI has issued guidelines via amendment in MCC in 2015. for the Political Parties and Candidates to adhere while releasing the election manifesto. These guidelines talk about the promises that political parties make in their manifesto.

Notably, the guidelines direct the political parties and candidates to "avoid making those promises which are likely to vitiate the purity of the election process or exert undue influence on the voters in exercising their franchise." Further, it also directed the parties and candidates to "reflect the rationale for the promises and broadly indicate the ways and means to meet the financial requirements for it."

8. With this end in view, and for the purposes of meaningful observance of the Model Code of Conduct for the Guidance of all National and recognized Political Parties and their Candidates, the Commission proposes to supplement existing MCC guidelines and mandate political parties to inform voters at large about financial ramifications of their promises in manifesto against well-defined quantifiable parameters aimed at assessing feasibility of implementation of such promises within the financial space available in the State/Union in the enclosed proforma which shall inter-alia capture the following:

  i) Extent and expanse of coverage (Ex. Individual, Family, Community, BPL or all population, etc.);
  ii) Quantification of physical coverage as in (i) above;
  iii) Quantification of financial implications of the promise (s) made;
  iv) Availability of the financial resources;
  v) Ways and means of raising resources for meeting the additional expenditure to be incurred in fulfilling the promises which could *inter-alia* include
      a. increase in tax and non-tax revenues,
      b. rationalization of expenditure,
      c. additional borrowings and
      d. any other sources to be specified.
  vi) Impact of the additional resource raising plan (for fulfilling promises) on fiscal sustainability of the State or the Union Government, as the case may be.

[*Excerpt from the ECI's letter*]

However, despite these guidelines in place, ECI found that the declarations made by the political parties and candidates do not provide adequate information to the voters. The ECI said, "The Commission notes that the consequences of inadequate disclosures by political parties get attenuated by the fact that elections are held frequently, providing opportunities for political parties to indulge in competitive electoral promises, particularly in multi-phase elections, without having to spell out their financial implications more particularly on committed expenditure. These declarations are also not submitted by most of the political parties in time."

The ECI further proposed that the parties should disclose the financial implications of the promises in terms of the "financial resources required and the ways of financing them on the one hand and the effect thereof on the fiscal sustainability of the State's or the Central Government's finances, as the case may be". The ECI added, "Given that the major objective of the disclosures is to facilitate informed choices, greater importance has been given to simplicity."

Proforma for Political Parties (Recognized National party and Recognized State party only) under Model Code of Conduct – Submission of details of physical coverage and financial implications of promises made in the manifesto

**PART-A: DETAILS OF ELECTORAL PROMISE WISE EXPENDITURE**

| Nomenclature of the promise made | Details of the promised scheme/welfare measures | Extent and expanse of coverage: | | | Financial Implication of the promise made: | | Remarks |
|---|---|---|---|---|---|---|---|
| | | Unit – individual/ family/ household (i) | Target – entire population/ specific group (ii) | Number of beneficiaries to be covered (iii) | Likely expenditure per beneficiary (to be rounded off to nearest ₹100/-) (i) | Likely total expenditure (₹ crore) (ii) | |
| Promise No.1 | | | | | | | |
| Promise No.2 | | | | | | | |
| Promise No. ...and so on[1] | | | | | | | |
| Total additional amount (₹ crore) required for all electoral promises [i.e., sum of the amounts indicated in column 4(ii)] | | | | | | | |

Note: Explanatory note for filling up Part A of Proforma—

1. For Column no. 2 – Promised schemes in the manifesto may include all such schemes/ welfare measures as distribution of free laptops for students, consumer durables, gadgets, waiver of loans, free water, free electricity, free transport, old pension schemes to employees, etc., which will have financial implications. Use a separate row for each promise.
2. The number of beneficiaries [as at 3(iii)] will be determined as under:
   i. Specify whether the unit of the target is an individual, household, family or a group.
   ii. Identify whether the target of the scheme is for entire population or a specified subset thereof such as farmers and within that small & marginal farmers or all farmers; MSMEs; women; senior citizens; persons below poverty line, etc.

[1] Please use one row for each promise

Proposed *proforma Part A*.

The Commission proposed to prescribe a proforma for the recognised National and State Political Parties to provide details of the financial implications of promises made in the election manifesto and the ways and means to finance them. ECI said, "To make the disclosures more meaningful, the proforma provides for certain fiscal information being prefilled by the respective State/Central Government."

**PART-B: FINANCING OF ELECTORAL PROMISES**  All Amounts in ₹ crores

| Sr.No. | To be filled in by the State/Centre as per the latest BE/RE | Sr.No. | To be filled in by the Political Party on financing of promise(s) | Remarks |
|---|---|---|---|---|
| | | 7 | Total additional amount required for all electoral promises (Brought forward from Part A) | |
| 1 | Revenue receipts:<br>a) Tax Revenue<br>b) Non tax revenue<br>c) Grants – in – aid<br>d) Others | 8 | Sources of financing the gap with reference to latest BE/RE: | |
| | | 8.1 | Increasing Revenue<br>a) Increasing rate of existing taxes<br>b) Levying of new taxes<br>c) Disinvestment/Monetization of assets | |
| 2 | Expenditure:<br>a) Revenue<br>   i. Interest Expenses    ii. Others<br>b) Capital | 8.2 | Rationalization of expenditure:<br>a) Revenue (excluding interest expenses)<br>b) Capital | |
| 3 | Net Borrowings[2] | 8.3 | Additional Borrowings | |
| 4 | Outstanding Liabilities[3] | | | |
| | | 8.4 | Others not covered in 8.1 to 8.3 above (to be specified) | |
| | | 8.5 | Total of additional resources mobilized for fulfilling all electoral promises (as at Sr.No. 7 above) | |
| 5 | Gross State Domestic Product – GSDP / GDP (in nominal terms) | 9 | GSDP or GDP as the case may be for the current year[4] (in nominal terms) | |
| 6 | Fiscal Sustainability Ratios: | 10 | Impact on Fiscal Sustainability Ratios: | |
| 6.1 | GFD/GSDP or GDP as the case may be | 10.1 | Additional borrowings/GSDP or GDP as the case may be [8.3 as % of 9] | |
| 6.2 | Debt/GSDP or GDP[5] as the case may be | 10.2 | Debt/GSDP or GDP as the case may be [(4+8.3) as % of 9][6] | |

Explanatory note for filling up Part B of Proforma–

1. General – Information w.r.t Sr 1 to 6.2 is to be provided by the Central/State governments based on the latest BE/RE. This is to enable the political parties to assess the reasonability of the resource raising plans and make the disclosures by various parties comparable
2. For serial no. 7 – Reproduce the amount from column 4 (ii) of Part A of Proforma.
3. For serial no. 8.4 – Please specify the sources through which additional resources will be mobilized/expenditure curtailed.

Abbreviations used:  **GFD**: Gross Fiscal Deficit; GSDP: Gross State Domestic Product; BE: Budget Estimate; RE: Revised Estimate

---

[2] Net of Repayments.
[3] As this may not be part of the Budget documents, Central/State governments to provide this information based on their records.
[4] To be based on average growth rate of GSDP/GDP of last three years.
[5] Please see footnote 3.
[6] For simplicity, it has not been required to be adjusted for repayments which have been made and to be made during the year.

Proposed proforma Part B.

EC's letter stated above also needs to be considered essential in the following context:

We talk of welfare of the people and freebies in the manifestos that have instant impact on the economic development. Where does the welfare or freebies come from? Both constitutionally, legally and legitimately come from the Consolidated Fund of India. Article in the constitution that deals with this Fund authorizes use of its funds for carrying out the objectives laid down in Part IV – Directive Principles of State Policy which mentions word 'free' only for legal aid. All the other objectives enunciated therein are linked to opening up or creating opportunities to the citizens through education that includes skill development etc. that should best serve the citizens to learn, earn and sustain on their own. This envisaged economic process generates wealth and revenue that add up to the said Fund. There is no via-media except effort, exertion; education and earning that contribute to self-sustainability of the citizens. Welfare and freebies have been misconstrued to maintain one's own personal and party desires. Both are like flying leaves in the wind, where the leaves ultimately land is unascertainable.

Economic development is the growth of the standard of living of a nation's people from a low-income (poor) economy to a high-income (rich) economy. When the local quality of life is improved, there is more economic development. When social scientists study economic development, they look at a lot of things. Economic development usually refers to the adoption of new technologies, transition from agriculture-based to industry-based economy, and general improvement in living standards. Put simply; economic development is all about improving living standards. 'Improved living standards' refers to higher levels of education and literacy, workers' income, health, and lifespan. Practically the way to accomplish economic development objectives is through advocating/influencing strategic choices in infrastructure and asset creation investment as well as public policies. Think of these choices as brand development, and they are articulated in a location's strategic plan.

There was further digression towards the start of the Twenty First Century. More and more socialized and personalized welfare schemes were considered to be best suited for the country and the people such as food security, free distribution of food grains, cash transfer to beneficiaries direct, few by way of illustration. The National Food Security Act, 2013 (NFSA) was launched to increase coverage to 75% of India's rural population and 50% of the urban population– a whopping 800 million people, as a magic wand against hunger not knowing even today flaws therein outweigh its benefits and program is sustainable for long. Such a wide-reaching program imposed significant financial costs. A conservative estimate places the costs at over 23 billion dollars a year, equivalent to about 0.72 percent of India's GDP. These costs don't just come from the grains themselves: setting up and maintaining distribution centres and government agencies to monitor the subsidies also creates extra costs. Critics argued that this money could have been better spent on generating employment, improving rural and urban infrastructure, investing in agriculture, and a number of other competing uses. This is the only way to create economic activity that helps sustain one.

India lives in rural areas whose positive change alone can change the face of India. Once that happens, development moves up in all the corners of the country with rising demand from rural consumers and the dawn of the cottage, small, medium and major industries, services and commercial hubs in and around the rural areas. This is for what the rural population has been yearning for all through. This did not the leaders of the ruling parties because their angle of economic development was not of the people but for own growth. Let a study be commissioned what were the economic and social conditions of the leaders that ruled the country during the last 45-50 years and what is their status that stands in the society, the state and country today; then we will know who travelled fast in economic and social development train, the people or the leaders of the ruling political parties.

In the light of the above submissions, I wish to state that freebies have no place under the Constitution of the country and, what was or is being done is inconsistent with the Constitutional provisions. The orders, directions, notifications on freebies, more so, on supply of free power, under the relevant law interpreting powers of the state specified therein permit such freebies do not stand to legal test, the reasons being they are outside purview of the Constitution itself and, if they have already considered as legally tenable by the courts of law and the regulatory authorities, with due respect to them, I wish to submit that such interpretation tantamount to misconstruing when the same are seen through the Constitutional touchstone. No law can be enacted which is outside the ambit the Constitution; Orders issued by the states for free supply of power etc. under an enabling provision of the governing Act are not valid considering that any such provision has no protection or within the purview of the Constitution.

# PART 04
# THE FISCAL DISASTER

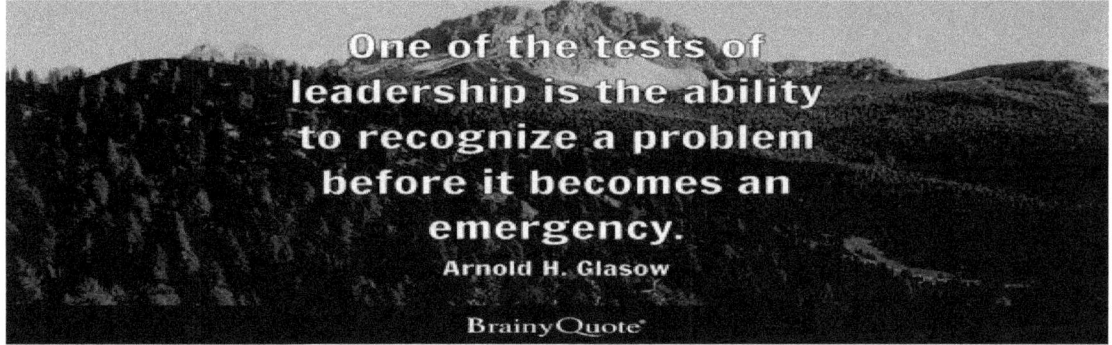

The welfare state has become a target of derision. Under this system, the welfare of its citizens is the responsibility of the state. Some countries take this to mean offering unemployment benefits and base level welfare payments, while others take it much further with universal healthcare, free college, and so on. Despite most nations falling on a spectrum of welfare state activity, with few holdouts among the most developed nations, there is a lot of charged rhetoric when the term comes up in conversation. A lot of this owes to the history of the welfare state. – Investopedia.

"It is a race to the bottom. Indeed, it is not the road to efficiency or prosperity, but a quick passport to fiscal disaster. It was not how cheap the freebies are but how expensive they are for the economy, for life quality and for social cohesion in the long run.

We must dread the thought of replicating the culture of competitive freebie politics. We must go to the route of achieving higher rates of economic growth. The race to efficiency is the race to prosperity," N. K. Singh, Chairman, Fifteenth Finance Commission.

Contributing factors to a financial crisis include systemic failures, unanticipated or uncontrollable human behavior, and incentives to take too much risk, regulatory absence or failures, or contagions that amount to a virus-like spread of problems from one institution or country to the next. Stages of financial crises are progressed in two and sometimes three stages: (1) Initiation of Financial Crisis. (2) Banking Crisis. (3) Debt Deflation. The major problems with fiscal policy are deficit spending, crowding out, timing, political considerations, and effects on international trade. What are some examples of fiscal responsibility? Preparation of a budget plan (including anticipated revenues and expenditures) Processing and Approving Financial Transactions. Financial Review. Internal Controls and Management Responsibilities. The 7 crises that will be presented are the Great Depression 1932; the Suez Crisis 1956; the International Debt Crisis 1982; the East Asian Economic Crisis 1997-2001; the Russian Economic Crisis 1992-97, the Latin American Debt Crisis in Mexico, Brazil and Argentina 1994-2002, and the Global Economic Recession 2007-09. What is one of the main problems of fiscal crisis? Crowding Out. Because an expansionary fiscal policy either increases government spending or reduces revenues, it increases the government budget deficit or reduces the surplus.

RBI Bulletin – June 16, 2022 notes, among others:

**State Subsidies and Freebies**

As per the latest available data from the Comptroller and Auditor General of India (CAG), the state governments' expenditure on subsidies has grown at 12.9 per cent and 11.2 per cent during 2020-21 and 2021-22, respectively, after contracting in 2019-20 (Chart 8a).14 Commensurately, the share of subsidies in total revenue expenditure by states has also risen from 7.8 per cent in 2019-20 to 8.2 per cent in 2021-22. At a disaggregated level, there are stark variations among states. For instance, Jharkhand, Kerala, Odisha, Telangana and Uttar Pradesh are the top five states with the largest rise in subsidies over the last three years. States like Gujarat, Punjab and Chhattisgarh spend more than 10 per cent of their revenue expenditure on subsidies (Chart 8b). Subsidies, however, are known to crowd out resources from other useful purposes (Gopalan, 2013).

In the recent period, state governments have started delivering a portion of their subsidies in the form of freebies.15 While there is no precise definition of freebies, it is necessary to distinguish them from public/merit goods, expenditure on which brings economic benefits, such as the public distribution system, employment guarantee schemes, states' support for education and health (Singh, 2022). On the other hand, provision of free electricity, free water, free public transportation, waiver of pending utility bills and farm loan waivers are often regarded as freebies, which potentially undermine credit culture, distort prices through cross-subsidisation eroding incentives for private investment, and disincentivise work at the current wage rate leading to a drop in labour force participation. Some freebies may benefit the poor if properly targeted with minimal leakages, but their advantages must be evaluated against the large fiscal costs and inefficiencies they cause by distorting prices and misallocating resources. Additionally, the provisions of free electricity and water are known to accelerate environmental degradation and depletion of water tables.

To derive an estimate of freebies, we have collated data on major financial assistance/ cash transfers, utility subsidies, loan or fee waivers and interest free loans announced by the states in their latest budget speeches (i.e., for 2022-23). As per these estimates, expenditure on freebies range from 0.1 - 2.7 per cent of GSDP for different states (Table 5). The freebies have exceeded 2 per cent of GSDP for some of the highly indebted states such as Andhra Pradesh and Punjab (Annex 1)[See the Bulletin]

| Table 5: Freebies Announced by the States in 2022-23 | | | |
|---|---|---|---|
| | (As a per cent of GSDP) | (As a per cent of Revenue Receipts) | (As a per cent of Own Tax Revenue) |
| 1 | 2 | 3 | 4 |
| Andhra Pradesh | 2.1 | 14.1 | 30.3 |
| Bihar | 0.1 | 0.6 | 2.7 |
| Haryana | 0.1 | 0.6 | 0.9 |
| Jharkhand | 1.7 | 8.0 | 26.7 |
| Kerala | 0 | 0 | 0.1 |
| Madhya Pradesh | 1.6 | 10.8 | 28.8 |
| Punjab* | 2.7 | 17.8 | 45.4 |
| Rajasthan | 0.6 | 3.9 | 8.6 |
| West Bengal | 1.1 | 9.5 | 23.8 |

*: Dhasmana, I. (2022). "Not all states are so financially weak that they can't announce freebies". Business Standard. April 2022.
Source: Budget documents of the state government.

The Centre's GST compensation pay-out will come to an end in June 2022, further reducing the headroom available for social sector expenditure. In such a situation, a multitude of social welfare schemes in the form of freebies will not only put a heavy burden on the exchequer but will also exert upward pressures on yields if they are financed through market borrowing. It will be important, therefore, for the state governments to reprioritise their expenditure to achieve optimum long-term welfare advantages by ensuring that the beneficiaries get empowered permanently and forego such benefits. Also, states should ensure that there is a sunset clause for each social sector scheme. Reducing the quantum of subsidies by ensuring that only the deserving receive them will free up resources to invest in health, education, agriculture, R&D and rural infrastructure, which will help create more jobs and reduce poverty on a sustainable basis (Gulati 2022).

Contingent Liabilities

Contingent liabilities are the contractual obligations of the government to pay in the event of a default by the borrower, either on the principal amount borrowed or interest payments on such amount or both. The contingent liabilities of states have been rising in recent years. As per the latest available information, the off-budget borrowings by states - loans raised by state-owned entities and guaranteed by the state governments - have reached around 4.5 per cent of GDP in 2022 (CRISIL, 2022). While the power sector accounts for almost 40 per cent of these guarantees, other beneficiaries include sectors like irrigation, infrastructure development, food and water supply. Contingent liabilities have surpassed 5 per cent of GSDP in states like Punjab, Rajasthan, Uttar Pradesh and Andhra Pradesh (Table 6).

DISCOMs Bailouts

The power sector accounts for much of the financial burden of state governments in India, both in terms of subsidies and contingent liabilities. Illustratively, many state governments provide subsidies, artificially depressing the cost of electricity for the farm sector and a section of the household sector. State governments also infuse capital into power distribution companies (DISCOMs) through equity and debt to enable them to undertake productive investments. Additionally, periodic bailouts (3 bailouts of DISCOMs in the last 20 years[16]) wherein states take over either the losses or the debt burden of the DISCOMs has substantial repercussion for state finances.

| Table 6: Guarantees issued by State Governments (Per cent of GSDP) | | | | | | | | |
|---|---|---|---|---|---|---|---|---|
| | Bihar | Kerala | Punjab | Rajasthan | West Bengal | Andhra Pradesh | Uttar Pradesh | Haryana |
| 2017-18 | 1.1 | 2.5 | 4.5 | 7.5 | 0.9 | 4.6 | 6.3 | 2.2 |
| 2018-19 | 1.0 | 3.4 | 0.9 | 7.6 | 0.6 | 6.2 | 6.9 | 2.6 |
| 2019-20 | 0.9 | 3.2 | 4.1 | 8.1 | 0.5 | 8.1 | 6.7 | 2.7 |
| 2020-21 (RE) | 3.4 | 3.9 | 5.3 | 8.6 | 0.6 | 9.0 | 8.0 | NA |

NA: Not Available
Sources: Budget documents of state government; state governments; and PRS Legislative Research (PRS).

Despite various financial restructuring measures[17], the performance of the DISCOMs has remained weak, with their losses surpassing the pre-UDAY level of 0.4 per cent of GDP in 2018-19 (Chart 9a). In addition, their long-term debt started increasing since 2017-18, surpassing the pre-UDAY level by 2018-19 and rising further in 2019-20 (Chart 9b). The combined losses of DISCOMs in the five most indebted states, viz., Bihar, Kerala, Punjab, Rajasthan and West Bengal, constituted 24.7 per cent of the total DISCOMs losses in 2019-20, while their combined long-term debt was 22.9 per cent of the total DISCOM debt in 2019-20 (Chart 9c). Furthermore, overdues of DISCOMs to power generating companies (GENCOs) have increased since March 2018 (with some moderation during November 2020 to April 2021 due to the additional liquidity provided to DISCOMs under the Atma Nirbhar Bharat Abhiyan)[18] which may require fresh Liquidity injections to ensure uninterrupted power supply [Chart 9d] {See Bulletin}. Liquidity injections to ensure uninterrupted power supply (Chart 9d) [See Bulletin].

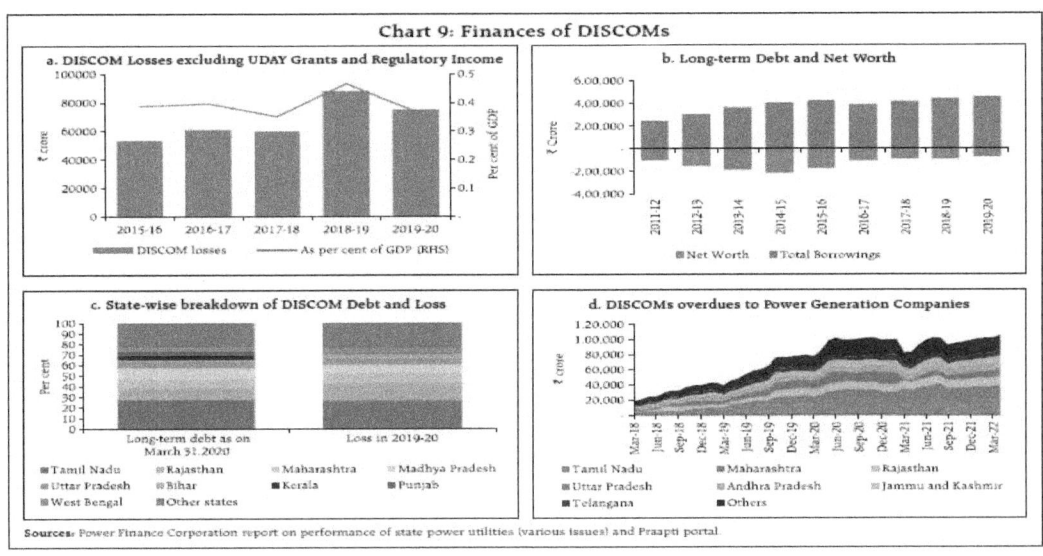

Chart 9: Finances of DISCOMs

a. DISCOM Losses excluding UDAY Grants and Regulatory Income
b. Long-term Debt and Net Worth
c. State-wise breakdown of DISCOM Debt and Loss
d. DISCOMs overdues to Power Generation Companies

Sources: Power Finance Corporation report on performance of state power utilities (various issues) and Praapti portal.

A rescue package for the DISCOMs may involve substantial financial burden for the states. For instance, if: (i) 75 per cent of the long-term debt of the DISCOMs (as at end-March 2020) is taken over by the state governments (similar to UDAY); and (ii) the states infuse liquidity (in the form of equity) into the DISCOMs to the tune of overdue outstanding to the GENCOs as of April 2022, the burden on the exchequer will be significant. For the 18 major states, the cost of the bailout will be 2.3 per cent of their combined GSDP, though there are significant differences amongst states. Tamil Nadu, Madhya Pradesh, Rajasthan and Punjab are most vulnerable to a possible bailout while Gujarat, Assam, Haryana and Odisha are relatively insulated from this risk (Table 7). For avoiding such bailouts, going forward, the DISCOMs need to undertake appropriate tariff revisions that reflect the underlying cost of power supply, keeping in view the rising cost of imported coal.

Table 7: Impact of Potential Bailout of DISCOMs in Major States

| State | Pre-bailout | | Size of the bailout | | Post-bailout | | Total bailout size | |
|---|---|---|---|---|---|---|---|---|
| | Long-term debt | Equity | Assumption of 75% of long-term debt | Liquidity infusion for power purchase overdues | Long-term debt | Equity | | |
| | ₹ Crore | ₹ Crore | ₹ Crore | ₹ Crore | ₹ Crore | ₹ Crore | ₹ Crore | Per cent of 2020-21 GSDP |
| Punjab | 16,258 | 22,417 | 12,194 | 1,404 | 4,065 | 36,015 | 13,598 | 2.5 |
| Rajasthan | 48,934 | 40,282 | 36,701 | 11,543 | 12,234 | 1,962 | 48,244 | 5.7 |
| West Bengal | 14,222 | 16,430 | 10,667 | 677 | 3,556 | 27,774 | 11,344 | 0.9 |
| Kerala | 20,310 | 9,961 | 15,233 | 493 | 5,078 | 10,145 | 15,726 | 1.8 |
| Bihar | 6,726 | 21,603 | 5,045 | 755 | 1,682 | 27,403 | 5,800 | 0.8 |
| Andhra Pradesh | 26,810 | 19,218 | 20,108 | 8,914 | 6,703 | 9,212 | 29,022 | 2.1 |
| Uttar Pradesh | 28,782 | 8,368 | 21,587 | 10,195 | 7,196 | 40,150 | 31,782 | 1.3 |
| Jharkhand | 10,530 | 2,889 | 7,898 | 3,643 | 2,633 | 14,430 | 11,541 | 2.5 |
| Haryana | 6,864 | 1,347 | 5,148 | 919 | 1,716 | 7,414 | 6,067 | 0.7 |
| Tamil Nadu | 1,24,413 | 22,413 | 93,310 | 21,038 | 31,103 | 41,937 | 1,14,348 | 5.2 |
| Odisha | 4,599 | 5,048 | 3,449 | 321 | 1,150 | 3,136 | 3,770 | 0.6 |
| Chattisgarh | 4,102 | 7,896 | 3,077 | 191 | 1,026 | 372 | 3,268 | 0.9 |
| Telangana | 21,948 | 21,703 | 16,461 | 7,201 | 5,487 | 299 | 23,662 | 1.7 |
| Madhya Pradesh | 49,112 | 11,190 | 36,834 | 5,240 | 12,278 | 10,984 | 42,074 | 3.9 |
| Assam | 2,429 | 8,457 | 1,822 | 45 | 607 | 10,324 | 1,867 | 0.5 |
| Karnataka | 22,767 | 3,232 | 17,075 | 4,304 | 5,692 | 24,611 | 21,379 | 1.0 |
| Gujarat | 563 | 16,607 | 422 | 715 | 141 | 17,744 | 1,137 | 0.0 |
| Maharashtra | 39,086 | 29,135 | 29,315 | 18,392 | 9,772 | 76,842 | 47,707 | 1.0 |
| Total for above states | 4,48,455 | -76,896 | 3,36,341 | 95,990 | 1,12,114 | 3,55,435 | 4,32,331 | 2.3 |

Sources: Power Finance Corporation report on performance of state power utilities (various issues), Praapti portal and RBI staff estimates.

Historical occurrences of whatever respect guide us to find a way for future betterment when we are in mid-sea. Those occurrences brought out the truth when an Inquiry Commission was appointed and went into in all the four corners of the subject matter. It so happened in USA in first decade of the twenty-first century which I could find on the website while in search of the causes for the origin of the financial and economic crisis or disasters. I had the benefit of studying the conclusions.

The report though relates to first decade of the twenty first century and, we may say of what relevance it could be now, its simple glancing through tells us how consciously and with conscience the National Commission considered the origin of the crisis, though it was for reasons different from the ones threatening in our country at present such as those stated before and for which purpose, this book is being presented. One would agree that regardless of the causes for origin of crisis, the traditionally in vogue financial and economic principles remain the parameters for subjecting such causes to inquiry. That was the guiding factor for me to proceed.

The common sense whether of politicians, professionals and the people also guides towards understanding what kind of bizarre has been in the process on the eve of elections or otherwise on one or the other excuse put forth by the governing authorities as an ointment to the burning skin. This skin does not burn because their mind itself propels them to keep the states' finances burning, recklessly spending giving illogical considerations, inimical economic reasoning and, that shows, how they set their thoughts once they decide to enter into the fray of the public life, rightly also as noted in one of the Articles stated below, the 'contemporary political leaders' whose wishful thinking of self-greediness under the one or the other guise overtakes their financial and economic sensibility to be applied when they are dealing about a subject matter such as the prudent financial and economic management of the state affairs for the public and country's good.

That not doing so means the field is open free for all. Even in the field of any sport, there are rules and regulations to be abided by, breach of which leads to penal action as laid down therein. That also means we expect the sports persons and other citizens who are subject to one or the other governance system, but we, as the political leaders, assume, there is no sunset clause [ a provision of a law that it will automatically be terminated after a fixed period unless.] in one or other part of the governance rather they feel as if they have to follow only the sun-rise clause.[A sunrise provision, also known as a sunrise clause, is a contract provision that extends coverage to events that occurred before the contract was signed.]. This also means the democracy we have adopted allows these kinds of attitudes and acts. It is not so. The public leaders when they sight coming of elections become blind to the Oath they have taken before assuming the office; perhaps thinking this is only a formality to be completed under the constitution of the country; whether we follow it in our thoughts, deeds and acts in real life is immaterial. Federalism does not mean that the State or its ministers, or the public leaders can make any promise, whether capable or not capable to be fulfilled in, without subjecting themselves to governing rules and regulations or the guidelines or the administrative protocol. So also is the position in the case of Union ministers. Due to lack of such understanding, the public leaders seem to be going beyond their own self-control when a citizen is compelled to seek legal intervention and redressal. That is where we stand today, each political party contesting with other how this is given and how that is given ignoring the fact that they themselves are public leaders and are supposed to self-regulate following whatever law, rules, regulation, guidelines, procedures and precedents or administrative hierarchal obligations they are governed with.

Assuming that there are not such obligations compelling them to be complied with, as submitted before, the entire process elections or of any nature of economic factor becomes meaningless to the essence of survival of the democracy with fiscal assurance and guarantee, the safeguarding of which is the primary responsibility of the public leaders and governance system. The governance system cannot up its hands when it is watching what is happening before its eyes that is causing grievous injury to the fiscal management of the country. If such measures are brought into the political field, in my personal view, such entry into the field amounts to forceful entry which suggests there are no governing rules for entry and exit of such field. This message has to be in ears and the eyes of the political leaders clearly warning that such entry and the games the political parties want to play not permissible under the constitution of the country, they being indiscriminate and lack of uniform application to the citizens. As noted hereunder, the constitution does not, other than free legal aid, despises utilization of the Consolidated Funds for freebies and free services, the creation of which costs the government or the corporate and such costs must and are liable to be recovered with provisions for concessions in the application of the burden to the weaker sections of the society but, under no circumstances, such making available of such services cannot be generalized. The constitution clearly lays down that "No moneys out of the Consolidated Fund of India or the Consolidated Fund of a State shall be appropriated except in accordance with law and for the purposes and in the manner provided in this Constitution. Even one thinks the various Acts made under the constitution such as Electricity Act, 2003 permit explicitly free or subsidized supply [other than for those specifically stipulated therein].

Section 108 - Directions by State Government.: (1) In the discharge of its functions, the State Commission shall be guided by such directions in matters of policy involving public interest as the State Government may give to it in writing. (2) If any question arises as to whether any such direction relates to a matter of policy involving public interest, the decision of the State Government thereon shall be final. What is the meaning of 'policy involving public interest'? Online Dictionary defines 'public interest' [which is relied upon in the absence of any specific definition under the laws in respect thereof] Public interest means any government action directed to protecting and benefiting citizens at large, whereby essential goods and services are provided for the welfare of the population. "Public Interest - Something in which the public, the community at large, has some pecuniary interest, or some interest. Supreme Court of India. Cites 95 - Cited by 134 - Full Document.[Indian Kanoon]. The public interest so stated does not explicitly or even implicitly include free services or freebies barring for those for whom explicitly specified. The Directions issued by the State Government to the State Electricity Regulatory Commission, compulsively if not deliberately including therein free supply of power to the consumers are overstretched the law and such inclusion cannot come under the protection that the decision of the state government shall be final. This is so because barring free legal aid enunciated under the Directive Principle of State Policy, the constitution does not contain connotation of 'free'.

On that basis also, the provisions of section referred to above cannot be construed to include 'free' under the state directions which, by its non-recognition under the constitution, renders itself unenforceable by the regulatory authority and is invalid. It is to be appreciated that a state cannot assume an extraordinary authority to say that what it has specified under its direction tantamount to 'final' inasmuch that itself is not consistent with the provisions of the constitution. This instant case is given as an example and the similar or identical provisions contained in any other law or laws have the same effect of non-maintainability with regard to the words public interest or final, if any, used therein. The intent of the constitution is not to drain out the public funds from the Consolidated Funds but to protect and preserve them after discharge of the state obligations of expenditure contemplated therein. Which other powers empower the political parties or the political leaders to undertake such services as generalized and available to all? Expenditure to be incurred out of the Consolidated Funds is self-governed when one reads the relevant provisions and governing Fiscal Rules and Accountability.

Another issue that pertinently arises is "Are we ready to appoint National Commission on the Causes of Financial and Economic Crisis or did we do it when there was crisis in 1991 or any other time like the one forced by the Americans? To my understanding, there was none. But we did one through the appointment of Joint Parliamentary Committee [JPC] when there was a break out of Securities Scam in 1992. JPC consisted of the representatives of both the Houses of Parliament. There is something known as "Lessons Learnt" sooner we noticed shades of crisis in the horizon. The Securities Scam 1992 was, if not whole, most part of it was identical to the causes of the financial crisis in the USA, the conclusions of the Inquiry Commission of which are given below to draw the kind attention of the governance and the readers to know how in depth the Commission went into to trace the truth. JPC in India went into the causes of securities scam with political overshadowing and, in that, lost the teeth to bite the real culprits who constructed the base for the scam and played the game behind the scenes fore fronting the Commercial Banks, leading Financial Institutions and major Brokers of the day in the stock market. Its origination was the brain child of the highly reputed experts who held high position in the organizations under the central government inventing the concept of Bank Receipts [BR].

The games played by the brokers with the Banks and FIs were rehearsed by the JPC which, with due respect to it, did not go into logic of creation of BR mode in place of physical possession mode that cheated the Banks and FIs whose officers and staff were made the culprits and victims while the real culprits and victims who included, besides the leading brokers, the bureaucrats holding high positions, the politicians, the corrupt bank and FIs high level officers whose names could have been known but for the seizure of the computers and gadgets overnight by the investigating agencies at the behest of higher authorities fearing their names would have been mentioned in the software maintained by the king pin broker. These were the findings of the JPC promptly welcomed by the government of the day whose orders for initiation of criminal proceedings even those against whom there was no recovery or any loss to the organization they were serving, were neatly executed and such innocent persons were hooked to the wooden plank by the investigating agencies leaving them to their own fate for periods even beyond twenty five years and continuing , trials are yet to start and on the day of the pronouncement of the judgment, the honourable trial courts would be informed that the accused persons are dead, thus the criminal cases against such persons stood automatically closed. Why JPC did not pursue with the same vigour the legality or illegality of BR, the origin of the scam or why JPC did not order opening and checking of the computers and software seized by the investigating agencies? The report is silent.

This was how the a large ground was created for playing the game of scam by the official and unofficial brokers camouflaging by which they mislead the Banks, Financial Institutions and large size investors into the stock market. This would not have happened but for the introduction of BR mode evolved and adopted with the knowledge and nodding of the central bank, that gave a false assurance to the Banks and FIs to believe and accept the mode so adopted, as if, was within the framework of securities market. More interesting to note was that the central government policies on investment of surplus funds by the Financial Institutions and government owned companies were retuned just before that period extending the hands of the above institutions to reach to the secondary market which opened up the window for scams day and night.

The day the scam broke out, the first line of instructions to the investigating agencies was to seize the computers and all the software material maintained by the major brokers which contained all the details of big fishes, overnight. The media coverage of the days stand testimony. They were subjected to scrutiny on selective basis within the walls of the investigating agencies, not even presented to the courts of law where they filed charge sheets against the small fishes, even twisting the texture and stitching the torn places by introducing the third elements. Those who were tried and sentenced are languishing in the jail while those other small fishes caught in web made to remain in the web for procrastinated period [s] stretching over more than twenty five years. They are languishing still in the web. This is how the securities scam came to end so far its character is concerned but the small fishes to which such character was attributed for charging continue to struggle within the web physically, financially and mentally. This is the sum and substance of the Indian securities scam

The size of the scam was enormous, about Rs. 55000 crores estimated by JPC that dent financial force and strength of the central government and its scheduled banks, Financial institutions as well as the public investors. The scheduled banks played a crucial role in using the base so built up that also enabled establishment of nexus between the scheduled commercial and foreign banks, more the foreign banks, got involved so deep believing they have their own sovereign access and control in attracting and managing the surplus funds with hands in gloves working together with the brokers often to do something dishonest that gave birth to the scam that spread like fire engulfing every corner and everyone in the way. The big fishes in the political, bureaucratic and high rich class fields made best of the opportunities during the course of scam and enriched wealth overnight while those small and middle level invested people lost everything and many of them committed suicide.

RBI appointed Janikiraman Committee to go into all aspects of the scam. The committee came out with reports in five volumes which also showed the shades of association of the officials of the central bank. Both JPC and the Janikiraman Committee findings found the middle and lower rung employees of the scheduled banks, the financial institutions and PSUs a most convenient category to indict with greater share of responsibility for the scam. The big fishes including the ministers, bureaucrats and political leaders sitting on fence who silently swam into the ocean of scam like big fishes and sharks do in the sea but none could come in the net because the net was of two sizes, one smaller and the other larger that facilitated the investigating agencies to ensure escaping of the big fishes to the shore, they were placed in a smaller size net with wide open space to escape whereas they put the medium and small fishes in the larger net with tightened space whereby they were forced to remain in the net and sink into the sea of investigation, trial and punishment. That group also covered most innocent fishes which the investigating agencies knew but could not help them to escape from the large net due to the strong undercurrents passing through to them from the high political figures and highly influential people. . That exhibited the quality of inquiry the government made in the securities scam of 1992.

Now, let us read the conclusions of the Commission which have bearing to any one time or all the time, the only difference being the causes for origin of the disease. This is how the National Commission diagnosed the disease. Such Inquiry lets the truth speak:

**THE FINANCIAL CRISIS INQUIRY REPORT FINAL REPORT OF THE NATIONAL COMMISSION ON THE CAUSES OF THE FINANCIAL AND ECONOMIC CRISIS IN THE UNITED STATES OFFICIAL GOVERNMENT EDITION THE FINANCIAL CRISIS INQUIRY COMMISSION Submitted by Pursuant to Public Law 111-21 January 2011: {Excerpts}:**

Now, let us read the conclusions of the Commission which have bearing to any one time but for all the time, the only difference being the causes for origin of the disease. This is how the National Commission diagnosed the disease. Such Inquiry lets the truth speak:

"The Financial Crisis Inquiry Commission has been called upon to examine the financial and economic crisis that has gripped our country and explain its causes to the American people. We are keenly aware of the significance of our charge, given the economic damage that America has suffered in the wake of the greatest financial crisis since the Great Depression.

Our task was first to determine what happened and how it happened so that we could understand why it happened. Here we present our conclusions. We encourage the American people to join us in making their own assessments based on the evidence gathered in our inquiry. If we do not learn from history, we are unlikely to fully recover from it. Some on Wall Street and in Washington with a stake in the status quo may be tempted to wipe from memory the events of this crisis, or to suggest that no one could have foreseen or prevented them. This report endeavours to expose the facts, identify responsibility, unravel myths, and help us understand how the crisis could have been avoided. It is an attempt to record history, not to rewrite it, nor allow it to be rewritten.

To help our fellow citizens better understand this crisis and its causes, we also present specific conclusions at the end of chapters in Parts III, IV, and V of this report.

The subject of this report is of no small consequence to this nation. The profound events of 2007 and 2008 were neither bumps in the road nor an accentuated dip in the financial and business cycles we have come to expect in a free market economic system. This was a fundamental disruption—a financial upheaval, if you will—that wreaked havoc in communities and neighborhoods across this country.

As this report goes to print, there are more than 26 million Americans who are out of work, cannot find full-time work, or have given up looking for work. About four million families have lost their homes to foreclosure and another four and a half million have slipped into the foreclosure process or are seriously behind on their mortgage payments. Nearly $11 trillion in household wealth has vanished, with retirement accounts and life savings swept away.

Businesses, large and small, have felt the sting of a deep recession. There is much anger about what has transpired, and justifiably so. Many people who abided by all the rules now find themselves out of work and uncertain about their future prospects. The collateral damage of this crisis has been real people and real communities. The impacts of this crisis are likely to be felt for a generation. And the nation faces no easy path to renewed economic strength.

Like so many Americans, we began our exploration with our own views and some preliminary knowledge about how the world's strongest financial system came to the brink of collapse. Even at the time of our appointment to this independent panel, much had already been written and said about the crisis. Yet all of us have been deeply affected by what we have learned in the course of our inquiry. We have been at various times fascinated, surprised, and even shocked by what we saw, heard, and read. Ours has been a journey of revelation.

Much attention over the past two years has been focused on the decisions by the federal government to provide massive financial assistance to stabilize the financial system and rescue large financial institutions that were deemed too systemically important to fail. Those decisions—and the deep emotions surrounding them—will be debated long into the future. But our mission was to ask and answer this central question: how did it come to pass that in 2008 our nation was forced to choose between two stark and painful alternatives—either risk the total collapse of our financial system and economy or inject trillions of taxpayer dollars into the financial system and an array of companies, as millions of Americans still lost their jobs, their savings, and their homes?

In this report, we detail the events of the crisis. But a simple summary, as we see it, is useful at the outset. While the vulnerabilities that created the potential for crisis were years in the making, it was the collapse of the housing bubble—fuelled by low interest rates, easy and available credit, scant regulation, and toxic mortgages— that was the spark that ignited a string of events, which led to a full-blown crisis in the fall of 2008. Trillions of dollars in risky mortgages had become embedded throughout the financial system, as mortgage-related securities were packaged, repackaged, and sold to investors around the world. When the bubble burst, hundreds of billions of dollars in losses in mortgages and mortgage-related securities shook markets as well as financial institutions that had significant exposures to those mortgages and had borrowed heavily against them. This happened not just in the United States but around the world. The losses were magnified by derivatives such as synthetic securities.

The crisis reached seismic proportions in September 2008 with the failure of Lehman Brothers and the impending collapse of the insurance giant American International Group (AIG). Panic fanned by a lack of transparency of the balance sheets of major financial institutions, coupled with a tangle of interconnections among institutions perceived to be "too big to fail," caused the credit markets to seize up. Trading ground to a halt. The stock market plummeted. The economy plunged into a deep recession.

The financial system we examined bears little resemblance to that of our parents' generation. The changes in the past three decades alone have been remarkable. The financial markets have become increasingly globalized. Technology has transformed the efficiency, speed, and complexity of financial instruments and transactions. There is broader access to and lower costs of financing than ever before. And the financial sector itself has become a much more dominant force in our economy.

From 1978 to 2007, the amount of debt held by the financial sector soared from $3 trillion to $36 trillion, more than doubling as a share of gross domestic product. The very nature of many Wall Street firms changed—from relatively staid private partnerships to publicly traded corporations taking greater and more diverse kinds of risks. By 2005, the 10 largest U.S. commercial banks held 55% of the industry's assets, more than double the level held in 2006. On the eve of the crisis in 27%, financial sector profits constituted 27% of all corporate profits in the United States, up from15% in 1980. Understanding this transformation has been critical to the Commission's analysis.

Now to our major findings and conclusions, which are based on the facts contained in this report: they are offered with the hope that lessons may be learned to help avoid future catastrophe.

• We conclude this financial crisis was avoidable. The crisis was the result of human action and inaction, not of Mother Nature or computer models gone haywire. The captains of finance and the public stewards of our financial system ignored warnings and failed to question, understand, and manage evolving risks within a system essential to the well-being of the American public. Theirs was a big miss, not a stumble. While the business cycle cannot be repealed, a crisis of this magnitude need not have occurred. To paraphrase Shakespeare, the fault lies not in the stars, but in us.

Despite the expressed view of many on Wall Street and in Washington that the crisis could not have been foreseen or avoided, there were warning signs. The tragedy was that they were ignored or discounted. There was an explosion in risky subprime lending and securitization, an unsustainable rise in housing prices, widespread reports of egregious and predatory lending practices, dramatic increases in household mortgage debt, and exponential growth in financial firms' trading activities, unregulated derivatives, and short-term "repo" lending markets, among many other red flags. Yet there was pervasive permissiveness; little meaningful action was taken to quell the threats in a timely manner.

The prime example is the Federal Reserve's pivotal failure to stem the flow of toxic mortgages, which it could have done by setting prudent mortgage-lending standards. The Federal Reserve was the one entity empowered to do so and it did not. The record of our examination is replete with evidence of other failures: financial institutions made, bought, and sold mortgage securities they never examined, did not care to examine, or knew to be defective; firms depended on tens of billions of dollars of borrowing that had to be renewed each and every night, secured by subprime mortgage securities; and major firms and investors blindly relied on credit rating agencies as their arbiters of risk. What else could one expect on a highway where there were neither speed limits nor neatly painted lines?

• We conclude widespread failures in financial regulation and supervision proved devastating to the stability of the nation's financial markets. The sentries were not at their posts, in no small part due to the widely accepted faith in the self-correcting nature of the markets and the ability of financial institutions to effectively police themselves. More than 30 years of deregulation and reliance on self-regulation by financial institutions, championed by former Federal Reserve chairman Alan Greenspan and others, supported by successive administrations and Congresses, and actively pushed by the powerful financial industry at every turn, had stripped away key safeguards, which could have helped avoid catastrophe. This approach had opened up gaps in oversight of critical areas with trillions of dollars at risk, such as the shadow banking system and over-the-counter derivatives markets. In addition, the government permitted financial firms to pick their preferred regulators in what became a race to the weakest supervisor.

Yet we do not accept the view that regulators lacked the power to protect the financial system. They had ample power in many arenas and they chose not to use it. To give just three examples: the Securities and Exchange Commission could have required more capital and halted risky practices at the big investment banks. It did not. The Federal Reserve Bank of New York and other regulators could have clamped down on Citigroup's excesses in the run-up to the crisis. They did not. Policy makers and regulators could have stopped the runaway mortgage securitization train. They did not. In case after case after case, regulators continued to rate the institutions they oversaw as safe and sound even in the face of mounting troubles, often downgrading them just before their collapse. And where regulators lacked authority, they could have sought it. Too often, they lacked the political will—in a political and ideological environment that constrained it—as well as the fortitude to critically challenge the institutions and the entire system they were entrusted to oversee.

Changes in the regulatory system occurred in many instances as financial markets evolved. But as the report will show, the financial industry itself played a key role in weakening regulatory constraints on institutions, markets, and products. It did not surprise the Commission that an industry of such wealth and power would exert pressure on policy makers and regulators. From 1998 to 2008, the financial sector expended $2.7 billion in reported federal lobbying expenses; individuals and political action committees in the sector made more than $1 billion in campaign contributions. What troubled us was the extent to which the nation was deprived of the necessary strength and independence of the oversight necessary to safeguard financial stability.

• We conclude dramatic failures of corporate governance and risk management at many systemically important financial institutions were a key cause of this crisis. There was a view that instincts for self-preservation inside major financial firms would shield them from fatal risk-taking without the need for a steady regulatory hand, which, the firms argued, would stifle innovation. Too many of these institutions acted recklessly, taking on too much risk, with too little capital, and with too much dependence on short-term funding. In many respects, this reflected a fundamental change in these institutions, particularly the large investment banks and bank holding companies, which focused their activities increasingly on risky trading activities that produced hefty profits. They took on enormous exposures in acquiring and supporting subprime lenders and creating, packaging, repackaging, and selling trillions of dollars in mortgage-related securities, including synthetic financial products. Like Icarus, they never feared flying ever closer to the sun.

Many of these institutions grew aggressively through poorly executed acquisition and integration strategies that made effective management more challenging. The CEO of Citigroup told the Commission that a $40 billion position in highly rated mortgage securities would "not in any way have excited my attention," and the cohead of Citigroup's investment bank said he spent "a small fraction of 1%" of his time on those securities. In this instance, too big to fail meant too big to manage.

Financial institutions and credit rating agencies embraced mathematical models as reliable predictors of risks, replacing judgment in too many instances. Too often, risk management became risk justification.

Compensation systems—designed in an environment of cheap money, intense competition, and light regulation—too often rewarded the quick deal, the short-term gain—without proper consideration of long-term consequences. Often, those systems encouraged the big bet—where the payoff on the upside could be huge and the downside limited. This was the case up and down the line—from the corporate boardroom to the mortgage broker on the street.

Our examination revealed stunning instances of governance breakdowns and irresponsibility. You will read, among other things, about AIG senior management's ignorance of the terms and risks of the company's $79 billion derivatives exposure to mortgage-related securities; Fannie Mae's quest for bigger market share, profits, and bonuses, which led it to ramp up its exposure to risky loans and securities as the housing market was peaking; and the costly surprise when Merrill Lynch's top management realized that the company held $55 billion in "super-senior" and supposedly "super-safe" mortgage-related securities that resulted in billions of dollars in losses.

• We conclude a combination of excessive borrowing, risky investments, and lack of transparency put the financial system on a collision course with crisis. Clearly, this vulnerability was related to failures of corporate governance and regulation, but it is significant enough by itself to warrant our attention here.

In the years leading up to the crisis, too many financial institutions, as well as too many households, borrowed to the hilt, leaving them vulnerable to financial distress or ruin if the value of their investments declined even modestly. For example, as of 2007, the five major investment banks—Bear Stearns, Goldman Sachs, Lehman Brothers, Merrill Lynch, and Morgan Stanley—were operating with extraordinarily thin capital. By one measure, their leverage ratios were as high as 40 to 1, meaning for every $40 in assets, there was only $1 in capital to cover losses. Less than a 3% drop in asset values could wipe out a firm. To make matters worse, much of their borrowing was short-term, in the overnight market—meaning the borrowing had to be renewed each and every day. For example, at the end of 2007, Bear Stearns had $11.8 billion equity and $383.6 billion in liabilities and was borrowing as much as $70 billion in the overnight market. It was the equivalent of a small business with $50,000 in equity borrowing $1.6 million, with $296,750 of that due each and every day. One can't really ask "What were they thinking?" when it seems that too many of them were thinking alike.

And the leverage was often hidden—in derivatives positions, in off-balance-sheet entities, and through "window dressing" of financial reports available to the investing public.

The kings of leverage were Fannie Mae and Freddie Mac, the two behemoth government-sponsored enterprises (GSEs). For example, by the end of 2007, Fannie's and Freddie's combined leverage ratio, including loans they owned and guaranteed, stood at 75 to 1.

But financial firms were not alone in the borrowing spree: from 2001 to2007, national mortgage debt almost doubled, and the amount of mortgage debt per household rose more than 63% from $91,500 to $149,500 even while wages were essentially stagnant. When the housing downturn hit, heavily indebted financial firms and families alike were walloped.

The heavy debt taken on by some financial institutions was exacerbated by the risky assets they were acquiring with that debt. As the mortgage and real estate markets churned out riskier and riskier loans and securities, many financial institutions loaded up on them. By the end of 2007, Lehman had amassed $111 billion in commercial and residential real estate holdings and securities, which was almost twice what it held just two years before, and more than four times its total equity. And again, the risk wasn't being taken on just by the big financial firms, but by families, too. Nearly one in10 mortgage borrowers in 2005 and 2006 took out "option ARM" loans, which meant they could choose to make payments so low that their mortgage balances rose every month.

Within the financial system, the dangers of this debt were magnified because transparency was not required or desired. Massive, short-term borrowing, combined with obligations unseen by others in the market, heightened the chances the system could rapidly unravel. In the early part of the 20th century, we erected a series of protections—the Federal Reserve as a lender of last resort, federal deposit insurance, ample regulations—to provide a bulwark against the panics that had regularly plagued America's banking system in the 19th century. Yet, over the past 30-plus years, we permitted the growth of a shadow banking system—opaque and laden with shortterm debt—that rivalled the size of the traditional banking system. Key components of the market—for example, the multitrillion-dollar repo lending market, off-balance-sheet entities, and the use of over-the-counter derivatives—were hidden from view, without the protections we had constructed to prevent financial meltdowns. We had a 21st-century financial system with 19th-century safeguards.

When the housing and mortgage markets cratered, the lack of transparency, the extraordinary debt loads, the short-term loans, and the risky assets all came home to roost. What resulted was panic. We had reaped what we had sown.

•We conclude the government was ill prepared for the crisis, and its inconsistent response added to the uncertainty and panic in the financial markets. As part of our charge, it was appropriate to review government actions taken in response to the developing crisis, not just those policies or actions that preceded it, to determine if any of those responses contributed to or exacerbated the crisis.

As our report shows, key policy makers—the Treasury Department, the Federal Reserve Board, and the Federal Reserve Bank of New York—who were best positioned to watch over our markets were ill prepared for the events of 2007 and 2008. Other agencies were also behind the curve. They were hampered because they did not have a clear grasp of the financial system they were charged with overseeing, particularly as it had evolved in the years leading up to the crisis. This was in no small measure due to the lack of transparency in key markets. They thought risk had been diversified when, in fact, it had been concentrated. Time and again, from the spring of 2007 on, policy makers and regulators were caught off guard as the contagion spread, responding on an ad hoc basis with specific programs to put fingers in the dike. There was no comprehensive and strategic plan for containment, because they lacked a full understanding of the risks and interconnections in the financial markets. Some regulators have conceded this error. We had allowed the system to race ahead of our ability to protect it.

While there was some awareness of or at least a debate about, the housing bubble, the record reflects that senior public officials did not recognize that a bursting of the bubble could threaten the entire financial system. Throughout the summer of 2007, both Federal Reserve Chairman Ben Bernanke and Treasury Secretary Henry Paulson offered public assurances that the turmoil in the subprime mortgage markets would be contained. When Bear Stearns's hedge funds, which were heavily invested in mortgage-related securities, imploded in June 2007, the Federal Reserve discussed the implications of the collapse. Despite the fact that so many other funds were exposed to the same risks as those hedge funds, the Bear Stearns funds were thought to be "relatively unique." Days before the collapse of Bear Stearns in March 2008, SEC Chairman Christopher Cox expressed "comfort about the capital cushions" at the big investment banks. It was not until August 2008, just weeks before the government takeover of Fannie Mae and Freddie Mac, that the Treasury Department understood the full measure of the dire financial conditions of those two institutions. And just a month before Lehman's collapse, the Federal Reserve Bank of New York was still seeking information on the exposures created by Lehman's more than 900,000 derivatives contracts.

In addition, the government's inconsistent handling of major financial institutions during the crisis—the decision to rescue Bear Stearns and then to place Fannie Mae and Freddie Mac into conservatorship, followed by its decision not to save Lehman Brothers and then to save AIG—increased uncertainty and panic in the market.

In making these observations, we deeply respect and appreciate the efforts made by Secretary Paulson, Chairman Bernanke, and Timothy Geithner, formerly president of the Federal Reserve Bank of New York and now treasury secretary, and so many others who laboured to stabilize our financial system and our economy in the most chaotic and challenging of circumstances.

• We conclude there was a systemic breakdown in accountability and ethics. The integrity of our financial markets and the public's trust in those markets are essential to the economic well-being of our nation. The soundness and the sustained prosperity of the financial system and our economy rely on the notions of fair dealing, responsibility, and transparency. In our economy, we expect businesses and individuals to pursue profits, at the same time that they produce products and services of quality and conduct themselves well.

Unfortunately—as has been the case in past speculative booms and busts—we witnessed an erosion of standards of responsibility and ethics that exacerbated the financial crisis. This was not universal, but these breaches stretched from the ground level to the corporate suites. They resulted not only in significant financial consequences but also in damage to the trust of investors, businesses, and the public in the financial system.

For example, our examination found, according to one measure, that the percentage of borrowers who defaulted on their mortgages within just a matter of months after taking a loan nearly doubled from the summer of 2006 to late 2007. This data indicates they likely took out mortgages that they never had the capacity or intention to pay. You will read about mortgage brokers who were paid "yield spread premiums" by lenders to put borrowers into higher-cost loans so they would get bigger fees, often never disclosed to borrowers. The report catalogues the rising incidence of mortgage fraud, which flourished in an environment of collapsing lending standards and lax regulation. The number of suspicious activity reports—reports of possible financial crimes filed by depository banks and their affiliates—related to mortgage fraud grew 20 fold between 1996 and 2005 and then more than doubled again between 2005 and 2009. One study places the losses resulting from fraud on mortgage loans made between 2005 and 2007 at $112 billion.

Lenders made loans that they knew borrowers could not afford and that could cause massive losses to investors in mortgage securities. As early as September 2004, countrywide executives recognized that many of the loans they were originating could result in "catastrophic consequences." Less than a year later, they noted that certain high-risk loans they were making could result not only in foreclosures but also in "financial and reputational catastrophe" for the firm. But they did not stop.

And the report documents that major financial institutions ineffectively sampled loans they were purchasing to package and sell to investors. They knew a significant percentage of the sampled loans did not meet their own underwriting standards or those of the originators. Nonetheless, they sold those securities to investors. The Commission's review of many prospectuses provided to investors found that this critical information was not disclosed.

THESE CONCLUSIONS must be viewed in the context of human nature and individual and societal responsibility. First, to pin this crisis on mortal flaws like greed and xxii FINANCIAL CRISIS INQUIRY COMMISSION REPORT hubris would be simplistic. It was the failure to account for human weakness that is relevant to this crisis. Second, we clearly believe the crisis was a result of human mistakes, misjudgements, and misdeeds that resulted in systemic failures for which our nation has paid dearly. As you read this report, you will see that specific firms and individuals acted irresponsibly. Yet a crisis of this magnitude cannot be the work of a few bad actors, and such was not the case here. At the same time, the breadth of this crisis does not mean that "everyone is at fault"; many firms and individuals did not participate in the excesses that spawned disaster. We do place special responsibility with the public leaders charged with protecting our financial system, those entrusted to run our regulatory agencies, and the chief executives of companies whose failures drove us to crisis. These individuals sought and accepted positions of significant responsibility and obligation. Tone at the top does matter and, in this instance, we were let down. No one said "no." But as a nation, we must also accept responsibility for what we permitted to occur. Collectively, but certainly not unanimously, we acquiesced to or embraced a system, a set of policies and actions, that gave rise to our present predicament. ................"

What the some of the leading Newspapers say about the freebies, the political parties are heavily leaning upon in their zealousness to the elections:

**"The Pioneer: Poll freebies: Road to economic disaster - 19 April 2022 | Uttam Gupta [Excerpts]:**

In recent years, this has occupied the centre-stage and holds the key to winning elections. For instance, in February 2020, the Aam Aadmi Party (AAP) ......mesmerised Delhi voters by promising freebies. They returned AAP to the seat of power with a thumping majority giving it 62 out of a total of 70 assembly seats.

Then, the freebies included free or heavily subsidised electricity and free water, free bus ride for women; free Wi-Fi, full reimbursement of hospitalisation expenses in case of accident, free testing and diagnostic services etc.

In the just-concluded Punjab elections, AAP was voted to power getting 92 out of a total of 117 assembly seats, the freebies promised included especially free electricity to each and every household for consumption up to 300 units per month, waiving off all outstanding power bills, depositing Rs 1000 per month in the account of every woman aged 18 or above, guaranteed treatment for every Punjabi regardless of the cost of the treatment or operation and so on have played a dominant role in AAP's victory.

In Uttar Pradesh too, the winning party, i.e., BJP had promised a host of freebies such as 20 million smartphones and tablets for poor students, two free LPG cylinders under 'Pradhan Mantri Ujjwala Yojana' every Holi and Diwali, free commute for women passengers above 60 years in public transport, financial assistance of up to Rs 100,000 for the marriage of girls belonging to poor families, free power to farmers for irrigation and so on.

A flood of negatives come to the fore the moment one starts introspecting on the subject. An overarching negative is abetment to corruption and erosion in governance ethics.

The Union Government's standards of financial propriety clearly lays down inter alia that "no authority shall exercise its powers of sanctioning expenditure to pass an order which will be directly or indirectly, to its advantage; and the expenditure from public moneys should not be incurred for the benefit of a particular person or a section of the people unless a claim for the amount could be enforced in a court of law or the expenditure is in pursuance of a recognised policy or custom".

The reckless spending of the tax payer's money on freebies is neither a recognised policy/custom nor it is sanctioned in a court of law. It is blatant financial irregularity that amounts to bribing voters using public money solely for gaining advantage in electoral politics. An individual candidate distributing cash or giving liquor bottles (using his own pocket money) to garner votes is treated as corrupt practice, and rightly so, whereas a party bribing voters that too using public money gets legitimacy (albeit de facto).

Second, unlike 'normal' budget expenses which are planned and backed by well-orchestrated efforts to garner revenue, additional financial liabilities imposed by the freebies promised in election manifesto affect the budgetary position of the State in a totally 'uncontrolled' and 'unplanned' manner. For instance, free power (consumption up to 300 units a month) and giving Rs 1000 per month to an adult woman will dent Punjab's budget by about Rs 20,000 crore annually.

There being no corresponding revenue generation against this liability (as the same is unplanned), this will be at the cost of slashing other essential expenditure including on development. Alternatively, this will result in additional borrowings and resultant increase in debt to unsustainable level. At the end of five years, the afore-mentioned freebies alone will increase State's debt by Rs 100,000 crore (this doesn't include interest; including it, the impact will be even higher) on top of existing around Rs 300,000 crore.

Third, any welfare measure is intended to help the poor as with meagre income, she can't afford to pay for basic facilities. But, the freebies given by contemporary breed of political parties defies this cardinal principle; for instance, free bus ride given by AAP in Delhi to 'all' women. This means, even a rich person is eligible if that person happens to be woman. Likewise, an adult woman in Punjab is entitled to Rs 1000 a month even if she is a millionaire. By contrast, a man won't be eligible even if he is poor.

Fourth, unlike a normal welfare scheme which has a sunset date and has a chance of getting terminated after the underlying purpose is achieved, the freebies offered by winning parties have none. This is because such doles are not backed by any well-defined objective; herein the sole consideration is to influence voters. Freebies being at the foundation on which victory is secured, the concerned parties are prone to promising them election-after-election.

Fifth, look at things from the perspective of tax payers. When, the tax revenue is used for giving subsidies to the poor sections of the society -for instance, beneficiaries under Ayushman Bharat which covers 100 million poor households - it passes muster as welfare measure. But, when it is used to give freebies to all including the rich, it may even trigger non-compliance amongst tax payers.

Finally, assured of financial help to meet most of their basic needs 'perpetually', the freebies cult is changing the mindset of people in a way that makes them complacent towards work. This can lead to a scenario whereby India's demographic dividend would be converted into a demographic liability.

In short, we will have a deadly cocktail of perpetual drain on the State exchequer leading to unsustainable debt, unfair and inequitable treatment leading to tension in the society, a negative orientation and unwillingness to work, non-compliance among tax payers, bureaucratic red tape and abetment to corruption. Put simply, freebies are a recipe for economic disaster. The only way to avoid it is to prohibit parties from promising doles.

In a judgment in S Subramaniam Balaji vs Government of Tamil Nadu &Ors in July, 2013, the Supreme Court had said that distribution of freebies of any kind influences all people; that "It shakes the root of free and fair elections to a large degree". Yet, it had held that promises in the election manifesto cannot be construed as "corrupt practice" under the Representation of People Act (RPA), or under any other prevailing law and, hence, distribution of freebies can't be stopped when the ruling party uses public funds for this purpose through the passage of Appropriation Acts in the state assembly.

After almost a decade, the matter has again come up before the SC - this time through a public interest litigation (PIL), filed by advocate Ashwani Dubey. On January 25, 2022 it observed "This is no doubt a serious issue. Budget for freebies is going above the regular budget. As the SC said before, this disturbs the level playing field,"

The top court recognizes that the problem is serious. Yet, thus far it has expressed helplessness. Whether, anything concrete will come out of the pending PIL, only time will tell."

**The Statesman - Way to Disaster - GOVIND BHATTACHARJEE | August 23, 2022**

"When faced with criticism, politicians are most adept at diverting attention to skirt the real issue, as seen once again in the ongoing debate on electoral freebies. The Aam Admi Party (AAP) led by Mr Arvind Kejriwal has been one of the biggest beneficiaries of electoral freebies in the country. It stormed into power in Punjab by promising a host of freebies which would drain the treasury by Rs 55000 crore, or almost 9 per cent of its GSDP ~ more than its own taxes of Rs 52000 crore. Punjab is almost bankrupt, staring at an impending financial implosion, but that didn't prevent the AAP from making and implementing its reckless promises of freebies like free electricity, farm loan waiver, allowances to unemployed and adult women, etc. Now that the debate has occupied centre-stage at the prodding of the Supreme Court, Mr Kejriwal has deftly deflected this issue by calling into question the so-called freebies provided by the state on education and healthcare. In doing so, he has conveniently forgotten the role of the state as well as the distinction between public goods and freebies.

To be fair, all parties including the BJP had promised freebies also, though none could match the AAP in the game. When populism is reckoned and resorted to as the only means to power, no party can afford to be left behind. The short-sightedness, irresponsibility and unreason that underpin our political system conveniently underplay the fact that the freebies will have to be financed by borrowing whose fiscal consequences would severely limit the state's development and growth. In a state with outstanding liabilities exceeding half its GSDP, this is a sure recipe for disaster. Mr Kejriwal knows this when his Chief Minister pleads with the Centre for a special package of Rs 1 lakh crore for Punjab, but that won't deter him from extending the same freebies all over India if he could, damned be economic growth.

There are plenty of lessons in our neighbourhood to learn from, but politicians would not listen to anything that may diminish their electoral prospects, come what may. The practice of offering freebies for votes makes a mockery of the fact that in a mature democracy, a political party only owes good and corruption-free governance and nothing else to the voters. While delivering good governance is difficult, fulfilling promises on freebies is simple. It also undermines the fact that relief offered by freebies is very temporary and completely ignores the larger problem of scarcity, input costs and capacity, which need to be addressed over a longer time-period using the same resources. Of course, like populism, freebies are not easy to define; besides, perception of what constitutes a freebie may also change over time. Promise of a welfare state held out by the Constitution makes this tricky, and it is understandable that both the Supreme Court and the Election Commission have so far trodden this prickly arena rather cautiously…………………..

The promises must also be credible. Wherever freebies are offered, parties must broadly state how they plan to gather the funds and finances to fulfil such promises." The wording of the guidelines thus rather legitimised this practice, leaving the field wide open for political parties. The present direction of the Supreme Court to address the issue collectively by all stakeholders is the next logical step. The primary role of the state ~ especially in a democracy ~ is to let the market function freely and to intervene only when there is a market failure. A state is supposed to provide public goods that benefit the largest number of people in the largest possible ways. Examples of public goods are clean air and water, quality healthcare and education, safety and security of life and property, etc. Public goods are non-excludable and non-rivalrous, which means that the use of any public good by one does not exclude others from using the same and there is no supply constraint, unlike private goods (groceries or durables) which are excludable and rivalrous ~ they are priced and subject to the laws of demand and supply in the market. Indeed, excludability is an essential condition for generating revenue streams for the state on their sale or use.

Public good creates a positive impact on individuals and society ~ reason why it is the state's duty to ensure that these are available to all citizens either free or at affordable cost. These cannot be confused with freebies. Free public education recognised by the Constitution as a fundamental right and made enforceable by the Right to Education Act, or free healthcare –

though not explicitly recognised as a fundamental right in the Constitution but asserted as one by numerous Supreme Court judgments ~ cannot be called freebies by any stretch of imagination. To provide these is the primary responsibility of the state and it does so everywhere. Differentiating between private and public goods may pose challenge; their status may also change over time. For example, there are fundamental rights in our constitution which are not enforceable because there is no enabling act. Access to internet is one such, and if a political party promises a smartphone or a laptop to every student to facilitate this, this cannot perhaps be considered a freebie any longer. Similarly the Midday Meal Programme initiated by the Tamil Nadu Government way back in the 1960s was once considered a populist scheme, but given its positive impact in education, nobody considers it populist any longer. Important is to note that public goods are available to all sections of society.

But a loan waiver to farmers or a subsidy to a specific section of voters, or free consumer durables so popular in Tamil Nadu cannot qualify as public good by any standards. The State also has a duty to provide relief to the disadvantaged and marginalised sections of society ~ but proper targeting is necessary for that to ensure that benefits reach only the deserving and not extended to those who can afford their costs. Since this is difficult to achieve, the easy way out is to make this universal and this is what makes the freebies unsustainable. They are not the same thing as providing relief to the needy and the vulnerable through carefully targeted government interventions like PDS. It is also to be noted that freebies inevitably distort the market and cause many other aberrations. Subsidy to fertiliser has contaminated the water bodies due to indiscriminate use, free electricity to farmers has depleted the groundwater tables because of over-drawal of water and loan waivers have completely perverted the repayment culture.

Doles don't serve any economic purpose; they offer temporary relief the opportunity cost of which is the creation of capacity in economy which alone can create the wealth necessary to sustain subsidies and freebies. All advanced countries keep their subsidy expenditure well under control ~ mostly below just 1 per cent of their GDP. It is only in the developing economies where corruption is endemic and both productivity and efficiency are low that subsidies and freebies thrive. Politicians benefit from them, while rest of the economy slides down the slippery slope of wasting resources and slowing growth. There is also the morality aspect, because freebies militate against the culture of hard work in society that brings its own social and economic rewards. We need to learn from history. Like all great empires, both Greek and Roman Empires were built on the edifice of hard work; both rose to unprecedented exuberance and prosperity in their times before losing their vitality in the end.

To contain civil unrest, the Roman Empire resorted to providing doles ~ free food to people and this "increased demand to live off the state" has been cited by Edward Gibbon, the author of the classic Decline and Fall of the Roman Empire, as one of the major reasons for its fall. As regards Greece, what Edith Hamilton said in The Echo of Greece should serve as a warning to all of us: "In the end, more than freedom, they wanted security. They wanted a comfortable life, and they lost it all ~ security, comfort, and freedom. When the Athenians finally wanted not to give to society but for society to give to them, when the freedom they wished for most was freedom from responsibility, then Athens ceased to be free and was never free again."

**Fiscal crisis Government – Britannica – by Simon Lee**: "**Fiscal crisis**, inability of the state to bridge a deficit between its expenditures and its tax revenues. Fiscal crises are characterized by a financial, economic, and technical dimension on the one hand and a political and social dimension on the other. The latter dimension tends to have the more important implication for governance, especially when a fiscal crisis necessitates painful and frequently simultaneous cuts in government expenditures and increases in taxes on individuals, households, and companies. A financial and economic crisis will tend to arise from a fiscal deficit if government debt levels contribute to a loss of market confidence in a national economy, reflected in turn in instability in currency and financial markets and stagnation in domestic output. A political and social crisis will tend to arise if both the fiscal deficit itself and the necessary corrective measure implemented to eliminate that deficit result in further losses of employment and output, falling living standards, and rising poverty.

The concept of a fiscal crisis first came to prominence in both developed and developing economies during the early 1970s, largely as a consequence of the breakdown of the Bretton Woods international economic order, the October 1973 Arab-Israeli war, and the resulting oil crisis. Those events combined to produce inflationary world energy and commodity prices, resulting in declining output and employment, and a simultaneous demand for higher government expenditure at a time of falling government revenues. The concept of a fiscal crisis of the state arose in relation to this fall in government revenues.

James O'Connor, a political economist influenced by Karl Marx, argued that the capitalist state was in crisis because of its need to fulfil two fundamental but contradictory functions, namely accumulation and legitimization. To promote profitable private capital accumulation, the state was required to finance expenditure on social capital—that is, investment in projects and services to enhance labour productivity, lower the reproduction costs of labour, and thereby increase the rate of profit. To promote legitimization, the state was required to finance expenditure on social expenses, notably on the welfare state, and thereby maintain social harmony among the workers and the unemployed. However, because of the private appropriation of profits, the capitalist state would experience a growing structural gap, or fiscal crisis, between its expenditures and revenues, which would lead in turn to an economic, social, and political crisis.

O'Connor asserted that the fiscal crisis of the state was actually a crisis of capitalism, for which the only lasting solution was socialism. Although the inflation and recession of the mid-1970s failed to deliver the downfall of capitalism, it did lead to a political crisis for the Keynesian social democratic welfare state. The increasing incidence of budget deficits became associated with the idea that government had become overloaded, that full employment was not a legitimate objective of macroeconomic policy, that the state had become unduly influenced by powerful interest groups, notably trade unions in the public sector, and that society had become ungovernable. The corrective action proposed was that the role of the public domain of the state should be rolled back, to thereby reduce the popular expectations on government, and the role of the private domain rolled forward, to enhance economic freedom and unleash the creative energy of the entrepreneur.

This ideological assault on big government was led by Margaret Thatcher in the United Kingdom and Ronald Reagan in the United States. Such thinking was given powerful credence by the fiscal crises and growing economic and political instability experienced in several major industrialized economies. This was most evident in the United Kingdom when, in September 1976, Chancellor of the Exchequer Denis Healey announced his application to the International Monetary Fund (IMF) for $3.9 billion, the largest credit that had been extended by the IMF. The conditionality that accompanied the IMF loan demanded cuts in government spending of £1 billion in 1977–78 and £1.5 billion in 1978–79 and the sale of £500 million of state assets to redress the fiscal crisis that had arisen largely as a consequence of the 12.5 percent real terms increase in government spending that had occurred in 1974–75.

In the subsequent era of increasingly liberalized financial markets, the consequences of fiscal crises for national economies, and their investors and creditors, including the IMF, have been even more severe, especially when government debt has been denominated in foreign currency and held by overseas investors, who in turn operate in volatile market conditions. When a fiscal crisis has combined with a currency crisis to create a systemic financial crisis, the consequences have been devastating. In Argentina, for example, weaknesses in fiscal policy and three years of recession led to the ratio of government debt to gross domestic product (GDP) increasing from 37.7 percent at the end of 1997 to 62 percent at the end of 2001. Despite the provision of no fewer than five successive IMF financing arrangements totalling $22 billion, and $39 billion of additional official and private finance, the loss of market confidence in the Argentine peso in January 2002 was so severe that, having been pegged at parity against the dollar since 1991, the peso's convertibility regime collapsed. Argentina defaulted on its sovereign debt, the economy contracted by 11 percent in 2002, unemployment rose higher than 20 percent, and the incidence of poverty increased dramatically. To avoid the risk of further expensive and destabilizing fiscal crises, the World Bank and IMF have built an extensive framework of best practice and transparency in fiscal policy into their frameworks for good governance in general and public-sector governance in particular."

**RBI Occasional Papers - Vol. 41, No. 2, 2020-** What it says about the fiscal crisis in the past and in the near future?

Fire fighting: The Financial Crisis and its Lessons by Ben S. Bernanke, Timothy F. Geithner and Henry M. Paulson, Jr., 230 pp., Profile Books Ltd, United Kingdom (2019):

"The global financial crisis of 2008 inflicted tremendous pain on the global economy by disrupting economic activity and causing intense pessimism in the financial system. The worst recession, also known as the 'Great Recession', was triggered by the bursting of the housing bubble in the United States (US) and its spillover effects contaminated the global economy. Much has been written on the 'crisis' covering its genesis, aftermath and policy responses. But this book titled Fire fighting: The Financial Crisis and its Lessons, written by the three architects of the American policy response to the crisis—Ben S. Bernanke, Chairman of the Federal Reserve (Fed); Henry M. Paulson, Jr., Treasury Secretary under George W. Bush, and Timothy F. Geithner, President of the Federal Reserve Bank of New York—provides a more authentic account of the way the crisis unfolded, its consequences, and the collaborative efforts made by the authors to deal with it. The authors also offer key lessons from their experience that might help to prevent and deal with future crises.

The authors argue that the turmoil in financial markets is usually self-adjusting, except for a few unusual cases, which require limited intervention by policymakers. However, the crisis of 2008 was the worst financial crisis since the Great Depression, which warranted extraordinary interventions from policymakers in the form of conventional and unconventional measures to stabilise the financial system. The crisis of 2008 was essentially a case of 'classic financial panic', a repeat occurrence since the dawn of modern banking. This time the crisis of confidence was triggered in mortgages. The authors profess that overleverage caused by excessive optimism during the period of boom coupled with risk transfer to non-banks, rapid financial innovations and absence of inter-regulatory coordination along with failure of regulatory authorities to keep up with changing market realities contributed to the financial shocks of 2008. As the invisible hand of free markets failed to stop the financial collapse, the visible hand of the government had to intervene to stop the panic, restore confidence and fix the broken financial system. Eventually, normalcy was restored in the system due to the deployment of all feasible range of financial and economic weapons at the disposal of the policymakers. While the implementation of sweeping financial reforms has reduced the probability of another financial crisis in the near future, the occurrence of another crisis cannot be ruled out given the inevitability of panic and overconfidence in human beings.

The book consists of five chapters, starting with the genesis of the crisis in Chapter 1. Chapters 2 through Chapter 5 cover the crisis and the various policy responses undertaken from August 2007 to May 2009, and offer lessons and warnings for the future. The financial system is inherently fragile and vulnerable to panic because of its dependence on investor confidence which is evanescent. The authors discuss how in the years prior to the crisis, the US economy was characterised by excessive optimism resulting in a credit boom in the mortgage market, unsustainable growth in household mortgage debt, reckless expansion in credit facilities to less creditworthy borrowers, securitisation of mortgages with low ratings, and spreading of risk through mortgage-backed securities through financial innovation to the financial system. Overexposure of the financial system to unanticipated risks in the mortgage market and overleverage of systemically important financial firms, especially short-term liabilities, became the triggers for panic market reaction. Furthermore, lack of tougher and more pro-active regulators, failure of the supervisors to recognise the actual level of leverage, a fragmented financial regulatory system with no agency responsible for monitoring systemic risk combined with the migration of the leverage to unregulated shadow banks or non-banks made the fragile financial system susceptible to a disaster. The authors acknowledge that it is exceptionally hard to predict a financial meltdown and they were not sufficiently creative or forceful in taking actions to prevent those risks. There was also a failure of institutional organisation structure within the government and the politics of boom time was not conducive to reforming the system before the crisis. The crisis started to make an appearance with the end of the housing bubble. Creditors and investors shunned not just subprime mortgages; they distanced themselves from anything associated with mortgages.

The authors emphasise that even though recognising a crisis is challenging, it is very important to assess the severity of the crisis, as an overreaction may create a real moral hazard problem, while under-reacting can be costlier and more damaging. In the initial period of the crisis, or during 'the first flames' as the book calls it, the Fed adhered to conventional tools like the discount window for providing emergency liquidity to commercial banks and reduction of federal funds rate. Subsequently, the Fed decided to launch unconventional monetary policy tools such as the Term Auction Facility (TAF) to provide long-term lending to eligible banks at a market determined rate and forex swap lines to increase dollar liquidity with foreign central banks to limit the panic. The US Department of the Treasury also devised fiscal stimulus in the form of temporary tax cuts to support the market. However, as the unusual market conditions persisted, the Fed, with the support of the US Congress, decided to extend liquidity support to non-banks through the Term Securities Lending Facility (TSLF) using emergency lending power. Subsequently, the Fed also created a new lending facility for investment banks called the Primary Dealer Credit

Facility (PDCF) for accepting a wider range of collaterals. The intervention through innovative lending facilities helped to rescue firms like Bear Stearns with the support of JP Morgan Chase. During the panic, some much criticised and unpopular interventions had to be resorted to by the authorities, including the nationalisation of systemic institutions Fannie Mae and Freddie Mac, which were constantly pushing the US Congress for more reforms to give more authority to the Fed and the Treasury.

The authors acknowledge that their aggressive interventions to stabilize the financial system also sent unintended messages to the market of higher fragility in the system and the market didn't breathe a sigh of relief. The demise of Lehman Brothers in September 2008 was the most consequential moment, which dramatically accelerated the crisis of confidence in every financial firm. Explaining the crises at Lehman and American International Group (AIG), the authors admit that failing to save AIG a day after Lehman's failure would have been calamitous. Despite concerted efforts from the Fed, the Lehman filed for bankruptcy because of its financial unviability and lack of acceptable collaterals at its disposal. At the peak of the crisis, with a worsening state of the broader economy, the passage of the Troubled Asset Relief Programme (TARP) gave remarkably expanded powers to the Treasury to purchase toxic mortgage-backed securities and quell the panic. Subsequently, it was decided to inject capital directly into financial institutions from TARP cash to adequately capitalise the system.

As the global financial system was still unstable and the economy was deteriorating, additional measures were taken including in the form of liquidity support to the commercial paper market through purchases of commercial papers from eligible issuers under the Commercial Paper Funding Facility (CPFF), a coordinated interest rate cut by the major central banks (led by Fed), and reducing the policy rate to zero by the Fed. The new US government pursued a variety of aggressive measures to bring the economy back to life, including the largest fiscal stimulus bill in American history and the Treasury's effort at forcing partnership with the private sector to buy troubled assets under the Public-Private Investment Programme (PPIP). The authors emphasise that the Supervisory Capital Assessment Programme, or 'the stress test', was the culmination of a long series of emergency interventions. The better than expected results of the stress test along with the previous series of intervention measures restored confidence in the health of the banking system and reassured the market that there would be no more Lehman.

The concluding chapter of the book is cautionary, and discusses the devastating effects of a financial crisis, irrespective of the aggressive nature of interventions and financial strength and credibility of the financial system. To not have another financial crisis is the best outcome for any financial system; however, the occurrence of another crisis is unpreventable. What can and must be ensured is preventing the deepening of a crisis by empowering crisis managers with necessary enabling provisions by the government. The authors acknowledge that their forceful and effective response was made possible by the expanded powers provided to them by the US Congress during the crisis, which eventually controlled the panic. While better regulations and supervisory standards such as the Basel III regulatory framework would be helpful to avoid panic in the future, the authors remain concerned about discontinuation of the new powers that were used to stabilize the system such as expiration of TARP, inoperative of 13(3) emergency authority of Fed, elimination of broad guarantee authority of Federal Deposit Insurance Corporation (FDIC), removal of Treasury's power to use the Exchange Stabilization Fund (ESF) to issue guarantees etc. Therefore, the authors insist on restoring the emergency tools of the authorities that helped to manage and contain the crisis of 2008.

The book provides an excellent narration of the 2008 financial crisis and the way it was managed. Beyond the narrative, the lessons drawn by the authors in battling the crisis can serve as an important guide to policymakers in general and central banks in particular. The advice related to the unconventional measures used in a crisis can supplement the Bagehot dictum for central banks. The authors are, however, at times appear prone to self-aggrandisement while responding to criticisms concerning their unpopular interventions. Nevertheless, their admission of not being sufficiently creative or forceful in their actions adds credibility to the analysis. The authors do offer a warning on the certainty of financial crises occurring in the future, and their advice to prepare better by providing stronger emergency time policy tools to the regulators should serve as a useful guide to contain vulnerability of the financial system."- Rasmi Ranjan Behera.

**INDIA TODAY - Recession is a certainty in 2023, but how much will it hurt India? - Samrat Sharma - New Delhi, UPDATED: Oct 12, 2022 13:31 IST:**

Major output loss in 2023

The global output would have risen 23 per cent since 2016 had the pandemic not happened. Now, however, it is projected to grow only 17 per cent. The global slowdown will leave real GDP still below its pre-pandemic trend and is expected to cost the world more than $17 trillion, which is nearly 20 per cent of the world's income.

Russia, Indonesia, India, the UK and Germany are among the countries that may contribute the most to this global output loss, a United Nations Conference on Trade and Development (UNCTAD) report observed.

While India may bear an output loss of 7.8 per cent in 2023, the Euro area is expected to lose 5.1 per cent, China 5.7 per cent, the U.K. 6.8 per cent, and Russia may bear 12.6 per cent output loss. Rising interest rates, weakening of currencies, mounting public debt — and all these factors raising food and fuel prices — have introduced uncertainty in the global markets.

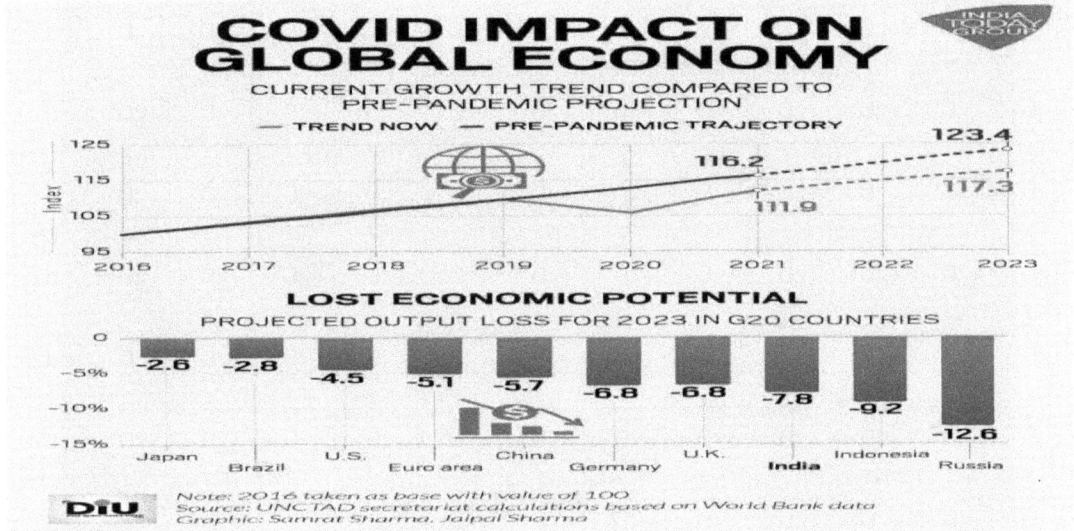

Rising interest rates to arrest inflation

A new World Bank study shows that central banks across the globe raising interest rates to curb inflation may not be a good idea. This can likely to lead to various financial crises along with the recession.

"Global growth is slowing sharply, with further slowing likely as more countries fall into recession. My deep concern is that these trends will persist, with long-lasting consequences that are devastating for people in emerging markets and developing economies," said World Bank Group President David Malpass.

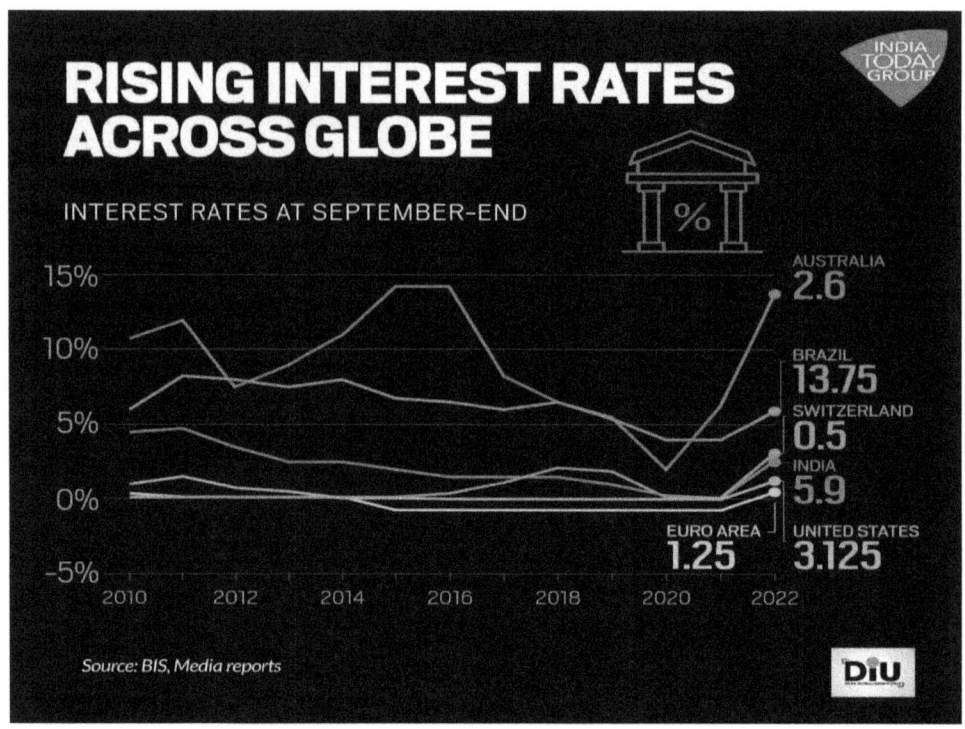

Mounting public debt

The International Monetary Fund (IMF) has pointed to the possibility of a recession next year as well. IMF's MD Kristalina Georgieva said earlier this week that the world economic growth may be lower by $4 trillion through 2026. Things are more likely to get worse before they get better, she added.

While all regions are expected to be affected, alarm bells are ringing the loudest for developing countries, many of which are edging closer to debt default. Lower-income and lower-middle-income countries are spending more money to service their public debt. Somalia, Sri Lanka, Angola, Gabon, and Laos are the countries with the highest proportion of revenue required to service their public debt.

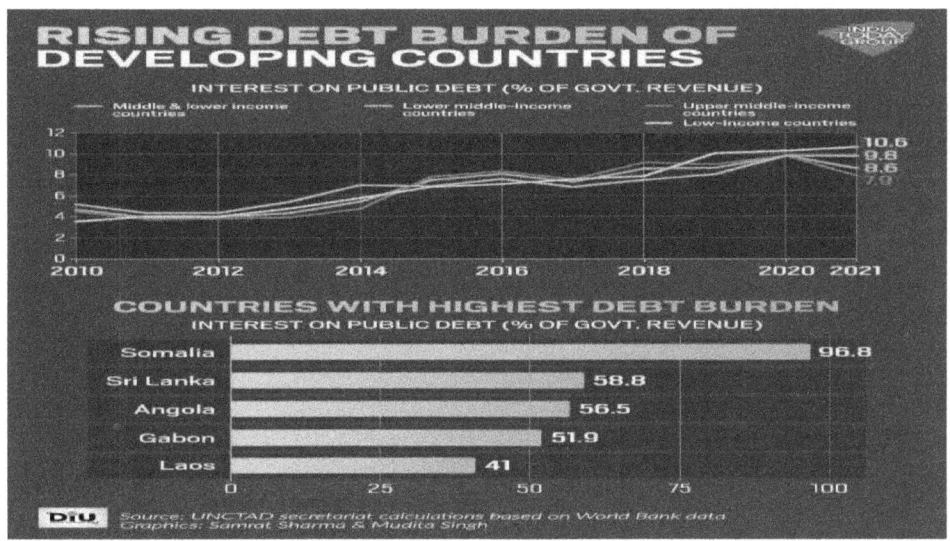

Weakening currencies

In an effort to cushion weakening currencies, developing countries have spent nearly $379 billion of their reserves, which is nearly double the amount of new Special Drawing Rights (SDR) by the IMF. The value of an SDR is based on a basket of the world's five leading currencies: the US dollar, euro, yuan, yen and the UK pound.

It is estimated that the interest rate hikes by advanced economies are hitting the most vulnerable hardest. Almost 90 developing countries have seen their currencies weaken against the dollar this year -- over a third of them by more than 10 per cent, the UNCTAD noted.

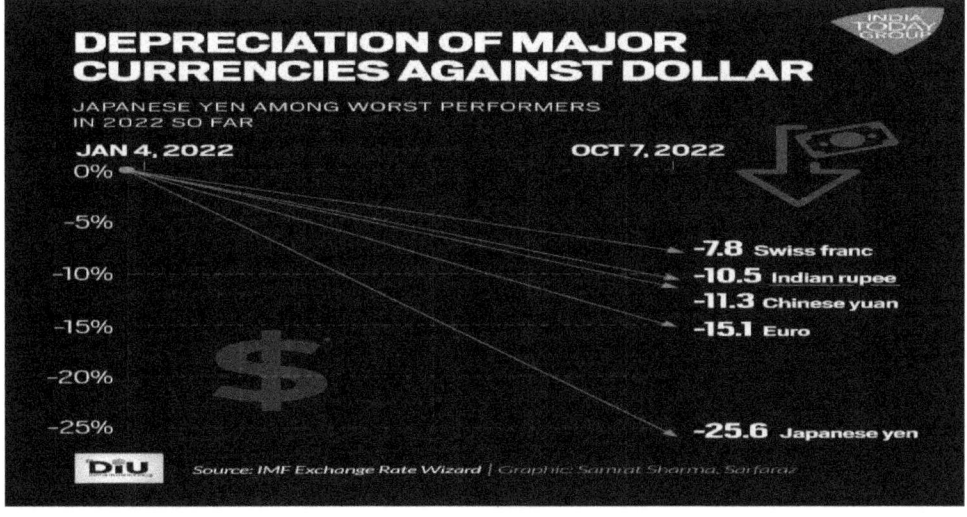

Costly food and fuel

Food and energy are two factors that directly affect the lives of common people. The year 2022 has seen a dramatic rise in food and fuel prices. While the food price index rose to a lifetime high of 125.7 in 2021 and further to 146.94 by September 2022, the Indian basket of crude oil prices averaged $102.14 a barrel from April-October 2022.

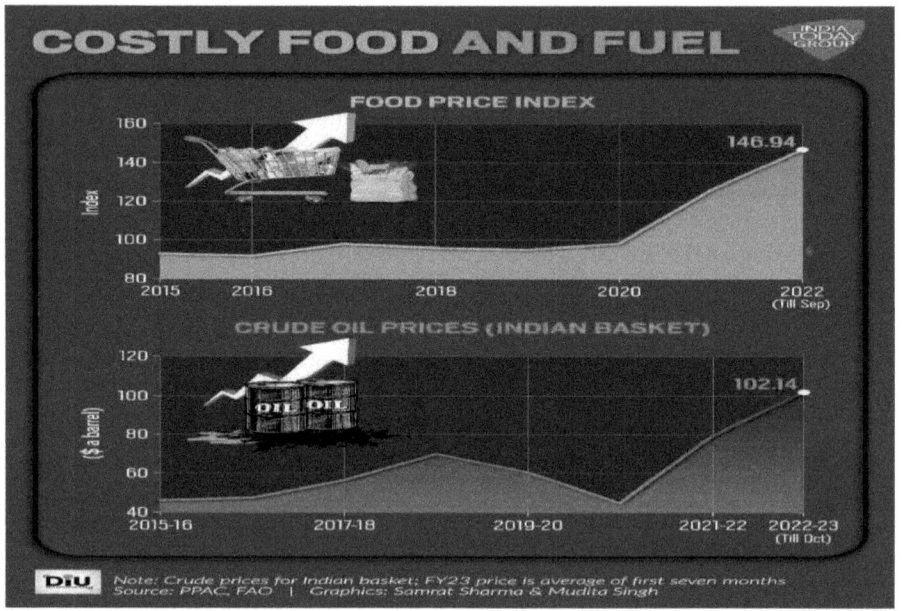

The price of the Indian basket of crude oil was $79.18 a barrel in 2021-22 and $44.82 a barrel in the previous financial year.

The basket of information and data stated before spell an uneasy financing and economic trends to follow in the near future. The government is aware of these developing scenarios. Chasing with too much anxiety since last a decade or so thinking welfare measures and freebies have great opportunity to convince the country that its economic parameters are resilient, the ground pattern of economic development underwent a sea change. In that, the government thought freebies and welfare schemes would have a greater appreciation by the people about what the government was doing for them. So also the government felt. This is the missing gap of how the real economic development could be achievable and what was actually thought of and being implemented has been widening. The main draw back that one could see in the economic development process followed since recent past is that it pinpoints more successes than weaknesses. The reality stands apart but not visible to the planners of the economic development. That is so because what was being claimed to have been achieved, as parameter to judge the mood of the people and not the economic development face of the country, lacked such claims going through the rigorous checks and balances including regular monitoring mechanism that offers one to reach at a realistic assessment of the achievements. This is the weakest bone in the body of economic development of the country presently compared with what was followed under five year plans subjecting the targets to actual achievements, analysis, identification of the causes for the shortfalls and measure to make up for prevention of such shortfalls. That gave self-confidence and self-strength to stand up and say why there were shortfalls in the implementation process like mirror to the peoples' eyes. These were in the report forms and were being placed in public domain, globally relied upon and used.

Time since when the planning concept and process changed, what we have been noticing are the announcements of the welfare schemes broken in different parts and holding out promises how such schemes were to benefit the people without any analytical process to show that the particular welfare benefits conferred were confirmable. It is one sided, in that the schemes in terms of numbers intended to be achieved are stated but whether or not achieved were not known. Such schemes, in the planning parlance, at best could be described as saying there is a well with full of water but the beneficiaries found unable to draw and get the water despite using longest available rope in their hand. Its impact and reaction do not become known immediately but after a gap of time when the people think they are living in fool's paradise.

Sounds and noises, the pictures and presentation and pushing up the print and electronic media in exhibiting the strength of our economic development is our greatest weakness of economic upliftment. Full size papers are in the print media focussing the photos of the state and central leaders the extent of economic achievements made for the benefit of the people, more and more for the poorer people. Also advocating that all their efforts for economic development are for pro people and particularly pro poorer people. The meaning of this is well coined in the popular Quote of Thomas Jefferson -

**"Nothing can now be believed which is seen in a newspaper. Truth itself becomes suspicious by being put into that polluted vehicle." Thomas Jefferson to John Norvell, June 11, 1807**

India is one, the central and state governments together represent the one governance, the people are one but how the basic principles and parameters universally accepted and adopted based on great research and books authored by the great Economists in the world? Does it mean to say the basic and primary concept of the economic development is variable according to one's whims and fancies? This is provoked here because the same country witnessed real and solid economic development during the first twenty five years of its becoming Republic, the governance being headed by the highly learned, experienced and competent political leaders who demonstrated their strength and grit during the freedom struggle, the aims and objects of all of which was sole consideration for building up the base and process for future economic development. This inculcated and imbibed the true sense and essence of the economic development tested laying down a path for future progress and welfare of the country and its people deriving its firmness from the established prime movers pronounced by the learned economic writers and scholars from time to time. This is unalterable, which could be alterable could be the size of the resources and changing technological advancements. These latter two considerations were to help push up the real and not rhetoric economic development.

Established economic parameters followed all over the world for centuries that enabled the most of the today's advancing countries in development to translate the parameters in reality for the benefits of the people, that having been done and achieved, these countries maintained advancement, now being known as advanced countries. They have achieved such status not through magical wand but through a sense of consensus, conciliation and reconciliation and placing before them the interests of the country and the people uppermost in their minds. This process has taken centuries to achieve their end objects and goals. That being the one side of the economic development, the other side consisted of the countries which believed more in propagation than in performance as if the administrators of the governance were different, the country's and the political parties interests were different and the real welfare of the people was different, though all of them were one. With such ill-conceived thoughts, the winds of the economic development also started changing the pattern whereby what one could see after twenty five years of the country's planning process was submerged in social and political slogans holding out high hopes of poverty removal through impractical welfarism as the satiating base for the people. This started in mid nineteen seventy fifth year and was considered it as most ideal way of economic development. This reached its peak beginning twenty-first centuries which witnessed mostly flying and floating economic benefits for the people that put back the wheels of the movement. The same concepts were further dressed up or refurbished and continued without assessment of the distance between the propagative and base achievements. That is what the economic development seems to have been understood and moving on.

It is extremely sad to note that the infrastructure development in the various sectors which alone has the enormous capacity to create wealth for the people and the country that includes welfare but breaking the same infrastructure earmarked resources into various parts highlighting them having inbuilt strength to augur welfare to the people is a misplaced economic development concept. The world moves through newer and newer creations and subjecting such creations to human exertions which has the urge and capacity of one having self-earned for self-survival with self-dignity, a perennial contentment and satisfaction. If this substantive and self-assured confidence and enthusiasm does not exist in every human effort, it is as good as a void effort. Humans live in this world that included our country and they know that without making their muscles moving and straining to the last breadth of the body, the body would not have resources and means to sustain itself. Newer Infrastructure Development Finance Corporation has been created being well aware rather ignoring the fact there were existing already sector specific such financing corporations which ought to have been reinvented, refurbished and financially strengthened with scope for undertaking large size of infrastructure projects with already proven experience and expertise built over the years ranging 25 to 50 years which would have delivered to the country much needed support for faster economic development instead of having a new body which is still stands in the stage of childhood. The decision to downgrade or defunct the existing DFIs of the central government based on the Narasimham Committee Report on Financial Sector Reforms followed by the Khan Committee Report were flawed decisions and put back the development clock back. It seems none applied their mind seriously in the central government and what was shining in the sky was Universal Banking that has least to do with the concept of the DFIs. The solidly standing infrastructure in the country today is the testimony of what the DFIs did during the period 1970 till the end of the Twelfth Five year Plan [2012]. The standing status of today's economic development is on the foundation of and strength derived from the performance of the older DFIs, some of which are in continuity while some others were became defunct.

In my personal view, if these glaring and staring omissions existing in the present economic development efforts are not seen as firebrands and urgent measures are not taken to revive and rejuvenate them earliest the possible, the chances are that the chaos will continue [such as in the power sector – the lifeline of economic development] and the possibility of the country landing in economic and financial crisis in the near future cannot be ruled out.

Even being aware of such circumstances prevailing in the country, the central government seems to be more interested in spurting the fiscal crisis as discernable from its recent decisions published in the newspapers that are dealt in the next Part.

# PART 05
# SPURRING THE FISCAL DISASTER

> As sure as the spring will follow the winter, prosperity and economic growth will follow recession.
> — Bo Bennett
> BrainyQuote

There is a strong voice and premonitions all over the world of the likely recession in the ensuing years that implicitly suggests slow building up financial crisis, the degree and size of which is not measurable at this hour of the countries undergoing economic development and whether it may be within or beyond the financial crisis occurred in 2008-2009 or prior thereto could be known only when the economic and financial signals start showing. There is, however, a broad understanding and consensual thinking that such a crisis is looking at the world that includes our country as well. It would be insensible to refuse to accept what is erupting around us rather than basking in the sun that our economic and financial parameters are straight, sustainable and resilient as not to be worried so much about the incoming hard times even when early warnings are emanating from the other countries, the IMF and the multilateral financing agencies. Assuming so is self-obsession to be caught unaware when it surfaces.

What was of importance at such time for any governance of a country is not to weigh the upcoming risks according one's own scale of measurement but the common scale that is being weighed upon in other countries of the world also needs to be considered to relook and review our economic and financial status whether what we are talking about ourselves has the built in strength to withstand the onslaught that may strike in the near future. We escaped with accepting the reality that stood staring at us in 1991 and did take timely sensible steps to avoid the Balance of Payment [BOP} crisis and saved the honour of the country. This happened because of our misplaced thoughts of managing the unmanageable while struggling against the time; according such long pause on international currency management was highly risky but managed to avoid the unpleasant confrontation.

The circumstances and situations that occurred that left negative impact and imprint on the sustainability our strength against the odd attacks should guide us to foresee what might happen if we were to stand up to the challenging circumstances, dare to dream or dare to act? The challenges whether in an individual's life or of the country don't look at the compassion and sympathy but attack with unkindness and crudeness. This is where the intelligence and tenability of the governing system seek for anticipation, indulgence, courage and confidence that emerge if one is mentally and physically prepared in advance of the arrival of such situations, whether or not that arrives is a different matter but certainly would not be upsetting the existing economic and financial order.

Constrained to note of what I have stated before because what I gathered from media information that our government seems to be more slackening day by day in initiating and attempting bolder steps and measures to meet the situation of the nature mentioned before regardless of the fact whether or not that would happen in a large or small scale which seems to be otherwise certain based on reading the mind of the other countries and international rating and multilateral agencies. That is not showing signs, what is being shown today is additional announcements to utilize as yet not attempted financial resources and wealth of the nation built over the years for some purpose [s] which are not asking for and managing smoothly with what is in hand, are being forced upon which suggests political motives. "An ounce of prevention is worth a pound of cure." — Benjamin Franklin. Views submitted before gain support from the media information mentioned below.

**New Industrial Policy seeks forex pile for financing companies: Report One of the proposals under the new industrial policy is to enable small businesses in accessing the corporate bond markets FP Trending December 15, 2022 17:51:49 IST**

"The Ministry of Commerce and Industry is working on a new industrial policy and is exploring the formation of a Development Finance Institution (DFI). The DFI could offer low-cost finance to companies and set up a technology fund to enable them in moving up the value chain, according to a Mint report. The draft "Industrial Policy 2022—Make in India for the world" has been disseminated for consultations with other ministries. The industrial policy which is being developed now intends to boost the access of companies to finance for rapid industrial growth. The policy contains a proposal for establishing a technology fund that would incentivise pioneer firms in areas of advanced technology and identify them for acquisitions.

The proposed industrial policy focuses on some key areas, such as achieving international scale, improving competitiveness, integration with global supply chains, improving the ease of doing business, and creating skills and employment. The policy also intends to facilitate the movement of the local industry up the value chain, and become an innovative knowledge economy.

But, not everyone is in agreement about the benefits of DFI. N.R. Bhanumurthy, vice-chancellor of Dr. B.R. Ambedkar School of Economics University, Bengaluru told Mint that "currency reserves are not assets to be used." He further said that the government cannot invest its forex anywhere.

Additionally, the policy contains a plan for developing mega clusters that can integrate with global supply chains and serves the requirements of key sectors like electronics, food processing, heavy engineering, drugs, semiconductors, and automobiles. One of the proposals under the new industrial policy is to help small businesses in accessing the corporate bond markets.

According to V.K. Agarwal, former president of the Federation of Indian Micro and Small & Medium Enterprises (FISME) and present chairman of its policy committee, financing is the biggest concern for micro, small & medium enterprises (MSMEs). He went on to add that banks look for collateral in order to offer funds to a growing medium-scale industry that eats into an MSME's working capital as most of them are unable to offer collateral over the years."

Purpose of keeping foreign exchange reserves

- To keep the value of their currencies at a fixed rate.
- Countries with a floating exchange rate system use forex reserves to keep the value of their currency lower than the US Dollar.
- To maintain liquidity in case of an economic crisis.
- The central bank (RBI) supplies foreign currency to keep markets steady.
- To ensure that a country meets its foreign obligations and liabilities.
- To know more about the Foreign Exchange Management Act, visit the linked article.

Reasons for High Forex Reserves

- Rise in investment by foreign portfolio investors and increased foreign direct investments (FDIs). Know in detail about the Foreign Direct Investment – FDI on the linked page.
- The sharp jump in reserves started with the Finance Ministry's announcement in 2019, cutting corporate tax rates.
- Fall in crude oil prices has brought down the oil import bill, saving precious foreign exchange.
- Dollar outflow from overseas remittances and foreign travels have fallen steeply.

Importance of foreign exchange reserves

- According to a report by Goldman Sachs, stronger foreign currency reserves will allow developing market central banks to "buffer their currencies against sharp declines by supplying dollars to the market" at times of volatility.

Importance of Increasing Foreign Exchange Reserves

- The government is in a comfortable position if there are rising forex reserves and the RBI in managing India's external and internal financial issues at a time of major contraction (23.9%) in economic growth.
- It Assist the government in meeting its foreign exchange needs and external debt obligations.
- Appreciation in Rupee – The rising foreign exchange reserves has helped the rupee to strengthen against the dollar.
- Crisis Management: Rising Forex Reserve serves as a cushion in the event of a Balance of Payment crisis on the economic front. It is enough to cover the import bill of the country for a year. Know more about the Balance of Payment on the linked page.
- Confidence in the Market: Forex Reserves will provide a level of confidence to markets and investors that a country can meet its external obligations

[Source: the+country&aqs=chrome..69i57j33i10i160.19039j0j7&sourceid=chrome&ie=UTF-8 – Byju's Exam Preparation]

**World Economic Forum Article posted on Website [Excerpts]:**

- Foreign currency or exchange reserves, otherwise known as forex reserves, comprise cash and other assets like gold that are held by central banks.
- Other developing countries are looking to shore up their foreign currency reserves in the face of escalating energy prices and supply chain issues.
- The dollar has reached an almost two-decade high as investors look for a 'safe haven' currency prompted by the global economic crisis.
- To meet a country's international finance obligations. These could include paying debts, financing imports and absorbing sudden capital movements.
- To fund internal projects. Infrastructure or industry programmes are sometimes financed this way.

- To reassure foreign investors. Wars or internal unrest can spook investors who may look to move their money out of the country. Holding forex reserves can project an air of confidence and calm investors' fears.

- To diversify their portfolio. By holding different currencies and assets in reserve, a central bank can diversify its risk and provide protection should one investment decline.

- During volatile periods for the world economy, investors and currency traders often seek to convert cash holdings into so-called 'safe haven' currencies for protection. Currencies such as the Swiss franc and the Japanese yen, but especially the US dollar are considered safe-haven assets.

- The dollar is particularly attractive, being the world's reserve currency and the one used in many international business deals. It is also backed by the world's largest gold reserves. The so-called 'Greenback' has recently been at its highest for two decades compared to major rival currencies. Investors have been flocking to it, encouraged by signs that the US Federal Reserve will increase interest rates faster than most.

- The World Economic Forum's Centre for the Fourth Industrial Revolution Network has built a global community of central banks, international organizations and leading blockchain experts to identify and leverage innovations in distributed ledger technologies (DLT) that could help usher in a new age for the global banking system.

- We are now helping central banks build, pilot and scale innovative policy frameworks for guiding the implementation of DLT, with a focus on central bank digital currencies (CBDCs). DLT has widespread implications for the financial and monetary systems of tomorrow, but decisions about its use require input from multiple sectors in order to realize the technology's full potential.

[Source:https://www.weforum.org/agenda/2022/08/foreign-currency-reserves-global-economic-crisis/

Foreign currency reserves are vital to a nation's economic well-being. Without adequate reserves, a country may be unable to pay for critical imports, such as crude oil, or service its external debt. Inadequate reserves can also limit a central bank's available responses in the event of an economic crisis. Objectives of Foreign Exchange Control include Restore the balance of payments equilibrium. The main objective of introducing exchange control regulations is to correct the balance of payments equilibrium, protect the value of the national currency, Prevent capital flight, Protect local industry and Build foreign exchange reserves. If a country cannot acquire additional reserves and if it does not change domestic policies in a way that causes excess demand for foreign currency to cease or reverse, then the country will run out of foreign reserves and will no longer be able to maintain a credible fixed exchange rate. The rising forex reserves give comfort to the government and the RBI in managing India's external and internal financial issues at a time of major contraction in economic growth. It serves as a cushion in the event of a crisis on the economic front, and is enough to cover the import bill of the country for a year.

**Should we employ our forex reserves to fund big infra push that can revive growth? - By Jyoti Prakash Gadia published in The New Indian Express - 06th September 2021 07:06 PM [Excerpts]:**

"………Financing of infrastructure is however a big challenge with limited fiscal resources available with the Government. The deployment of our 'Foreign Exchange Reserves, as one of the resources for infra development has recently come up as per media reports. Here we discuss the broad modalities and options available:

….NHAI is looking at dollar funding and the highways minister has spoken of plans to explore the possibilities of deploying foreign exchange reserves for long-term infrastructure funding.

Use of forex reserves to fund the infrastructure sector: Foreign exchange reserves are held and managed by the Reserve Bank of India as part of its assets. These primarily consist of foreign currencies, mainly US dollar, gold etc. During the 1991 crisis, India was in a very precarious position when it came to forex reserves, with just US$ 5.8 billion to show. This constituted less than a fortnight of the total import bill. Over time, India has built its kitty of reserves and we are now at a comfortable position of US$ 620.576 billion as of July 30. This constitutes about 15 months' worth of import bills.

The possibility of using foreign exchange reserves for funding infrastructure is a debatable proposition and all the pros and cons in going down this route need to be understood.

These reserves are primarily meant to act as a cushion or backup against external stress triggered by various economic factors and to protect our currency and handle various issues relating to international trade. Earlier, the availability of these reserves helped us in withstanding global events like the Asian financial crisis of 1997, the global financial crisis of 2008, and the taper tantrums of 2013. With possible volatility emerging due to the current geopolitical situation, whether the quantum of reserves we have is a surplus at all for usage other than required for international transactions itself needs to be assessed……..

For infrastructure development, we require long-term funds and carving out the funds out of reserves will involve a 'trade off' against the availability of cushion, as these funds are not in the nature of long-term surplus available. Asset-liability management issues similar to those faced by banks will also need to be assessed.

Alternate Avenues: While the possible usage of foreign reserves for infrastructure development funding and the modalities evolve over time, we should continue to rely upon instruments/sources like INVITs, Infrastructure debt funds, credit enhancement guarantee funds etc. This will facilitate the timely availability of crucial funding of infrastructure."

Balance of Payment Crisis (1991), India. India faced the Balance of Payment crisis in 1991 due to huge macroeconomic imbalance. Balance of Payment (BoP) Crisis is also called currency crisis. It occurs when a nation is unable to pay for essential imports or service its external debt payments. The 1991 crisis in India is believed to have been caused mainly by high fiscal deficits, the loss of confidence in the government, and mounting current account deficits. What was the 1990-91 Indian economic crisis known as?

"1991 CRISIS

Towards the end of 1980s, India was facing a Balance of Payments (BoP) crisis, due to unsustainable borrowing and high expenditure. The Current Account Deficit (3.5 percent) in 1990-91 massively weakened the ability to finance deficit.

**Macroeconomic Indicators and Balance of Payments Situation in 1990-1991:**

The trade deficit increased from Rs. 12,400 crore in 1989-90 to Rs. 16,900 crore in 1990-91.

The current account deficit increased from Rs. 11,350 crore in 1989-90 to Rs. 17,350 crore in 1990-91.

The CAD/GDP ratio increased from 2.3 in 1989-90 to 3.1 percent in 1990-91. Besides this, the fiscal deficit to GDP ratio was more than 7 percent during the two years 1989-90 and 1990-91. The foreign exchange reserves, meant to cover import costs for two years (1989-1991), were just sufficient to cover close to two and half months of imports.

The average rate of inflation was 7.5 percent in 1989-90, which went up to 10 percent in the year 1990-91. In 1991-92, it crossed 13 percent. The GDP growth rate which was 6.5 percent in 1989-90, went down to 5.5 percent in 1990-91.

The Balance of Payments crisis also affected the performance of industrial sector. The average industrial growth rate was 8 percent in the second half of 1980s. In 1989-90, it was 8.6 percent and in 1990-91 it was 8.2 percent.

India's foreign exchange reserves stood at Rs. 5,277 crore on 31 December 1989, which declined to Rs. 2,152 crore by the end of December 1990. Between May and July 1991, these reserves ranged between Rs. 2,500 crore to 3,300 crore.

1991 Economic Crisis:

The main causes behind the Balance of Payments crisis of 1990-91 were as follows:

Break-up of the Soviet Bloc: Rupee trade (payment for trade was made in rupees) with the Soviet Bloc was an important element of India's total trade up to the 1980s. However, the introduction of Glasnost and Perestroika and the break-up of the Eastern European countries led to termination of several rupee payment agreements in 1990-91. As a consequence, the flow of new rupee trade credits declined abruptly in 1990-91. Further, there was also a decline in our exports to Eastern Europe—these exports constituted 22 .1 percent of total exports in 1980 and 19.3 percent in 1989; but they declined to 17.9 percent in 1990-91 and further to 10.9 percent in 1991-92.

Iraq-Kuwait War: The Gulf crisis began with the invasion of Kuwait by Iraq at the beginning of August 1990. Crude oil prices rose rapidly thereafter–from USD 15 per barrel in July 1990 to USD 35 per barrel in October 1990. Iraq and Kuwait were the major sources of India's oil imports and the war made it necessary to buy oil from the spot market. Short term purchases from the spot market had to be followed up by new long term contracts at higher prices. As a result, the oil import bill increased by about 60 percent in 1990-91 and remained 40 percent above the 1989-90 level the next year. As noted in Economic Survey (1991-92):

"The immediate cause of the loss of reserves beginning in September 1990 was a sharp rise in the imports of oil and petroleum products (from an average of $ 287 million in June-August 1990, petroleum products imports rose sharply to $ 671 million in 6 months). This accounted for rise in trade deficit from an average of $ 356 million per month in June-August 1990 to $ 677 million per month in the following 6 months."

Slow Growth of Important Trading Partners: The deterioration of the current account was also induced by slow growth in economies of important trading partners. Export markets were weak in the period leading up to India's crisis, as the world growth declined steadily from 4.5 percent in 1988 to 2.25 percent in 1991. The decline was even greater for the U.S., India's single largest export destination. In the United States, growth fell from 3.9 percent in 1988 to 0.8 percent in 1990 and to -1 percent in 1991.

Political Uncertainty and Instability: The period from November 1989 to May 1991 was marked with political uncertainty and instability in India. In fact, within a span of one and half years there were three coalition governments and three Prime Ministers. This led to delay in tackling the ongoing balance of payment crisis, and also led to a loss of investor confidence.

Loss of Investors' Confidence: The widening current account deficits and reserve losses contributed to low investor confidence, which was further weakened by political uncertainty. This was aggravated by the downgrade of India's credit rating by credit rating agencies. By March 1991, the International Credit Rating agencies Standard & Poor's, and Moody's, had downgraded India's long term foreign debt rating to the bottom of investment grade. Due to the loss of investors' confidence, commercial bank financing became hard to obtain, and outflows began to take place on short-term external debt, as creditors became reluctant to roll over maturing loans.

Fiscal Indiscipline: The Economic Survey (1991-92) had categorically remarked that: "Throughout the eighties, all the important indicators of fiscal imbalances were on the rise. These were the conventional budgetary deficit, the revenue deficit, the monetized deficit and gross fiscal deficit. Moreover, the concept of fiscal deficit is a more complete measure of macroeconomic imbalance as it reflects the indebtedness of the Government. This gross fiscal deficit of the Central Government has been more than 8 percent of GDP since 1985 – 86, as compared with 6 percent in the beginning of 1980s and 4 percent in the mid – 1970s."

Increase in Non-oil Imports: The trends in imports and exports show that imports rose much faster than exports during the eighties. Imports increased by 2.3 percent of GDP, while exports increased by only 0.3 percent of GDP. As a consequence, trade deficit increased from an average of 1.2 percent of GDP in the seventies, to 3.2 percent of GDP in eighties.

| Period | Oil Imports | Non – Oil Imports | Total Imports |
|---|---|---|---|
| 1981- 82 to 1985 - 86 | 26041.61 (32.00) | 54491.03 (68.00) | 80532.64 (100.00) |
| 1986 – 87 to 1990 - 91 | 28299.75 (19.00) | 120796.18 (81.00) | 149095.93 (100.00) |

Note: Figures in brackets are percent to total.

Source: Reserve Bank of India – *Handbook of Statistics on Indian Economy,*
*2005 – 06*

Rise in External Debt: In the second half of the 1980s, the current account deficit was showing a rising trend and was becoming unsustainable. An important issue was the way in which this deficit was being financed. The current account deficit was mainly financed with costly sources of external finance such as external commercial borrowings, NRI deposits, etc.

In the context of external debt the following observations are worth considering:

- The period of eighties was marked by a reduction in flows of concessional assistance to India, principally from the World Bank Group. In 1980, disbursements on concessional terms constituted more than 89 percent of assistance to India from multilateral sources; in 1990, this proportion declined to about 35 percent

- Due to a decline in concessional assistance there was a rise in average interest cost of external borrowing

- There was a change in the composition of debt as it shifted from official (like bilateral sources) to private sources like external commercial borrowings (ECBs) and NRI deposits. These private sources were costlier

- The external debt was funneled into financing the government's deficit

- India's external debt increased from Rs. 194.70 crore (USD 23.50 billion) in 1980-81 to Rs. 459.61 crore (USD 37.50 billion) in 1985 – 86. It went up to Rs. 1,003.76 crore (USD 58.63 billion) in 1989-90. In 1990-91, it was Rs. 1,229.50 crore (USD 63.40 billion)

Thus, the balance of payments situation came to the verge of collapse in 1991, mainly because the current account deficits were mainly financed by borrowing from abroad. The economic situation of India was critical; the government was close to default. With India's foreign exchange reserves at USD 1.2 billion in January 1991 and depleted by half by June, an amount barely enough to cover roughly three weeks of essential imports, India was only weeks way from defaulting on its external balance of payment obligations.

Government of India's immediate response was to secure an emergency loan of USD 2.2 billion from the International Monetary Fund by pledging 67 tons of India's gold reserves as collateral. The Reserve Bank of India had to airlift 47 tons of gold to the Bank of England and 20 tons of gold to the Union Bank of Switzerland to raise USD 600 million.

These moves helped tide over the balance of payment crisis temporarily and kick-started P V Narasimha Rao's economic reform process."

Why is India borrowing in external markets in external currency?

1. Indian government's domestic borrowing is crowding out private investment and preventing the interest rates from falling even when inflation has cooled off and the RBI is cutting policy rates.

2. If the government was to borrow some of its loans from outside India, there will be investable money left for private companies to borrow; not to mention that interest rates could start coming down.

3. A sovereign bond issue will provide a yield curve — a benchmark — for Indian corporates who wish to raise loans in foreign markets. This will help Indian businesses that have increasingly looked towards foreign economies to borrow money.

4. Globally, and especially in the advanced economies where the government is likely to go to borrow, the interest rates are low and, thanks to the easy monetary policies

of foreign central banks, there are a lot of surplus funds waiting for a product that pays more.

5. In an ideal scenario, it could be win-win for all: Indian government raises loans at interest rates much cheaper than domestic interest rates, while foreign investors get a much higher return than is available in their own markets.

What is the controversial part?

- The current controversy relates to India's sovereign bonds that will be floated in foreign countries and will be denominated in foreign currencies.

- This would differentiate these proposed bonds from either government securities (or G-secs, wherein the Indian government raises loans within India and in Indian rupee) or Masala bonds (wherein Indian entities — not the government — raise money overseas in rupee terms).

- The difference between issuing a bond denominated in rupees and issuing it in a foreign currency (say US dollar) is the incidence of exchange rate risk.

- If the loan is in terms of dollars, and the rupee weakens against the dollar during the bond's tenure, the government would have to return more rupees to pay back the same amount of dollars. If, however, the initial loan is denominated in rupee terms, then the negative fallout would be on the foreign investor.

Why are so many cautioning against this move?

1. The volatility in India's exchange rate is far more than the volatility in the yields of India's G-secs (the yields are the interest rate that the government pays when it borrows domestically). This means that although the government would be borrowing at "cheaper" rates than domestically, the eventual rates (after incorporating the possible weakening of rupee against the dollar) might make the deal costlier.

2. Borrowing outside would not necessarily reduce the number of government bonds the domestic market will have to absorb. That's because if fresh foreign currency comes into the economy, the RBI would have to "neutralise" it by sucking the exact amount out of the money supply. This, in turn, will require selling more bonds. If the RBI doesn't do it then the excess money supply will create inflation and push up the interest rates, thus disincentivising private investments.

3. Based on the unpleasant experience of other emerging economies, many argue that a small initial borrowing is the thin end of the wedge. It is quite likely that the government will be tempted to dip into the foreign markets for more loans every time it runs out of money. At some point, especially if India does not take care of its

fiscal health, the foreign investors will pull the plug on fresh investments, creating dire consequences for India.

**The impact of public debt on foreign exchange reserves and central bank profitability: the case of Hungary Gergely Baksay, Ferenc Karvalits and Zsolt Kuti1 [Posted on the Website] [Excerpts]:**

"……….Foreign currency issuances can fall short in times of market stress, resulting in a lower-than-expected level of foreign exchange reserves Evidently, foreign currency debt issuance can be a continuous net contributor to reserve growth only if new issues exceed the amounts maturing in a given year. At times of crisis this might be difficult to achieve, especially for countries with weak economic fundamentals. Even to renew maturing debt can be hard and, even if market access is possible, the increased funding cost can be punitive. In the worst case of a sudden stop, the country is unable to obtain market funding at any rate. As a consequence, market debt issuance usually cannot work as an automatic stabilizer for foreign exchange reserves. Since the expected level of foreign reserves generally increases in times of stress, any shortfall in foreign currency funding can exacerbate the problem of inadequate foreign currency reserves…………..

Heavy public indebtedness can cause significant interest rate differentials which can push up carry trader's demand for short-term assets Again, tendencies can vary from country to country, but emerging economies with heavier public debt burdens and weaker fundamentals usually need to offer higher interest rates on their public debt. However, high interest rates can attract carry traders especially when the interest rates offered by the "safe haven" currencies are low and there is abundant liquidity in the global financial system. Such flows directly push up reserve requirements but, since they do not contribute to the foreign exchange reserves themselves, reserve adequacy is eroded……………………………….

Lessons from the viewpoint of foreign reserve management:

As we have seen, the level and dynamics of foreign currency public debt can heavily affect the central bank's ability to formulate its own strategy on foreign reserves. This section summarises the most relevant constraints and policy conclusions.

Growing public debt tends to increase the level of uncertainty in the dynamics of foreign exchange reserves Foreign currency debt issuance can contribute significantly to the growth of foreign exchange reserves. Yet, reserve accumulation via this channel is strongly countercyclical: during periods of abundant market liquidity and low risk awareness, there are practically no constraints. In bad times, however, when the need to use these reserves arises, an emerging economy has very limited scope to issue new debt in the necessary amounts. Furthermore, hot money investors tend to become more active as public debt grows, causing an everincreasing volume of short-term funding to flow in and out of the country.

The central bank needs to have a buffer above necessary level of reserves All the above factors tend to increase the uncertainties in the dynamics of foreign exchange reserves: that is, reserves are likely to fall below the expected level when sudden and large shifts occur in reserve requirements. In such a situation, simply targeting the reserve level at the precautionary level (ie at the level indicated by the Guidotti-Greenspan rule or similar) can create difficulties, given that the replenishment of reserves will take time and that, especially during a period of market disorder, the required funds will be difficult to obtain from the market. This suggests that the central bank will be better off if it maintains an additional buffer, over and above the precautionary level of reserves.

However, maintaining excess reserves implies extra costs too. The size of these costs is determined by the differential between the financing cost and the yield on reserve assets. This gap is usually positive and during an episode of market disorder it tends to widen……………………..

Efficient coordination between government agencies is vital. Serious conflicts of interest can arise between different government institutions (such as the debt management agency, finance ministry or central bank) which can strongly influence the evolution of the foreign exchange reserves. For example, changes in the preferences of policymakers regarding the structure of the public debt can greatly affect the reserves accumulation process. A particularly crucial decision is the level at which the target ratio of the foreign component in total debt is determined. Any move to reduce this ratio can easily conflict with policy targets related to foreign exchange reserves. Furthermore, any early repayment of foreign currency public debt can have a negative side effect on foreign exchange reserves. Clearly, swings in debt management policy can cause major difficulties for the management of foreign exchange reserves. In addition, if the issue of foreign exchange reserve adequacy has only a limited weight in the decision-making process, foreign currency debt management may lead to suboptimal results at the consolidated level. In order to avoid such an outcome and to optimally coordinate the different interests, we believe that a long-term debt issuance strategy should be defined in which both the central government and the central bank have a say in determining the size and the timing of foreign exchange issuance – a strategy which would also be binding on the debt management agency…………………………………."

"The important point is to understand how high levels of debt are likely to affect the subsequent performance of an economy. Excessive debt can undermine economic performance when it is followed by transfers that are economically suboptimal. More importantly, these transfers can set off financial distress behavior that undermines subsequent growth, in many cases substantially. In addition, to the extent that excessive debt creates fictitious wealth, it can boost current growth in suboptimal ways and harm future growth as the trend reverses. And finally, excessive debt can set off unpredictable hysteresis effects.

What is often forgotten (until it becomes obvious, by which time it is too late) is how highly self-reinforcing these effects can be. As the impact of a high debt burden eventually causes growth to slow, this slower growth in turn raises the existing debt burden and causes new debt problems to emerge in sectors once though relatively safe. These dynamics in turn reinforce factors that caused growth to slow. It is notable that in almost every case in history when a country's rapid growth has been associated with even more rapid growth in its debt burden, the subsequent adjustment has always turned out to far more difficult than even pessimists had predicted. People have always systematically underestimated the positive impact on economic activity of rising debt and the negative (and asymmetrical) impact on economic activity of the subsequent adjustment. There is little reason to believe that the future will be much different." [Excerpts from How Does Excessive Debt Hurt an Economy? - MICHAEL PETTIS - 2022 Carnegie Endowment for International Peace.

Above back up information and data is included herein to understand the extent of distance and distinction the BOP Crisis 1991 confronted the country and the extant state of economic crises the country is confronted with. Forex is a build flowing from the quantitative and qualitative strength of economic development and, when we measure the forex reserve at a given time, its stability and insurability needs to be seen what was behind us, what is before us and what would be the incoming future scenario. Cyclones and hurricanes whether related to humans or the financial and economic health of the country and its ability to sustain the high pressure that is absorbed to be best possible extent through natural disaster management of the modern age where such dangers are of natural nature but their occurrence in the nature of economic and financial crisis unpredictable. The past events all over the world including our own country support this understanding. Any long view of any significant policy matter has to embrace the past and capable to foresee the sudden and eruptive nature of events likely to stand staring at us not only in the near future, also all the time because the blow of such eruptions could be severe and serious, possibly fatal to the developing countries. These are apprehensive but not apprehensible.

The news that is circulating in the air today is the utilization of the forex reserve for financing companies. The just preceding Article has attempted to explain how such reserve could be used, specific to the country of writer. First question is whether or not to use it for purposes other than those specified under the governing laws and regulations. To my understanding, there was no occasion in the past or so far when the country diverted its forex reserves other than the purpose for which it is intended. This is new foliage opened for debate; how and why it prompted when the companies and the government entities are capable of garnering the financial resources to their own requirements and for financing the infrastructure and other activities in the country. Is there any change now in the policies and programs of the central and state governments that is warranting use of forex reserve for financing the companies or high ways, a new thought emerging from the central government think-tanks and the minister[s]? There is none, to my mind. Things with respect to this matter are going through as usual and now, an injection is intended to be administered to forex reserves holdings of the country, to begin with and gradually puncture it to the bare minimum leaving the central bank in a state of shocks surprises if there happens to be financial threatening on economic or forex considerations, both are uncertain but always believed to exist in the governance and central banking system. The news items on the subject matter, however, do not contain the views of the RBI or the consultation process between central government and RBI on such crucial aspect, being considered for being opened up. This is a worrying matter.

Second question is would it be possible for the RBI to consider, assuming there is an agreement between the central government and RBI, use of the forex reserve for financing companies or highways when the forex reserves consist of basket of currencies and gold and how, average weighted average cost of interest for financing the companies could be worked out, plus the minimum margin for the risks involved? Assuming there could be possibility to do so, the rate has to be designated in dollar currency that is strong and sustainable in the world and if that is done so, the interest rate to the companies or for high ways and tenor of repayment [presuming it would be in the form of loan] would have to be operationally in INR arrived at according to the prevailing exchange rate. Would such rate be cheaper than borrowing in INR from the domestic financial market? Also, how the repayment mechanism could be worked out considering the forex being in a set of foreign currencies baskets with the serious risks as to exchange rate variations at the time of the repayment by the companies to the RBI or any other designated agency? Face of it, these are unmatchable and unworkable. Someone somewhere seems to have thought why to hold forex reserve in excess of the anticipated requirement, as if this method much cheaper than the domestic borrowings?

This seems to be the brain child of some interest groups or on quid pro quo considerations. Britannica defines 'interest group' as follows:

"An interest group is usually a formally organized association that seeks to influence public policy. This broad definition, increasingly used by scholars, contrasts with older, narrower ones that include only private associations that have a distinct, formal organization, such as Italy's Confindustria (General Confederation of Industry), the United States's National Education Association, and Guatemala's Mutual Support Group (human rights organization). One problem with such a narrow definition is that many formally organized entities are not private. The most important lobbying forces in any society are the various entities of government: national, regional, and local government agencies and institutions such as the military. Another reason to opt for a broad definition is that in all societies there are many informal groups that are, in effect, interest groups but would not be covered by the narrower definition. For example, in all political systems there are influential groups of political and professional elites that may not be recognized as formal groups but are nonetheless crucial in informally influencing public policy.

Some interest groups consist of individuals such as ranchers or fruit growers who may form farm commodity organizations. In other instances, an interest group consists not of individuals but of organizations or businesses, such as the Histadrut (General Federation of Labour) in Israel and Amazon Watch, which includes environmental and indigenous organizations in several South American countries. These types of organizations are called peak associations, as they are, in effect, the major groups in their area of interest in a country.

The term interest rather than interest group is often used to denote broad or less-formalized political constituencies, such as the agricultural interest and the environmental interest—segments of society that may include many formal interest groups. Similarly, *interest* is often used when considering government entities working to influence other governments (e.g., a local government seeking to secure funding from the national government). In authoritarian and developing societies, where formal interest groups are restricted or not as well developed, *interest* is often used to designate broader groupings such as government elites and tribal leaders............"

Investopedia states the meaning of 'quid pro quo' as follows: "The key to a quid pro quo business agreement is a *consideration*, which may take the form of a good, service, money, or, financial instrument. Such considerations are attached to a contract in which something is provided and something of equal value is hence returned in exchange. Without such considerations, a court may find a contract to be invalid or nonbinding.

Additionally, if the agreement appears to be unfair or overly one-sided, the courts may rule that the contract is null and void. Any individual, business, or other transacting entity should know what is expected of both parties to enter into a contract.

A bartering arrangement between two parties is an example of a quid pro quo business agreement where one exchanges something for something else of similar value. In other contexts, a quid pro quo may involve something along the lines of a more questionably ethical situation involving a "favor for a favor" arrangement rather than a balanced exchange of equally valued goods or services."

One may ask what relevance both the above terms has to do with the matter under consideration. Somethings sometimes occur in individual's life or in a national life that baffles one to understand because what happened is something never happened in the past and blushes out suddenly on the face one considers difficult to find a solution other than extraordinary development. When that is so, one also feels such development is the outcome of pressure or special interest. That is what happened in the present case. It was like a bolt from blue.

I adverted before as to which is cheaper - economical and safeguards the currency interests of the country – foreign debt or sovereign debt or using Forex Reserve for meeting and matching the domestic financial calls irrespective of the purpose it is intended for. Ordinarily, such situations arise where there is scope of technology transfer and the benefits overweigh the indigenous technology. It is worth the purpose. But when there vast and widening space within the country for raising the additional financial resources whether by the central or state government or the corporate, it is prudent to explore and exploit the domestically available scope rather than substituting it by the foreign debts or sovereign debt or use of Forex Reserve. It is like holding in hand a gold plate with full of gold coins and, at the same time searching for gold coins elsewhere outside the country. What does it show? Our inability to invent new ways and means to assess and arrange financial resources within the country in various forms including those parked by the citizens of the country in foreign banks. It is also like something we are in need which is available in the neighboring shop, our desire to search for it from far distant shops which adds cartage for carrying to the home. This is also a kind of science that should work in the financial sector, more so, in capital formation and high rate savings.

"If there is one common theme to the vast range of the world's financial crises, it is that excessive debt accumulation, whether by the government, banks, corporations, or consumers, often poses greater systemic risks than it seems during a boom." — Carmen Reinhart

Carnegie India in its Website post of November 16, 2016 on Raising Financial Resources notes [Excerpts]:

"……..Even India's current savings rate is deceptive since the share of household savings locked up in illiquid and unproductive investments such as real estate and gold has grown in recent years.38 A study from Credit Lyonnais Securities Asia, a group of brokerage and investment houses focused on institutional services and asset management, found that as of the end of 2012, land and gold together made up 71 percent of all household assets.39 The limited market for housing mortgages and gold funds means that savings in these forms contribute very little to India's investment needs, and the share of equity and other nonbank financial investments is marginal. This is in sharp contrast to global trends, which show the bulk of savings invested directly in financial assets. The investment proclivities of Indians therefore shrink the pool of savings available for investments.

Thus another challenge emerges. High growth rates cannot be sustained without high investment rates, but high investment rates require a high domestic savings rate. The alternative, namely, to use foreign capital, risks creating large current account deficits, which would leave the country vulnerable to sudden stops of capital inflow and capital flight.

………………………

As India explores various alternatives for financing infrastructure, it would do well to keep in mind the dominant experience from across the world and understand that domestic bank loans should form the lion's share of infrastructure financing. Alternative sources, such as structured debt and equity, can contribute only marginally. This again underscores the importance of immediately restoring bank balance sheets and recapitalizing banks. The size of the banking sector imposes another constraint. The small size of the banking sector calls for prioritized action to expand the breadth and depth of financial intermediation by the country's banking sector, including privatization and liberalization to allow foreign investments.

To finance infrastructure, then, India will have to embrace all available financial intermediation channels—domestic and foreign, equity and debt, bank and capital markets. In each case, policy action should expedite a market deepening and broadening by expanding market participation, both on the demand side and on the supply side."

Foreign invaders from seventh century till the mid-nineteenth century looted the wealth of our country. What is country's wealth. The wealth held by the governments and that collective held by its population is country's wealth. It has not come from any part of Universe. This much should be clear to us. When something is stolen from someone's home, the police take its cognizance as theft or stealing, an offence under the relevant law of the land. It is more pinching when we are told that the corruption within the country and black money parking in foreign banks by our own people are increasing year after year and the central government informed the parliament at one time that black money is not amenable to any assessment. Central government has obtained list of Indians parking black money in foreign banks but hesitant to place it in public domain. Stealing generally refers to the activity to take away belongings of the other without permission or legal right, whereas looting is a kind of stealing typically during a war, riot etc.

The reasons for this also seem to be the involvement of 'interest groups'. When in a mood of hesitation either to dig out the corrupt practices and illegally created and held or to retrieve the black money lying in the foreign banks. What does it suggest? Easy financial resources lie outside the country such as foreign debt, sovereign debt, bilateral and multilateral borrowings more beneficial to the country than to search our own pocket to find how much money is lying therein. What should we say when our own people are engaged in looting the public wealth in various forms stated before. Stealing generally refers to the activity to take away belongings of the other without permission or legal right, whereas looting is a kind of stealing typically during a war, riot, etc.

In: Developing Economies: Innovation, Investment... ISBN: 978-1-61122-541-9

Editor: Joanne M. Carcillo © 2010 Nova Science Publishers, Inc.

Chapter 7

# BLACK MONEY AND CORRUPTION IN INDIA: NECESSARY EVILS TO SURVIVE?: A COMMENTARY

Pradeep Chaudhry *

Arid Forest Research Institute, Jodhpur, India

## ABSTRACT

Black money is the actual flowing blood in the veins of traditional Indian business and commerce. It is the real fuel of high-pitched central, state and local election campaigns, the high-octane of most of the bollywood star contracts, the blowing fire of real-estate deals and the dynamics of the bulk of the Indian share-market. The salaried middle and lower middle-class, intellectuals with integrity and principles are condemned to irrelevance and very often laughed upon in the society. Underground income is so widespread in Indian society that its existence no longer shocks or surprises anyone.

Barring few exceptions, it is difficult to find political leaders, high profile government officers and self-earning professionals; not having wealth disproportionate to their known sources of income. Before independence, foreigners looted this country and sent the booty across seven seas but now the same task is being performed by a class of politicians, high flying officers, businessmen and industrialists by looting the country and depositing black money in to Swiss and Caribbean banks. Some innovative ways to arrest the spreading the black money in Indian society, checking corruption; means to sustain the social and economic system have been discussed at the end of the commentary

"Black money is the actual flowing blood in the veins of traditional Indian business and commerce. It is the real fuel of high-pitched central, state and local election campaigns, the high-octane of most of the Bollywood star contracts, the blowing fire of real-estate deals and the dynamics of the bulk of the Indian share-market. The salaried middle and lower middle-class, intellectuals with integrity and principles are condemned to irrelevance and very often laughed upon in the society. Underground income is so widespread in Indian society that its existence no longer shocks or surprises anyone. Barring few exceptions, it is difficult to find political leaders, high profile government officers and self-earning professionals; not having wealth disproportionate to their known sources of income. Before independence, foreigners looted this country and sent the booty across seven seas but now the same task is being performed by a class of politicians, high flying officers, businessmen and industrialists by looting the country and depositing black money in to Swiss and Caribbean banks. Some innovative ways to arrest the spreading the black money in Indian society, checking corruption; means to sustain the social and economic system have been discussed at the end of the commentary......."[Black money and corruption in India-necessary evils to survive?: A commentary - January 2011 - Authors: Pradeep Chaudhry, Indian Institute of Forest Management, Bhopal, India.

God is within and not outside us. Belief we cultivated that God resides somewhere above the Mother Earth is a misplaced belief. If there is no Soul, there is no body. If there is no Conscience, that creates more and jungles than inhabitations. We visit Holy Places to worship or offer prayers. What is worship or offering prayers? We mundanely believe it to be continuing since several civilizations. There is no denial that there exist on Mother Earth Temples, Gurdwara, Mosques and Churches that house Idols or Holy Scripts of God or Holy Saints. We believe by visiting such holy places daily or periodically believing that would secure us peace of mind and a spiritual satisfaction. We make with all humbleness offers according to one's capacity and one's Faith. Our knowledge limits us not think beyond this perfunctory performance. It may be true to follow and adhere to. That is one part. God does not need offerings but desires humans to see Him or His Holy Scriptures with an intent eye, the benevolence and generosity of which behind those eyes. Our ancestors introduced the concept of offerings at Holy Place for their maintenance and given opportunities to millions of those who are serving the Holy Place to enable them to self-sustain and keep moving on generations after generations.

Other part is let us also think why at all the Holy Places such as those mentioned before have made their place on Mother Earth through our ancestors one civilization after another. There is no doubt making offers is supreme whether HIM or to HIS less fortune children. There is also another purpose besides this. That is, the Holy Places mentioned before exist on Mother Earth to remind us of those Great Incarnations in various forms including Idols and Holy Scriptures existed on Mother Earth, all of whom acquired that holy and spiritual status and character of holiness not by their birth or arrival on Mother Earth just to live like others but to evolve into a godly life that is reflected from the very way they lived their lives, loved the people, taught the people about good, righteousness and bad to create a sense of urge among humans to understand their essence and meaning; they are not meant only for making offerings and reciting holy scriptures but mainly to enable the humans to reminiscent themselves their blessings to humans in various forms and to insistently remind them that humans should endeavor their best in their life to practice how they lived, what they attained at the end of the day and what preaching they made for seeking solace and happiness in one's life. This, we seem to have overlooked doing and practicing in our lives of what the Idols and Holy Scriptures manifested within them, the holy messages, acts, deeds and things hoping the humans would continue to follow them for ever and ever. That we seem to have put aside assuaging ourselves what we are speaking about, acting about and doing about are right. That is how we landed in an abysmal depth of depravity and greediness that blinding us to understand that doing against the very interests of the country to which we belong is against Conscience and sinful. That gave birth to corruption, black money for one's own enjoyment at the extreme and extinctive cost of others especially the poorest of the poor who have been made naked physically, mentally and financially. Do we realize the consequences to follow? No. They will come according to their own times. This is the Ordain of God and Law of Nature. We will know the effects of the consequences. "Earn your success based on service to others, not at the expense of others." H. Jackson Brown, Jr.

Tax on agricultural income from the high agricultural land holders has the capacity to create sizeable financial resources for economic development but that is forgotten forever not because of desire to do it but because of the same theory of 'interest groups'. Then what is the difference between the outside and inside invaders in so far as treating and maintaining the wealth of the nation.

In: Developing Economies: Innovation, Investment... ISBN: 978-1-61122-541-9

Editor: Joanne M. Carcillo © 2010 Nova Science Publishers, Inc.

## Chapter 7

## BLACK MONEY AND CORRUPTION IN INDIA:

## NECESSARY EVILS TO SURVIVE?: A COMMENTARY

Pradeep Chaudhry *

Arid Forest Research Institute, Jodhpur, India

## ABSTRACT

Black money is the actual flowing blood in the veins of traditional Indian business and commerce. It is the real fuel of high-pitched central, state and local election campaigns, the high-octane of most of the bollywood star contracts, the blowing fire of real-estate deals and the dynamics of the bulk of the Indian share-market. The salaried middle and lower middle-class, intellectuals with integrity and principles are condemned to irrelevance and very often laughed upon in the society. Underground income is so widespread in Indian society that its existence no longer shocks or surprises anyone.

Barring few exceptions, it is difficult to find political leaders, high profile government officers and self-earning professionals; not having wealth disproportionate to their known sources of income. Before independence, foreigners looted this country and sent the booty across seven seas but now the same task is being performed by a class of politicians, high flying officers, businessmen and industrialists by looting the country and depositing black money in to Swiss and Caribbean banks. Some innovative ways to arrest the spreading the black money in Indian society, checking corruption; means to sustain the social and economic system have been discussed at the end of the commentary."[Black money and corruption in India-necessary evils to survive?: A commentary - January 2011 - Authors: Pradeep Chaudhry, Indian Institute of Forest Management, Bhopal, India.

Tax on agricultural income from the high agricultural land holders has the capacity to create sizeable financial resources for economic development but that is forgotten forever not because of desire to do it but because of the same theory of 'interest groups'. Then what is the difference between the outside and inside invaders in so far as treating and maintaining the wealth of the nation.

Consequences of black money will have an adverse impact on the Indian economy. Along with the economic effects, black money also has social consequences. Some of them are mentioned below:-

- Loss of revenue to the government and running of parallel economy in the country– The increase and spread of black money has a serious impact on the economy as it results in the reduction if government revenues. The black money is in such amount that it is said that a separate economy including only black money is running parallel to the current Indian economy. If only some part of the black money which has been in circulation in the economy could have been paid as taxes to the government, it would have benefitted the Indian economy to a large extent.

- Vicious circle as a result of black money and corruption– As a known fact India already has a number of corrupt practices going on. Black money has added to this corruption by the illegal transactions which are made to hide the black money. The bribes are given by the people to the bureaucrats, government officials, etc. for getting their work done go to the unaccounted books and is never shown as income which adds more black money to the society. Therefore black money is the result of corruption and the already existing corruption is the result of black money which forms a vicious circle which is never going to end unless some serious step is taken by the government.

- Effects on national income and real capita income– Black money is a result of revealing low income to the government while paying tax by the people which also results in low national income of the country. The national income of the country will take a big jump if the amount of black money in circulation is backed up to the national economy of the country. This will also increase the quality of life for the whole country.

- Decrease in the quality of public goods & services– This is somewhat related to the existing corruption in the country. The people who give bribe to the producers and marketing staff or the services provider will naturally get good quality products and services in comparison to the general public who will not be provided with the same products and quality of services has to suffer. The real-life example which is experienced by almost every person that if one goes to any government official for getting some work done, the one who will pay him some bribe will get his work done faster when compared to the one who did not pay anything and will have to wait. This wait can be in days, weeks, months and sometimes even in years. Bribing the government official is quite popular and is popularly known as "the easy way out".

- Higher taxation and inflation– The main reason behind the taxation is to earn revenues for the expenditures done by the government in order to make a balanced budget. Therefore it is obvious that if the amount of black money which the people are hiding from the government is revealed and included in the budget of the government then the tax rate will surely come down as the revenues which the government wants to earn from the people by imposing high taxes will already be with the government. Similarly, rising prices are the result of too much money in circulation for some particular goods in the market. The Reserve Bank of India itself has admitted that the amount of money in circulation in the Indian economy is quite more than the money inflow on papers. According to the accounts, there is a particular amount circulating in the market but apparently, the market also includes black money which has not been included as a fact of being black money which leads to more money than the calculated amount. Therefore the amount of goods and services which were there in the market according to the accounted money gets a hike in their prices which results in inflation.

- Difficulty in the formation of monetary and fiscal policy– This is an obvious impact as the government while making these policies is not able to count the exact national income because of the hidden black money which makes such policies unrealistic. Such policies can only have some impact on the Indian economy if these are made with exact calculation keeping in mind the consequences and needs of the people.

- Increased criminal activities in the society– The illegally earned or the black usually gives rise to various illegal activities in society and corruption is one of them. The duration of elections is also the time when the illegal use of black money can be seen. Various terrorist activities have backup power of hoarders of black money which is even harmful to the whole country. The illegal weapons with various groups of unsocial elements are usually bought up by the use of black money. Drugs are the biggest enemy for the youth of the country. The smuggling of drugs in various colleges, hostels, hotels, clubs and bars is done with the help of black money which further leads to various criminal activities. Various murders are the result of black money which are done for political revenge and are done by the contractors engaged by the various political leaders. It is usually said money corrupts the life of even a normal person, and money in excess corrupts excessively. The situation is worse when that money is black money. This black money is a type of excessive money which is spent carelessly and lavishly by the owners of this money. The law sometimes has no effect at a situation which involves black money as money shuts off even the high ranked government officials.

"The biggest risk of all is not taking one." — Mellody Hobson

Setting right of the Election Financing Method is the only way to move away the 'Interests Group' from the political shadowing.

**Business Line of December 13, 2020 states in an Article by B. Prasanna on 'What to do with forex reserve riches' [Excerpts]:**

"……Currently the forex reserves are tilting towards adequate or more than adequate, as suggested by various metrics. Moreover, given the central bank's focus on safety and liquidity of these reserves, the current investment portfolio generates low returns.

So what are the possible avenues of usage of the portion of 'excess reserves' and options to maximize returns for the central. One common advice is to use these funds for financing infrastructure development. Funding infrastructure development using excess foreign capital could lead to questions over the independence of the central bank, with the fine line of distinction between aligning its objectives with that of the government and maintenance of credibility.

Moreover, using forex reserves for infrastructure funding could lead to difficulties in monetary management and lead to the increase in government debt.

Since a portion of forex reserves would have to be converted to rupees that would lead to an increase in money supply. The dollars would ultimately be bought by the RBI to maintain stability in its exchange rates and prevent further appreciation, leading to increase in monetary base.

This would generally call for sterilization operations by the RBI (to stabilize price levels), which would lead to issuances of government bonds, thus leading to increase in costs and higher debt…

A more constructive option would be to use the excess reserves to import goods thus leading to dollar payments abroad. The target import goods could be pre-decided in consultation with the government aimed at improving productive capacities of the economy, enhancing infrastructure development or towards building capabilities of strategically important technology and defence sectors.

This would solve the dual objectives of acquiring growth enhancing assets as well as mitigating any adverse complications to monetary management.

An alternative fund - Another option would be to park a certain portion of the excess reserves to an alternative fund that then utilizes these to invest in possibly lesser liquid avenues but those that generate higher returns. This could be in line with the 'heritage funds' of the likes established in Singapore and Korea. Given the contradictory or conflicting objectives of reserve holdings by the central bank and the use of excess reserves to generate higher returns, it would be prudent to create a separate legal entity for investment management akin to a Sovereign Wealth Fund.

This could be managed by independent investment managers with the profits from these investments being transferred to the Reserve Bank, which would then feed into dividend pay-outs to the government, addressing the problems of apt use of excessive forex built-up and appropriate and more desirable returns on investment of these reserves.

So, to conclude, the excessive build-up of forex reserves calls for an opportune time for the central bank, in consultation with the government, to look at alternative ways to use these funds.

The two most feasible options include either import of capital goods directed towards building long-term productive capacities in the country or setting up an investment entity with the objective of maximizing returns.

These options would create alternative avenues of garnering long-term returns/income or funding development in the country without the risks and inherent complications and implications on monetary management and central bank independence of usage of reserves within the country."

Use of excess forex reserve for the purposes mentioned in the Article stated before seems to be advisable and feasible if the central government and the central bank stand on the same platform. First priority of safeguarding and protecting the Forex Reserves rests with the central bank and anything the central governments proposes to spur up the matter; both of them need to reach an outline of agreement with legal acceptability under the governing laws and rules.

From the information submitted before, there is no mention anywhere therein for using the Forex Reserve for financing the companies. This looks like an 'Out of the Box' idea. The policy considerations in hand with the central government as have been brought in the newspapers stated before likely to hasten spurring of the Fiscal Disaster

**World Bank Press Release 'Risk of Global Recession in 2023 Rises Amid Simultaneous Rate Hikes – 15 September, 2022 - Washington: Nandita Roy**: "Study Highlights Need for Policies to Curb Inflation without Exacerbating Recession Risk.

As central banks across the world simultaneously hike interest rates in response to inflation, the world may be edging toward a global recession in 2023 and a string of financial crises in emerging market and developing economies that would do them lasting harm, according to a comprehensive new study by the World Bank.

Central banks around the world have been raising interest rates this year with a degree of synchronicity not seen over the past five decades—a trend that is likely to continue well into next year, according to the report. Yet the currently expected trajectory of interest-rate increases and other policy actions may not be sufficient to bring global inflation back down to levels seen before the pandemic. Investors expect central banks to raise global monetary-policy rates to almost 4 percent through 2023—an increase of more than 2 percentage points over their 2021 average.

Unless supply disruptions and labor-market pressures subside, those interest-rate increases could leave the global core inflation rate (excluding energy) at about 5 percent in 2023—nearly double the five-year average before the pandemic, the study finds. To cut global inflation to a rate consistent with their targets, central banks may need to raise interest rates by an additional 2 percentage points, according to the report's model. If this were accompanied by financial-market stress, global GDP growth would slow to 0.5 percent in 2023—a 0.4 percent contraction in per–capita terms that would meet the technical definition of a global recession.

"Global growth is slowing sharply, with further slowing likely as more countries fall into recession. My deep concern is that these trends will persist, with long-lasting consequences that are devastating for people in emerging market and developing economies," said **World Bank Group President David Malpass.** "To achieve low inflation rates, currency stability and faster growth, policymakers could shift their focus from reducing consumption to boosting production. Policies should seek to generate additional investment and improve productivity and capital allocation, which are critical for growth and poverty reduction."

The study highlights the unusually fraught circumstances under which central banks are fighting inflation today. Several historical indicators of global recessions are already flashing warnings. The global economy is now in its steepest slowdown following a post-recession recovery since 1970. Global consumer confidence has already suffered a much sharper decline than in the run-up to previous global recessions. The world's three largest economies—the United States, China, and the euro area—have been slowing sharply. Under the circumstances, even a moderate hit to the global economy over the next year could tip it into recession.

The study relies on insights from previous global recessions to analyze the recent evolution of economic activity and presents scenarios for 2022–24. A slowdown—such that the one now underway—typically calls for countercyclical policy to support activity. However, the threat of inflation and limited fiscal space are spurring policymakers in many countries to withdraw policy support even as the global economy slows sharply.

The experience of the 1970s, the policy responses to the 1975 global recession, the subsequent period of stagflation, and the global recession of 1982 illustrate the risk of allowing inflation to remain elevated for long while growth is weak. The 1982 global recession coincided with the second-lowest growth rate in developing economies over the past five decades, second only to 2020. It triggered more than 40 debt crises] and was followed by a decade of lost growth in many developing economies.

"Recent tightening of monetary and fiscal policies will likely prove helpful in reducing inflation," said **Ayhan Kose, the World Bank's Acting Vice President** for Equitable Growth, Finance, and Institutions. "But because they are highly synchronous across countries, they could be mutually compounding in tightening financial conditions and steepening the global growth slowdown. Policymakers in emerging market and developing economies need to stand ready to manage the potential spillovers from globally synchronous tightening of policies."

Central banks should persist in their efforts to control inflation—and it can be done without touching off a global recession, the study finds. But it will require concerted action by a variety of policymakers:

**Central banks** must communicate policy decisions clearly while safeguarding their independence. This could help anchor inflation expectations and reduce the degree of tightening needed. In advanced economies, central banks should keep in mind the cross-border spillover effects of monetary tightening. In emerging market and developing economies, they should strengthen macro prudential regulations and build foreign-exchange reserves.

**Fiscal authorities** will need to carefully calibrate the withdrawal of fiscal support measures while ensuring consistency with monetary-policy objectives. The fraction of countries tightening fiscal policies next year is expected to reach its highest level since the early 1990s. This could amplify the effects of monetary policy on growth. Policymakers should also put in place credible medium-term fiscal plans and provide targeted relief to vulnerable households.

**Other economic policymakers** will need to join in the fight against inflation—particularly by taking strong steps to boost global supply. These include:

- Easing labor-market constraints. Policy measures need to help increase labor-force participation and reduce price pressures. Labor-market policies can facilitate the reallocation of displaced workers.

- Boosting the global supply of commodities. Global coordination can go a long way in increasing food and energy supply. For energy commodities, policymakers should accelerate the transition to low–carbon energy sources and introduce measures to reduce energy consumption.

- Strengthening global trade networks. Policymakers should cooperate to alleviate global supply bottlenecks. They should support a rules-based international economic order, one that guards against the threat of protectionism and fragmentation that could further disrupt trade networks. It's better to keep what you have than to risk it and lose it. [Proverb].

The World Bank Paper on the impending Recession is a timely warning for the central government and the central bank; both of whom must heed the call and take credible measures and make best efforts to deal with the foreseeable eventuality and the accompanying consequences.

## "TAKE TIME FOR ALL THINGS: GREAT HASTE MAKES GREAT WASTE". BENJAMIN FRANKLIN.

"The Indian rupee's most appealing trait for traders is fast deteriorating, helping turn the currency into emerging Asia's worst performer over the past month.

Twelve-month implied rupee yields—typically a reflection of interest rate differentials with the US—fell to the lowest since 2009 last week. That's bad news for carry traders, who seek profits from capturing the difference between the rates of high-yielding versus low-yielding currencies.

With the Reserve Bank of India widely expected to end a rate-hike cycle early next year, and the Federal Reserve seen peaking toward the middle, the interest-rate differentials are expected to worsen, further pressuring the carry trade and ultimately the rupee.

"Such lower forward premiums could become self-perpetuating for the rupee, making carry trades less attractive for foreign investors, implying fears of unwinding these trades," said Madhavi Arora, an economist at Emkay Global Financial Services Ltd.

The rupee is down about 2 per cent over the past month to around 82.5375 per dollar Monday and is seen falling to 84 per dollar next quarter, according to the likes of Australia and New Zealand Bank and Barclays Plc.

**Dwindling dollars**

A shortage of dollars and the RBI's intervention in the FX market have also led to lower premiums, according to Gaura Sen Gupta, an economist at IDFC First Bank. The RBI's forward dollar book fell to $10.4 billion in September from $65.8 billion in March — the lowest since 2020.

"The combination of global risk-off sentiment and reducing interest rate differentials between India and US supports our expectation that the rupee should weaken against the dollar next year," she added.

**Market deviation**

Shorter tenor rates in the money and FX markets tend to follow each other. However, a higher-than-usual trade and balance-of-payment deficit have exacerbated the cash dollar shortage and the forward premia have deviated from other money markets like onshore rate swaps, said Emkay's Arora.

**High volatility**

Rupee's historical volatility continues to climb, with the one-month measure now well above the level that marked Russia's invasion of Ukraine in February. That can weigh on demand from some carry investors." [Source: Caution ahead. Indian rupee's most appealing trait for traders vanishing by BLOOMBERG published in Business Line in its Edition of December 13, 2022 - Updated 11:32 am IST].

**CEOInsights [Upcoming Global Recession and Its Impact on India Sthitaprajnya Panigrahi [Excerpts]:**

…………Amidst the ongoing geopolitical developments happening around the globe, exports have slowed down globally, and central banks have tightened their fiscal policy. And considering these ongoing scenarios, it is widely expected that India may experience an economic downfall in the medium term.

Moody's Investors Service recently shared a report, where it lowered India's economic growth projection to 8.8% for 2022 from 9.1%, which was projected earlier by citing high inflation. However, the bond credit rating business of Moody's Corporation, which represents the company's traditional line of business and its historical name, has also stated that it has maintained its growth forecasts for 2023 at 5.4 percent.

Since India's economic fundamentals are much sturdier as compared to other countries, therefore, despite some short-term turbulence, the impact on the long-term outlook will be minimal. In terms of good news, the fear of an upcoming recession is now bringing commodity prices down. Prices of most commodities are dipping, starting from crude to metal and edible oil. This might come as an opportunity for India, which is one of the foremost importers of these commodities.

Similarly, across the retail market, edible oil prices have started declining with the depletion in international rates. India will be immensely benefitted from this trend as it imports more than 60 percent of its edible oil requirement from abroad.

Since April of this year, the global prices of base metals have been witnessing a sharp fall as well. This phenomenon is expected to boost consumption in India because user industries, such as white goods and automobiles, would be able to cut their input costs and pass on the profits to their consumers.

The crude oil, otherwise known as the black gold, is trading below $100 for the first time since May 11th of this year, and this fall in prices is majorly driven by recession fears. It is expected that crude prices might touch $65 a barrel by the end of this year and could even fall to as low as $45 by the end of 2023 if the recession hits. Though this might affect the advanced economies adversely, it will be a relief for India, which is regarded as the world's third largest oil-consuming and importing nation.

According to recent data, the crude oil import bill of India nearly doubled to $119 billion in the last financial year as energy prices soared globally following the return of demand post-pandemic and war in Ukraine. As India's soaring import bill of crude prices will come down, India can push demand fiscally and monetarily to recover a bleeding economy.

The Silver Lining

Most economic stalwarts believe that the global recession won't affect the Indian economy severely, as our economy is strong enough to maintain solid growth momentum. Not all businesses and industries go through the same pain during economic downturns. There are few silver linings, as some businesses benefit from the recession. The reason behind this is that the consumers cut back on substitute products. Strong businesses can take this opportunity to thrive as labor and capital become economical.

New Year Gift for Poor:

"Centre Makes Food grain Free of Cost for 81.35 Cr People under NFSA for 1 Year according to Outlook dated December 254, 2022. Currently, the beneficiaries covered under the NFSA pay Rs 1-3 per kg. The decision comes days ahead of the Pradhan Mantri Garib Kalyan Anna Yojana (PMGKAY) ending on December 31, 2022. The move will entail an expenditure of about Rs 2 lakh crore for the exchequer, he said, adding the entire cost will be borne by the Union government.

The beneficiaries will not have to pay a single rupee to get food grains…The Centre enacted NFSA in July 2013, giving legal entitlement to 67 per cent of the population (75 per cent in rural areas and 50 per cent in urban areas) to receive highly subsidized food grain. The coverage under the Act is based on the population figures of Census 2011. The NFSA is being implemented in all 36 states/UTs and covers about 81.35 crore person. ………………………..

Recently, in a written reply in the Lok Sabha, Goyal had said that under the PMGKAY, the government has allocated a total of almost 1,118 lakh tonnes of food grains to the states/UTs (total allocation from Phase I to Phase VII). The total sanctioned outlay for food subsidy and central assistance for all phases I-VII is about Rs 3.91 lakh crore.

With the government deciding not to provide extra food grains over and above NFSA quota, experts said the decision will ease the pressure on food grain stocks under the central pool.

The government had to ban wheat exports in May to control inflation after its procurement fell sharply. Domestic production of wheat also fell slightly in 2021-22. About 159 lakh tonnes of wheat and 104 lakh tonnes of rice will be available as on January 1, 2023, as against the respective buffer norms requirement of 138 lakh tonnes of wheat and 76 lakh tonnes of rice as on January 1, the government recently said."

Food production is the base for food security. Internationally accepted definition of food security given by the Food and Agriculture Organization of the UN (FAO) in the Rome Declaration on World Food Security, 1996, further refined in the FAO's State of Food Insecurity in the World, 2001 states: "Food security [is] a situation that exists when all people, at all times, have physical, social and economic access to sufficient, safe and nutritious food that meets their dietary needs and food preferences for an active and healthy life".

Various kinds of subsidies and benefits are good to appreciate when these are read in Budget Papers but most disappointing when one reads news items of frauds and malpractices in the system of administration of subsidies preventing benefits to reach the beneficiaries. Agriculturists today are those who are rich in themselves at the cost of their own less fortune brothers and sisters by virtue of seeking and having most of the agricultural benefits to themselves depriving the class that needs such help. Most of industries and corporate are surviving from the bye products of agriculture industry but people who provide the bye products are least compensated retaining thriving profits by the corporate.

The National Food Security Act, 2013 (NFSA) was launched to increase coverage to 75% of India's rural population and 50% of the urban population – a whopping 800 million people, as a magic wand against hunger not knowing even today flaws therein outweigh its benefits and program is sustainable for long. Such a wide-reaching program imposed significant financial costs. A conservative estimate places the costs at over 23 billion dollars a year, equivalent to about 0.72 percent of India's GDP.[Estimated in 2013]. These costs don't just come from the grains themselves: setting up and maintaining distribution centers and government agencies to monitor the subsidies also create extra costs. Critics argue that this money could have been better spent on generating employment, improving rural and urban infrastructure, investing in agriculture, and a number of other competing uses. This is the only way to create economic activity that helps sustain one-self.

India is a dominant agricultural country and food production has been increasing year by year as per official announcements. Barring few rural rich people holding large scale agricultural control, ordinary agriculturist continues to reel under the yoke of poverty, bankruptcy and suicides. It is not known whether the central or state governments have gone into the root cause of such sad situations which is imperative to cure the ills of the poverty in the villages. Various Committees had been set up in the past and continue to be set up on ways and means for increasing further the agricultural production but there does not seem any report that would have gone into causes of the villagers tragedies.

Announcement of higher food grain production the government holds out to the people year after year is a contradiction when seen from the availability of food grain for ordinary citizens in the market and the price at which available. It is hardly seen the price of food grain once shot up returned downward. It rather further moves up and up with anxiety and panicky among the ordinary citizens impacting more on poorer and rural people. Is it not a paradoxical situation where on one hand, there is increase year after year in food grain production , on the other hand, there is shortage of food grain in the market – the cause for high prices? Import of short food grains is order of the day whenever there is increasing hoarding and high prices. Are we sincere to ourselves when we talk of import when we know whole sale distributors and commodities exchanges are playing havoc in creating artificial scarcity and scare among the people. What is needed is sternly dealing with hoarders rather resorting to imports necessitating additional costs. Situation as is growing seems to be perplexed while law abiders continue to bear the burden and the law enforcement agencies remain silent spectators. Vegetables and fruits production and availability also speak the same language as of food grain. It has become a matter of habit for the governments to wake up only when there are demonstrations and protestations on shortage and high prices of vegetables and fruits in the retail market. Sometimes it looks like a political swinging among the political parties. – PLENTY OF FOOD BUT SCARCITY FOR ALL AND DON'T PART UNLESS PRICES FLY HIGH OR LET THE FOOD ROT.

How should we define pro poor? Pro-poor growth is a term used for primarily national policies to stimulate economic growth for the benefit of poor people (primarily in the economic sense of poverty). Pro-poor growth can be defined as absolute, where the poor benefits from overall growth in the economy, or relative - which refers to targeted efforts to increase the growth specifically among poor people. - Year: 2011 - [Source: https://www.grida.no/resources/7948]

What is Pro-poor Growth and why do We Need to Know?

Economic growth that is good for the poor is known as 'pro-poor growth'. But what exactly does the term mean? This briefing note from the Department for International Development (DFID) examines the relationship between growth and poverty. Given DFID's aim of eliminating absolute poverty, it argues that the most appropriate measure of pro-poor growth is the average growth rate of the incomes of the poor.

The Millennium Development Goals (MDGs) will only be achieved if developing countries experience rapid and sustained growth. Poverty reduction strategies would benefit from clearer analysis of the links between growth and poverty alleviation. As a basis for this, it is important to establish what is meant by 'pro-poor growth'. There are two main approaches: the absolute definition considers only the incomes of the poor, and the relative definition compares changes in the incomes of the poor with those who are not poor. If the objective is to reduce absolute poverty, then the former definition is preferable. Higher rates of growth usually result in more rapid poverty reduction. However this relationship varies between countries, mainly due to differences in what happens to income inequality.

According to the relative definition, growth is only pro-poor if the incomes of poor people grow faster than those of the overall population. However, DFID is committed to the MDG of halving absolute poverty income by 2015, and thus prefers to judge whether growth is pro-poor by how fast on average the incomes of the poor rise. [Source: DFID Policy Division, 2004, 'What is Pro-poor Growth and Why do We Need to Know?', Pro-Poor Growth Briefing Note 1, Department for International Development, London.]

Understanding Pro-poor Policy Processes:

'Pro-poor' is a term that has become widely used in the development literature. The general understanding that can be drawn from this literature is that pro-poor policies are those that directly target poor people, or that are more generally aimed at reducing poverty. There is also a general consensus that pro-poor policy processes are those that allow poor people to be directly involved in the policy process, or that by their nature and structure lead to pro-poor outcomes. The current definition used by the Civil Society Partnership Programme is that 'the aim of pro-poor policies is to improve the assets and capabilities of the poor'. [Source: https://odi.org/en/about/our-work/understanding-pro-poor-policy-processes/] .

Neither National Food Security Act, 2013 nor Pradhan Mantri Garib Kalyan Anna Yojana [PMGKY} defines the words 'pro poor' though it provides for eligibility conditions etc. I have stated before authoritative definitions or understanding of the words 'pro poor' as have been laid down by the different international agencies accepted and adopted worldwide. Free supply or distribution of food grains does not come within the meaning of 'pro poor' policies, programs or schemes. The Directive Principles of State Policy in the Constitution of the country do not envisage such free supply or distribution of food grains except for free legal services. Thus, it seems that the governing political parties are making a misconceived application of the provisions of the said Principles. Those look like brightening the future of the poor but in reality those are in a bleak status.

My understanding is that wherever any policy or program or scheme envisages one or more social welfare or social benefits, the ruling political parties think that once the word 'pro poor' or 'poor' is included, it should be either free or highly subsidized. The definitions of pro poor speak otherwise. All the definitions spell out same or similar meaning of 'pro poor'. Most appropriate and appealing definition which I could find is 'Pro-poor growth is a term used for primarily national policies to stimulate economic growth for the benefit of poor people (primarily in the economic sense of poverty). Pro-poor growth can be defined as absolute, where the poor benefits from overall growth in the economy, or relative - which refers to targeted efforts to increase the growth specifically among poor people. The current definition used by the Civil Society Partnership Programme is that 'the aim of pro-poor policies is to improve the assets and capabilities of the poor. It is a comparison of what existed at a given time, what is envisaged under the policy or program or scheme and whether at the end of the period of such policy or program as slated, the earning or income capacity has been increased compared to what existed on the eve of the launch of the policy. This is the core content for bringing up the poor gradually to stage higher than existing to the next higher stage of their economic status and improvements in their wellbeing. This should be the yardstick for measurement of the efforts made for upliftment of pro poor. This is an indication of moving towards the improving the pro poor growth. This is possible only through creative efforts supported by the financial aid and assistance and not through free distribution of the food grains and so on. Such understanding is beyond the concept of the social welfare and social justice enunciated under the said Principles but considered on face of as most impressive which hides the chasing shadow of the ruling parties interests, the politicians and the middlemen.

Instead of making such moves, it would be have been saner and sanitized if the existing prices of the food grains, vegetables and fruits commonly used by the poor for survival was further reduced by 50% [Fifty percent] that would have met both the ends of social welfare or justice contemplated in the said Principles. Those pro poor, as we know, are now paying the fixed lower prices for food grains and surviving and they would have much more happy if the prices were reduced as suggested before in place of free distribution which in fact denies the intended benefit because of long channel and loopholes in the way. There is nothing free other than free legal aid. This needs to be clearly understood and a line needs to be drawn on the concept of freebies that weaken the fiscal capacity of the government, the strength and stability of which is much more greater than anything else in the interests of the financial security of the nation. Fiscal management of the country does not admit such measures irrespective of whatsoever shown as attractive from the poverty point of view, a populist measure to serve mainly the psychological comfort of the people. Let us not do such things for; that acta against our own Conscience.

India gave birth to populist economic development in mid-nineteen seventies. It created more sounds than the substance. Economic development, prior thereto, was pragmatic and practical to the eyes. Now it has assumed monstrous size and dominating political game among the political parties easy to play than real economic game for the benefit of the people and for the overall interests of the country. Understanding essence of economic development in these terms will ever shine the face of the nation and of its people; otherwise we will be entering into thickening forest where darkness prevails over the sunrise. Online Dictionary explains it in a more lucid language 'The foliage's of trees are very close to each other and form a very thick canopy. Only approximately 1% of the light that gets to the canopy reaches the ground and so the lower branches are too dark to let leaves develop and there's virtually no undergrowth.'

"The rise of populism in the past two decades has motivated much work on its drivers, but less is known about its economic and political consequences. This column uses a comprehensive cross-country database on populism dating back to 1900 to offer a historical, long-run perspective. It shows that (1) populism has a long history and is serial in nature – if countries have been governed by a populist once, they are much more likely to see another populist coming to office in the future; (2) populist leadership is economically costly, with a notable long-run decline in consumption and output; and (3) populism is politically disruptive, fostering instability and institutional decay. The analysis suggests that populism is here to stay." - Moritz Schularick, Christoph Trebesch, Manuel Funke – 16 Feb 2021.

The freebies and welfare schemes which the central and state governments have launched have no protection of the accountability and deliverability mandates mentioned before that constrains one to think whether loud voice we have been making about our economic and financial strengths are backed up with the reality or are flying balloons in the air. The order and discipline are the first lessons of the development. Erratic thinking lends hands to making more errors in one's life. Eulogization and personalized attachment to the concept of development weakens individual and national strength inasmuch as such attachment is shown more aggressively in the print and electronic media everyday by one or other central and state leaders believing it tastes good for the readers knowing that such propaganda and presentations remain illusory because the method should have been the other way where the people held the performance with high esteem and vouched by the media and critics as facts and not fictions.

# REFERENCES

01. Welfare Schemes for a cross section of the society of Government of India. https://www.india.gov.in/my-government/schemes for updated schemes and programs - D82/A, NANGAL DEWAT VILLAGE, VASANT KUNJ, NEW DELHI – 110070.
02. Government Schemes in India - %20BYJUS%20List%20of%20Schermes.htm.
03. Reinforcing social welfare schemes to withstand crises. - RITUPARNA SANYAL, SHRADDHA SHRIVASTAVA – April 15, 2021 – IDR Website.
04. List of important Schemes launched by the Government of India.
05. Freebies can lead to fiscal disaster: 15th Finance Commission chief - ET Online
06. Last Updated: Apr 20, 2022, 12:27 AM IST.
07. Fiscal crisis - government by Simon Lee – Britannica - Fiscal%20Disaster/fiscal-crisis%20Britinicca.htm
08. Poll freebies: Road to economic disaster - Tuesday, 19 April 2022 | Uttam Gupta – The Pioneer – 10 December, 2022.
09. Way to Disaster - GOVIND BHATTACHARJEE | August 23, 2022 12:58 pm – The Statesman.
10. 26 important schemes launched by Narendra Modi government – India Today - New Delhi, UPDATED: Aug 27, 2019 15:48 IST.
11. Pro-poor growth, absolute and relative definition - 2022 GRID-Arendal.
12. Spurring%20Fiscal%20Disaster/86397%20Carniege%20Internationl%20Peace%20-Debt%20Impact.htm.
13. ResearchGate Recovery Of NPAS Through Debt Recovery Channels In Indian Banks - An Analysis - August 2019 Restaurant Business 118(8):245-254 DOI:10.26643/rb.v118i8.7683 Project: ICSSR Major research project - Authors: R. Alamelumangai, B. Sudha.
14. New Year Gift for Poor: Centre Makes Food grain Free of Cost for 81.35 Cr People under NFSA for 1 Year – Outlook - Updated: 24 Dec 2022 8:50 am.
15. Why is India opting for overseas bonds? - The government plans to raise a part of its gross borrowing in external markets. What are the advantages and risks? - July 13, 2019 07:22 pm | Updated July 14, 2019 03:36 pm IST - T.C.A. Sharad Raghavan.
16. BusinessLine: All you wanted to know about... Foreign sovereign bonds December 06, 2021 - Updated 06:14 pm IST.

17. BusinessLine: What to do with forex reserve riches - December 13, 2020 - Updated 08:32 pm IST - By B Prasanna.
18. BusinessLine: Caution ahead. Indian rupee's most appealing trait for traders vanishing December 13, 2022 - Updated 11:32 am IST - By Bloomberg.
19. BusinessLine: Bad debts. Over 5 years, banks recovered just 13% of ₹10-lakh-cr loan write-off: FinMin data December 14, 2022 - Updated 12:28 pm IST – Shishir Sinha.
20. The impact of public debt on foreign exchange reserves and central bank profitability: the case of Hungary Gergely Baksay, Ferenc Karvalits and Zsolt Kuti.
21. Forex Reserves - d%20(3) %20[Importance%20of%20FER%20-%20Buyj's].htm.
22. GK Padho.com: Achievements Of Modi Government Sarkar Till Date All Scheme Current Affairs October 23, 2022 8:46 am by Namniyata Osh.
23. InstaPedia: What are sovereign bonds, and what are their risks and rewards?
24. World Economic Forum: What are foreign currency reserves and can they help combat the global economic crisis? Aug 9, 2022.
25. GSDRC- DFID Policy Davison 2004 - What is Pro-poor Growth and Why do We Need to Know?
26. Business Standard: Forex reserves for hedging, can't use them to fund projects: Experts - Abhijit Lele | Mumbai - Last Updated at August 13, 2021 02:22 IST.
27. India Today: Recession is a certainty in 2023, but how much will it hurt India? - Samrat Sharma - New Delhi, UPDATED: Oct 12, 2022 13:31 IST.
28. India needs very serious reforms: IMF's Gita Gopinath - Furquan Moharkan, DHNS, Bengaluru - Dec 30 2019, 01:15 IST updated: Dec 30 2019, 01:24 IST.
29. Firstpost. New Industrial Policy seeks forex pile for financing companies: Report - FP Trending December 15, 2022 17:51:49 IST.
30. Sovereign Gold Bond Scheme 2022-23 – Ministry of Finance - DEC 2022 7:06PM by PIB Delhi.
31. World Bank - Risk of Global Recession in 2023 Rises Amid Simultaneous Rate Hikes - PRESS RELEASE September 15, 2022.
32. The New Indian Express: Should we employ our forex reserves to fund big infra push that can revive growth? - By Jyoti Prakash Gadia - Last Updated: 06th September 2021 07:35 PM.
33. Mint: The world is looking at India as a destination for investment: Gita Gopinath - Updated: 15 Dec 2022, 06:14 AM IST Gireesh Chandra Prasad, Sruthijith K.K.
34. The Daily Star: What to do with rising foreign exchange reserves? Sharjil Haque - Tue Jan 5, 2016 12:00 AM Last update on: Tue Jan 5, 2016 12:00 AM.
35. THE REPRESENTATION OF THE PEOPLE ACT, 1951.

36. Cory Contini (Author), 2008, Political Accountability and Responsibility in the Government, Munich, GRIN Verlag, https://www.grin.com/document/230610.
37. Explained: What are 'freebies' and how they may burden state finances
38. About welfarism - About%20Welfarism.pdf.
39. Accountability – Wikipedia.
40. Outlook: Appointment Of Chief Election Commissioner: Why SC Cites T N Seshan? All you need To Know - Written By Abhik Bhattacharya UPDATED: 23 NOV 2022 12:36 PM.
41. The Hindu Centre: Interview: The IAS officers' loyalty has to be to the people, the Constitution and the nation: K. Sujatha Rao Smita Gupta - Jun 25, 2018 14:20 IST - Updated: Jun 26, 2018 16:07 IST.
42. BLOCK: BusinessLine on campus: Freebies walk a thin line between welfare and wasteful - B Bhaskar **-** 02 September 2022 14:52:30 IST.
43. Reserve Bank of India – RBI Bulletin - State Finances: A Risk Analysis - Date : Jun 16, 2022.
44. Hindustan Times News: Can't couch all freebies as welfare schemes: Supreme Court – Shrikant Singh - **India News** - Updated on Aug 12, 2022 05:22 AM IST.
45. GS SCORE - Civil Services Reforms: Historical Underpinnings Governance: Doing the rights things in the right way – Published - 29th Jun, 2022.
46. Rhode, Carla (2017) : An OECD Framework for Financing Democracy, ifo DICE Report, ISSN 2511-7823, ifo Institut - Leibniz-Institut für Wirtschaftsforschung an der Universität München, München, Vol. 15, Iss. 2, pp. 55-60.
47. Drishti IAS: English: Directive Principles of State Policy (DPSP) - 05 Jul 2021.
48. Difference between NITI Aayog and the Planning Commission - %20(3)[Difference%20-Niti%20Aayog%20and%20Planning%20Commission].htm
49. GeeksforGeeks – riya90654 - Importance of Five Year Plan in India Last Updated : 22 Nov, 2022.
50. ECI comes down heavily on freebie culture, proposes proforma for political parties to explain how they will fulfill poll promises – 4 October, 2022 - %20%7BECI%20%20Guidelines%20Freebies.htm
51. Law Commission Report - Report No.255 On Electoral Reforms - GOVERNMENT OF INDIA - LAW COMMISSION - OF INDIA
52. CONSTITUENT ASSEMBLY OF INDIA - VOLUME VII Friday, the 19th November, 1948 The Constituent Assembly of India met in the Constitution Hall, New Delhi, at Ten of the Clock Mr. Vice-President (Dr. H. C. Mookherjee) in the Chair.
53. Pleaders - Directive Principles of State Policy - August 9, 2019.

54. Election Commission of India - MODEL CODE OF CONDUCT FOR THE GUIDANCE OF POLITICAL PARTIES AND CANDIDATES.
55. Government of India – NITI Aayog DEMO.
56. Electoral reform in India – Wikipedia.
57. Principles of Democracy – Government Accountability - overnment-dem%20(1).htm.
58. THE FINANCIAL CRISIS INQUIRY REPORT - Final Report of the National Commission on the Causes of the Financial and ISBN 978-0-16-087727-8 Economic Crisis in the United States.
59. Business Standard: NITI's new 3-year strategic paper: How different is it from a 5-year plan? - BS Reporter | New Delhi - Last Updated at April 13, 2017 10:00 IST.
60. Social and Economic Justice under Constitution of India: A Critical Analysis Mahantesh G. S. Principal and Coordinator, ABBS School of Law, Bangalore Karnataka, India.
61. Political Funding - Unconfirmed 58415 Political Funding (1).crdownload.
62. CEO Insights - Upcoming Global Recession and Its Impact on India - Sthitaprajnya Panigrahi.
63. UPSC WITH NIKHIL - Utilization Of Public Funds - Last Updated : 15-Dec-2022.
64. Business Standard: What is the Consolidated Fund of India? - Krishna Veera Vanamali | New Delhi - Last Updated at January 7, 2022 08:45 IST.
65. Carnegie India – Raising Financial Resources - Published November 16, 2016.

# ABOUT THE AUTHOR

Graduate in Commerce 1961. Completed short Vigilance Course organized by the Institute of Secretariat Training & Management and in Parliamentary Procedures and Practices organized by the Bureau of Parliamentary Studies & Training, Ten days on job training in World Bank (1990), Washington and was a Team Member of the World Bank and ADB Teams for Project Appraisal and Special Studies. Was a member of the Loan Negotiation Team of the Government of India for ADB Loan for power projects.

Served Rural Electrification Corporation Limited {REC} for 18 years and Power Finance Corporation Limited {PFC} for 12 years, overall 30 years.

While I was working in Rural Electrification Corporation Limited (REC) as Deputy Secretary, my services were sought by the erstwhile Ministry of Energy for drafting MOA and AOA, other related documents and for incorporating PFC. PFC was incorporated on 16 July, 1986 under the Companies Act, 1956 after due approvals and as per the procedure prescribed under company law. My services were again sought by the Ministry on immediate basis in the first week of September, 1987. Joined PFC on 17$^{th}$ September, 1987 on deputation for one year, from REC for raising Rs. 100 Cr. from the financial market including its utilization for critical power projects selected by the erstwhile Planning Commission before 31$^{st}$ March, 1988, as per the mandate to the Ministry from the MOF/PMO. CMD was yet to be appointed. I was reporting to Joint Secretary (F) in the Ministry.

CMD assumed office on 14$^{th}$ January, 1988. The entire amount mobilized was utilized for the projects stated before the mandated date after due approvals and loan documentation. Awarded honorarium and commendation letter. Absorbed in the services of PFC after one year as per the desire of the CMD as Employee Number One (001) of PFC.

As my moral duty, I wish to state that at fag end of my service in PFC, I was implicated in a politically motivated criminal case when the security scam broke out in 1992, in connection with investment transactions of around Rs. 419 Cr. made with a UCO Bank, Hamam Street, Mumbai, even though the fact being that the investment transactions related to 1988-90 and had no relationship with security scam.

PFC did not file any complaint with the CBI. CBI registered the case suomoto.

The then CMD appeared before the Joint Parliamentary Committee (JPC) in connection with investment of Rs. 300 Cr in March, 1992 made by him, the period covered under Securities Scam.

Due to tremendous political pressure, soon thereafter, I was placed under suspension in November 1992. On appeal in the Hon'ble High Court of Delhi and the orders passed by the Hon'ble High Court, the suspension order was revoked in May; 1996.

The charge sheet doesn't mention a word about any allegation against me of corruption or recovery from me or any of my relatives or of any financial loss to PFC.

Even though PFC did not file complaint with CBI as stated before, sanction for prosecution was accorded by the then CMD which was suggestive of bias, if not malicious. The Statutory Auditor's Report incorporated in the Annual Report of PFC for 1992-93 {P 39, Para 1. Page 40 Para 11.6 and Page 41 Para 4, 5, 9 Point 26.1} regarding investment of Rs. 300 Cr. stated above supports the mala-fide intention of the then CMD. PFC suffered financial loss of Rs.15 Cr under the above investment. After due process of inquiry, the amount is stated to have been written off in the books of accounts while there was no financial loss whatsoever in the transactions made by me with the approval of the then CMD. There was no criminal or departmental action against those who caused financial loss of Rs. 15 cr. which was rather written off?

PFC then being newly established company; there was no procedure on investment of surplus funds laid down by the Board of Directors (BOD). In its absence, a procedure was established by me with the approval of the CMD who had the powers on all matters of investment of funds as per delegated powers by the BOD. All the transactions of investment of surplus funds were accordingly made with the approval of CMD. PFC did not deal investment transactions with any Broker's firm as a matter of policy though its Articles permitted to deal with brokers.

The New Delhi Main Branch of the UCO Bank, Hamam Street, Mumbai which was approached to offer the quotes for investment of surplus funds advised PFC to approach their Branch at Mumbai which was solely dealing in securities transactions through its Official Brokers. On the mandate of the Nationalized Bank at Mumbai with whom the investment transactions were done, PFC obtained quotes from the Representative of their Official Broker's firm in New Delhi and all the investments, were based on merits of rate and absorbing capacity, duly approved by the then CMD were made in the name of UCO Bank, Hamam Street, Mumbai as advised by the New Delhi Main Branch of the UCO Bank.

All the investment transactions with the aforesaid Bank were made by RBI Cheques (Banker's Cheques) initially through the New Delhi Main Branch and later, as mandated by the UCO Bank, Hamam Street, Mumbai, the investments were routed through a designated foreign Bank (ANZ Grindlays Bank, Parliament Street, New Delhi) which had the online money transfer facility (SWIFT facility) since investment amount was to be transferred on the same day as the interest thereon was to start from the date of the cheque.

PFC had given specific written mandate along with the Banker's Cheque to the said foreign Bank with copy to the said Bank at Mumbai for transfer of money to the invested Bank at Mumbai. The designated foreign bank for transfer, as per the Charge Sheet, credited the proceeds of the banker's cheque to the account of the Broker's firm. It is also stated in the Charge Sheet the forwarding letters and the banker's cheques were handed over by the concerned Officers in PFC to the local representative of the broker's firm. The practice followed was to handover to the letters and cheques to the duly authorized representatives of the banks and the same procedure was followed as per such authorization letter given by the UCO Bank, Hamam Street at Mumbai to PFC.

I was not aware of crediting the banker's cheque proceeds to the account of Broker's firm by the said foreign bank since all the monies invested together with interest due and payable were received back by PFC on due dates with no loss of funds, thus leaving no scope for suspicion on misuse. The charge is undue favour to the Broker's Firm when, as stated before, no investment transaction was done with that Broker's Firm or any other Broker's Firm by PFC.As stated before, there was no recovery from me or any of my relatives as per the Search Report of CBI which I submitted to the then CMD of PFC. Under these circumstances, there was no undue favour to the Broker's firm, whatsoever.

The then CMD ordered special audit of the investment transactions of the value stated before. The special audit report contains the complete procedure followed by the investment department with no adverse comments or qualifications, thus authenticated the investment procedure followed with the approval of the then CMD. The special audit report also specifically confirmed in Part III to the specific queries of CMD to the effect there were no deviations in the investment procedure followed with the said UCO Bank and the transactions had the approval of the competent authority i.e. the then CMD.

This report was considered by the Central Vigilance Commission (CV) which requested the Ministry of Energy to forward it to the Director of CBI for taking into consideration while investigating the case. This was accordingly done by the Ministry of Energy (now Power). CBI, except attaching a copy of the same with Charge Sheet as part of the documents (D23), did not mention a single word about the same in the Charge Sheet, thus had not taken the report into consideration during the investigation. The report would have bared the allegations made in the Charge Sheet had CBI taken same into consideration during investigation and had dealt it also in the Charge Sheet. This was biased and prejudicial on the part of the CBI.

I was under depression for about six months after the suspension. I made written submissions to the CMD, PFC, then Secretary in the Ministry and the Hon'ble Minister of Energy but there was no response from any one. My wife developed hypertension in 1993 which could not be controlled despite best medical treatment. She suffered brain stroke $12^{th}$ May, 2005 midnight, admitted to the hospital, remained in coma for 28 days. On regaining on the 29th day, the Doctors found her having completely paralyzed right side and loss of speech. She remained bed ridden for eight years and passed away on $7^{th}$ Dec 2013. I and my family came under social stigma and the social standing of the family was ruined.

The case was transferred to Special Court in Mumbai on the petitions filed by some of the accused persons residing in Mumbai sometime in 2017. On appeal by CBI in Hon'ble Court of Delhi, in 2017, the transfer of case was stayed. Final Order is still awaited. The regular trial at the Trial Court is yet to commence. The case has thus been pending for the last 28 years. I have been struggling in managing the legal and travel expenses. I have been living since then with loss of face, reputation and integrity built over 30 years of my service both in REC and PFC.

I was due for retirement on $31^{st}$ December, 1996; my service was extended up to $31^{st}$ July, 1997, the date on which I retired from the services of PFC. There being no Pension Scheme in PFC at that time, I served as Consultant in Multinational Consultancy Organizations for 18 years post retirement to financially support myself and my family. PFC engaged me as consultant in May, 2006 on policy, procedural and compliance matters of SPVs set up by PFC under Ultra Mega Power Projects, an Initiative launched by the GOI/MOP in 2005-06, served PFC in that position for two years on contract basis. In June, 2008 joined another multinational subsidiary company (a Subsidiary of German based Parent Company) as Senior Advisor. Best Professional Employee and Special Contribution Awards were given while working in this company.

I am now aged 85 years and, on that ground and there being no allegation of any recovery nor financial loss to PFC, filed petition for discharge in the Hon'ble High Court of Delhi permissible under the law which, though appreciated the facts, dismissed the petition as not a fit case on the ground that other accused had not filed any such petition. Among the accused persons in the case, I was the only person eldest of all others.

On completion of the contract in 2018, I took up writing of books. So far, I have authored "Time We Change for a Better India"(Jan 2017), "A Wake up Call for Every Indian"(Oct 2019) and "Jammu & Kashmir – The Truth of The Matter" (Nov. 2019), "The Living God on Earth" (Jan 2020), "Sounds of Silences in India's Constitution – Dangers Ahead" (December, 2020), "COVID-19 not a Natural Calamity – An analysis of its Origin and the Fallout" (January, 2021), "India's Political Blunders Bleeding Its Borders {May, 2021), "Socialist, Secular and Religion in India – The Misconceptions" (June, 2021), "India's

Stressed Assets Conundrum-Suggested Way-Out" (Oct, 2021), "Anyone who can tell where did Covid-19 come from that killed millions humans in the world-Is silence an answer" (Nov 2021), "Indian Parliament Monsoon Session {2021} Ruckus – Time to think about course of action" (Dec 2021) and "About the correctness of Tariff decisions under the Electricity Act, 2003 – in retrospect" 2021.

www.ingramcontent.com/pod-product-compliance
Lightning Source LLC
LaVergne TN
LVHW070526070526
838199LV00073B/6708

9 789357 049702